QUANTITATIVE ANALYSIS IN MARKETING MANAGEMENT

Quantitative Analysis in Marketing Management

Luiz Moutinho, Mark Goode and Fiona Davies

John Wiley & Sons
Chichester • New York • Weinheim • Brisbane • Singapore • Toronto

Other Wiley Editorial Offices

John Wiley & Sons, Inc., 605 Third Avenue,
New York, NY 10158-0012, USA

WILEY-VCH Verlag GmbH, Pappelallee 3,
D-69469 Weinheim, Germany

Jacaranda Wiley Ltd, 33 Park Road, Milton,
Queensland 4064, Australia

John Wiley & Sons (Asia) Pte Ltd, 2 Clementi Loop #02-01,
Jin Xing Distripark, Singapore 129809

John Wiley & Sons (Canada) Ltd, 22 Worcester Road,
Rexdale, Ontario M9W 1L1, Canada

Library of Congress Cataloging-in-Publication Data

Moutinho, Luiz
    Quantitative analysis in marketing management/by Luiz Moutinho,
Mark Goode, Fiona Davies.
      p.   cm.
    Includes bibliographical references and index.
    ISBN 0-471-96339-9 (cloth: alk. paper). – ISBN 0-471-96430-1
(pbk. : alk. paper)
    1. Marketing – Management – Statistical methods. 2. Marketing – Management – Mathematical models. I. Goode, Mark. II. Davies, Fiona. III. Title
HF5415.13.M695 1998   97-49694
658.8'001'51–dc21   CIP

British Library Cataloguing in Publication Data

A catalogue record for this book is available from the British Library

ISBN 0-471-96339-9 (cloth) 0-471-96430-1 (paperback)

Typeset in 10/12pt Times by MHL Typesetting, Coventry.
Printed and bound in Great Britain by Bookcraft, Midsomer Norton.
This book is printed on acid-free paper responsibly manufactured from sustainable forestry, in which at least two trees are planted for each one used for paper production.

This book is dedicated to our children

Hannah, Rachel, Nathan

and in loving memory of

Duncan

Contents

Preface

This book is the result of many years of doing research and teaching marketing using quantitative methods. The students on these courses were primarily from business and social sciences, and were interested in getting a good working knowledge of the quantitative techniques which are most relevant to marketing management without getting bogged down with derivations and/or rigorous proofs. That is, consistent with the needs of today's marketing managers, the students were more interested in knowing when correctly to use a particular technique and its interpretation rather than the mechanics of the technique.

Our approach here is to make statistics and quantitative methods applied to marketing management a 'kinder and gentler' subject by introducing students to the various techniques used in business without intimidating them with mathematical derivations. The main emphasis is on when to use the various data-analytic and decision-making techniques, and how to interpret the resulting output obtained from the most widely used statistical and quantitative tools in marketing. The book tries to achieve these objectives by using the strategy of dividing the chapters into two parts. The text provides a conceptual understanding of techniques, with relevant concepts illustrated by real or hypothetical data sets. Short case studies and analytical marketing problems are then included in the chapter to allow students to test their knowledge and understanding of the concepts, techniques and quantitative marketing tools.

Chapter 1 provides an introductory discussion of the need for the use of quantitative analysis in marketing management as well as an overview of the structure of the text content. Chapter 2 is focused on the area of marketing research and includes a comprehensive discussion of data collection methods as well as sampling issues and procedures. Chapter 3 provides an analytical discussion of elementary and advanced statistics. The statistical techniques introduced range from ANOVA, regression analysis, factor analysis, parametric and non-parametric tests to multivariate data analysis techniques, such as path analysis, LISREL, Logit and Probit. Chapter 4 deals with demand analysis and contains discussion of key issues such as elasticity of demand, demand schedules, market potentials and different market demand measurement methods. Chapter 5 introduces forecasting methods ranging from judgemental approaches and statistical methods to environmental forecasting and econometric modelling. Chapter 6 introduces a discussion of the financial techniques widely used in marketing management, such as pricing models, investment appraisal tools and cash flow analysis. Chapter 7 deals with concepts and techniques related to marketing budgeting and control. Concepts covered include response functions, profitability analysis, resource allocation and the measurement of marketing effectiveness. Chapter 8 is devoted to the discussion of specific decision techniques, such as PERT/CPM, game theory, queuing and linear programming. Chapter 9 introduces techniques and concepts related to production/operations management. The areas of discussion range from capacity management and inventory control to quality management and just-in-time. Finally, Chapter 10 introduces new developments in the area of quantitative analysis in marketing management. The topics covered include marketing decision support systems, knowledge based systems, neural networks and approximate algorithms.

The analytical approach used in designing the book's content essentially reinforces the concepts introduced. Detailed discussions of the interpretation of results are provided and, wherever necessary, computations of the various interpretative statistics and calculations are illustrated in order to give a better understanding of the techniques.

We hope you like the end result ...!

Luiz Moutinho
Mark Goode
Fiona Davies

Acknowledgements

We would like to thank Mr Steve Hardman, Ms See Hanson and Mr Iain Gibson at *John Wiley & Sons* for their encouragement to undertake and complete this book. Thanks also go to Professor Mick Silver, Dr Peter Morgan and Miss Helena Snee for useful comments on early drafts of some of the chapters in the book, and also to the anonymous reviewers, whose insightful comments led to rewrites which substantially improved the clarity and readability of the book. We would also like to thank all the MBA students at Cardiff Business School who took the Market Analysis and Forecasting elective in 1997 for testing the software and making numerous helpful suggestions.

We would like to thank all the publishers and authors who have given their permission for pieces of diagrams, statistical tables and case studies to be used in this book. We feel the quality of the book has been greatly enhanced by the inclusion of these pieces of work. Every effort has been made to trace and acknowledge ownership of copyright. The publishers will be glad to hear from any copyright holders whom it has not been possible to contact.

Finally, we would like to thank the following secretaries: Miss Debbie Hughes, Miss Cath Colgan and Miss Julie Roberts from Cardiff Business School, and Mrs Sylvia Kerrigan from Glasgow Business School, for typing and editing the manuscript.

1
Introduction

In recent years, more and more organisations the world over have been developing a marketing orientation. Greater consumer power and sophistication, increasing competition and technological innovation are some of the main factors which have led (or in some cases, forced) companies to realise the importance of researching and satisfying consumer needs and wants. Thus, the old days when the main task of marketers was to sell what was produced, are long gone. Then, marketing focused mainly on promotions, and was often considered as a purely creative function, with little need for hard figures or quantitative methods. Nowadays, the marketing department in a marketing-oriented company is involved in decisions on research, forecasting, production, personnel, sales, organisational strategy and operations management, as well as decisions on marketing strategy and marketing mix.

The increasing complexity of organisations means that decisions in all these areas are becoming increasingly complex. This has led to the demand for more scientific, rational, systematic methods of decision making, which are more consistent, where the reasoning behind the decision can be logically explained, and which can be analysed after the event in order to improve future decision making. This book sets out some of these methods which are suitable for marketing. However, such methods should not be seen as a substitute for managerial knowledge and experience, rather as a means by which knowledge of the market can be expressed objectively rather than subjectively. Indeed, it often helps to clarify thinking on a decision if managers can analyse their intuitive and experience-based ideas on the problem, to discover what underlying factors lead them to think that way. Marketers need to think both qualitatively and quantitatively.

The discipline of marketing draws from several quantitative areas, such as accounting, economics, operations management and statistics, and borrows techniques from these areas to be used in the main marketing functions of market analysis and forecasting, designing a marketing strategy and marketing mix, and controlling operations. Thus the marketer needs to be familiar with many different ways of thinking.

The following chapters of this book aim to guide the reader through the various techniques which can be useful to the marketer. The emphasis is on how to use these techniques and interpret the results, and how they should be integrated with other marketing considerations, rather than on detailed derivation of formulae. Students wishing to know more on the background or derivation of specific techniques should consult books on business statistics or operations management, as appropriate – references for some of these are given at the end of the relevant chapters.

The book commences by addressing market research issues. A customer-oriented company needs to hold reliable and detailed information on customers and potential customers, and Chapter 2 discusses methods of communication, observation, experimentation and sampling. It will guide readers to the type of market research which is most appropriate for the situation – for instance: should reactions to the new advertising campaign be investigated through personal interview, telephone interview, mail or e-mail survey, or in a series of small focus groups? In order to find out likely sales of a new product, should we be setting up a simulated shopping situation to find out who buys and at what price, or should we be 'test marketing' by selling it in certain areas – and if so, which?

The section on sampling compares different methods and their advantages and disadvantages, enabling marketers to achieve the best balance between amount of data obtained, reliability of extending these findings to the whole market, and time and cost factors. The various forms of probability sampling are illustrated with a worked example, which could be used as a model.

Chapter 3 moves on to describe the many statistical tests which can be used in such areas as the analysis of consumer preferences, comparison of test markets, and analysis of advertising effectiveness. Many times, marketers face questions such as 'Are the differences in our results (e.g. between sales in different test market areas) meaningful?' or 'Which product attributes/marketing mix variables/buyer charac-teristics have most influence on customer satisfaction?' The statistical methods provide numerical measures which can be used to determine the significance of particular results, and thus guide marketers in answering such questions.

A car factory produces two-seater sports cars, small hatchbacks, family cars and executive models. But how does it decide how many of each to make in a year? The company needs to estimate market demand for each model in order to optimise production. Chapter 4 discusses market demand, how it can be predicted, and what factors may affect it. It continues by describing methods by which a company may analyse market demand for its products or services, e.g. the internal and external data sources that this car company could use to forecast demand, and shows how the statistical method of regression analysis could use previous sales data to forecast next year's sales of each model of car.

The theme of forecasting continues in Chapter 5, which describes judgemental approaches to forecasting before continuing with a detailed section on statistical forecasting methods, each illustrated by an example. Some other forecasting methods are also briefly described. Marketers will find these techniques helpful not only in forecasting future sales, but in forecasting other important variables such as share or commodity prices, and looking at questions such as 'Are our sales seasonal?' and 'When should we use discounting or couponing to boost sales?'. The chapter also discusses how forecasting methods can be compared, and the situations in which specific methods are most suitable, so that marketers can make an informed decision on the best method for their circumstances.

Setting the price for a product or service can be a tricky decision. A manufacturer of electric fires may look for a 10% profit margin over costs, but find that this makes their model substantially more expensive than the competition. A new car may have features which make it superior to rivals – what price premium should be put on these? If a biscuit manufacturer reduces prices to undercut competitors, how can the company be sure that they are not led into a price war which results in the product making a loss? Chapter 6 looks at such important pricing issues. Having introduced the concept of the break even point, it discusses how this can be of use not just in setting prices so that a profit can be made, but in analysing effects of price changes and in comparing competitors. The chapter also looks at marginal analysis – what is the optimum output for profit maximisation? This is a concept which the marketer can apply in other areas, for instance to decide on the optimal amount of advertising spending. This chapter also discusses the advantages, disadvantages and likely uses of various pricing methods. Finally, Chapter 6 looks at investment appraisal techniques – answering questions such as 'Should we build this new factory?' or 'If we buy a new machine, are we likely to recoup this expenditure within an acceptable time?'

With a limited marketing budget at its disposal, a firm needs to ensure that it is shared in the most effective way among functions such as advertising, public relations, sponsorship, etc. Chapter 7 looks at the allocation of the marketing budget, and relationships between the marketing mix and levels of sales. The chapter then discusses the important issues of control and evaluation – ways in which companies can measure their performance against their objectives, take corrective action if necessary, and constantly monitor their products, services, promotional activities, staff and distribution systems to ensure that they are both effective and responsive to the needs of the market.

Chapter 8 introduces the reader to four main types of decision technique – critical path analysis, queuing theory, linear programming and game theory. Critical path analysis helps the marketer in areas such as new product development and launch, where there are many different activities to be carried out, some of which are dependent on others and all of which must be completed by the product launch date. Queuing theory is of particular help to services marketers, as it can help to achieve an acceptable balance between the standard of customer service (e.g. how long customers have to wait for service in a supermarket queue) and costs (e.g. of employing extra checkout operators to ensure shorter waiting times). Linear programming helps a company to optimise its procedures in order to maximise or minimise a single goal, such as profits, costs, revenue or advertising effectiveness. Game theory, finally, aids companies in their choice of strategy in a competitive market by modelling likely strategic actions (e.g. washing powder manufacturer brings out 'new improved version') and responses (e.g. competitor also brings out improved version, competitor cuts price of existing product, competitor steps up advertising), and the likelihood of specific outcomes (e.g. gain/loss of market share/ profit).

The next chapter, Chapter 9, provides an introduction to the area of operations management by looking at some of the problems which are of most concern to the marketer, especially in a mass production situation – capacity management, inventory control, quality control and production management systems. Effectiveness in these areas will increase the likelihood of customer satisfaction, as the company will be able to produce high quality products in sufficient numbers to satisfy demand, minimising sources of dissatisfaction such as non-functioning products which have to be returned, non-availability of products or non-availability of spare parts.

One of today's marketers' main aims is to know customers better, to develop a relationship with them and foster customer loyalty – the major supermarkets, for instance, have all introduced types of loyalty card which reward customers for shopping with them, while enabling the company to gain detailed information on their purchasing behaviour. Increasing sophistication of computer databases and information systems plays a crucial part in this. So Chapter 10 looks at future trends in the use of quantitative methods in marketing. Most of these relate to the increased use of computers – databases to hold more and better information on customers, decision support systems of various types, neural networks for customer analysis, and methods of optimising marketing effectiveness in areas such as segmentation, distribution and sales.

After each of Chapters 2 to 9, a few problems and/or case studies are included to illustrate some of the concepts covered in the chapter and how they can be applied in a real marketing situation.

PART 1

Statistical Analysis, Demand Analysis and Forecasting in Marketing

2
Data collection and sampling

This chapter is divided into two main sections, the first on data collection and the second on sampling.

Contents

Data collection
Sampling

Objectives

After reading this chapter you should:
- Know how to select an appropriate method of data collection for a given situation.
- Know the advantages and disadvantages of different data collection methods.
- Know how to select an appropriate sampling method for a given situation.
- Know the advantages and disadvantages of different sampling methods.

DATA COLLECTION

How does a car manufacturer know which aspects of its cars appeal most to its customers (economy, safety, spaciousness, speed...)? How does a biscuit manufacturer know if its new line of biscuits is proving more popular with children or adults? How does a bank know if its customers are satisfied with the services it provides? How does an advertiser know if its campaign has reached the desired targets and achieved the desired objectives?

Sales figures and patterns can throw some light on these questions, but to gain real, in-depth knowledge of customers, we have to contact them more directly. Acquiring data from respondents is a major part of marketing research. Data may

7

be required concerning respondents' past behaviour (e.g. what brands they have purchased), attitudes (what beliefs and feelings they have about a product) and characteristics (demographic, socio-economic, psychological or psychographic). The two basic ways of collecting data from respondents are by communication and by observation. We shall first look at methods of communication.

Communication Methods

A useful way to classify communication methods is by their degree of directness and degree of structure, as shown in Figure 2.1. A direct approach is one where the objectives of the research are obvious to the respondent from the questions asked, while an indirect approach asks questions in such a way as to disguise these objectives. The degree of structure may be seen as a continuum, from the highly structured formal questionnaire where the respondent must choose from predetermined responses, through semi-structured questionnaires where responses may be open-ended, to sets of questions which are no more than guidelines, to the completely unstructured discussion in which respondents express their views freely. We shall now consider the uses, advantages and disadvantages of different methods.

Structured-Direct

This is the most commonly used method – the standardised questionnaire where responses require selection of one or more alternatives from a set of predetermined responses. Questions are asked with exactly the same wording and in exactly the same order for each respondent. This type of approach is most appropriate where

	Structured	Semi-structured	Unstructured
Direct	Structured questionnaire	Semi-structured questionnaire	Focus-group interview Depth interview
Indirect	Performance of objective task technique		Thematic Apperception Test Role playing Cartoon completion Word association Sentence completion

Figure 2.1 Classification of communication methods

the data required from the respondent are easily articulated, clear-cut and limited in scope, but less appropriate where researchers want more in-depth information related to the formation and evolution of attitudes. Structured-direct questionnaires require time and skill to develop effectively, and generally also need extensive pre-testing to ensure that the questionnaire is correctly interpreted by respondents and that the questions measure what they are designed to measure.

The advantages of this method are its ease of administration (by mail, telephone, e-mail or personal interview) and ease of data processing and analysis. The format is designed to control response bias and thus increase the data reliability. Disadvantages are that respondents may not be willing or able to provide the required data, or the interviewing process may bias their responses, e.g. they may give socially acceptable responses rather than true ones.

Unstructured-Direct

The two main techniques using this approach are the depth interview and the focus group. The depth interview is an unstructured personal interview where the respondent is encouraged to express freely his or her detailed beliefs and feelings on the subject in question. The interviewer will have a note of the general areas for discussion but no fixed sequence in which they must be covered, and will use probing questions to fully explore the respondent's ideas and attitudes. This approach is used when the object of the research is to get below surface reactions to the more fundamental reasons for respondents' beliefs and feelings.

The advantage of the depth interview is the depth of insight which can be gained into the respondents' feelings and motivations, and so it is used mainly in *exploratory research*. Disadvantages include the high degree of reliance on the interviewer, who must create an environment in which the respondent is comfortable to discuss the topic freely. Interviewers with the skills and experience to create a high level of rapport, while also probing to get the required level of information, are relatively few in number and generally highly paid. The high cost per interview and the length of interview required imply a small sample size, and this, coupled with the lack of structure, means that analysis will be qualitative rather than quantitative.

The focus group interview is a frequently used technique in marketing research. It is a loosely structured interview conducted simultaneously with a group of respondents, who all have something in common (e.g. all full-time housewives, or teenagers who are still at school, or members of a particular profession). The interviewer, usually called a *moderator*, must be highly skilled and experienced in order to establish rapport among the group, to keep the discussion relevant to the topic and ensure the required depth of discussion, and create interaction within the group rather than seem to be interviewing participants individually. The selection of respondents and the physical setting of the group are also important. Focus group interviews can be used for several purposes – to stimulate new ideas on products or concepts, to get impressions of new product concepts, to generate hypotheses for further quantitative testing, or to interpret previously obtained quantitative results.

The advantages of well-conducted focus group interviews are many. They are a chance for marketers to listen directly to the consumer's opinions, thus gaining a valuable insight into how their product is actually perceived. The combined group is likely to produce more ideas than the same number of respondents interviewed individually, due to participant interaction, a higher level of involvement in the discussion, and more spontaneous responses. As with the depth interview, a highly-trained and experienced interviewer is required, but is used more efficiently in 'interviewing' several people at once. Group sessions are often recorded to allow further analysis at a later date.

The major disadvantage of the focus group is that the data gathered cannot be used in a conclusive manner; no quantitative information can be elicited which can be extended to target markets, and findings are highly dependent upon the perception of the moderator and others who interpret them. Other disadvantages relate to the risk that groups will be poorly recruited or conducted.

Semi-Structured-Direct

This category covers questionnaires which are less formally structured than the standardised questionnaire, but do not offer the complete flexibility of the depth interview. They would typically be used in a personal interview where a range of information is required, some of which is easily classified into categories and some of which requires more detail.

The advantages of a semi-structured approach are the possiblity of generating both quantitative and qualitative data, and the flexibility of the approach – for instance, some or all of the standardised questions may be mailed to the respondent prior to the interview date, so they are already answered and the interviewer only needs to probe where explanations and more detail are required. Disadvantages are that interviews still require a fair amount of interviewer time, so samples are likely to be fairly small, and, as in the depth interview, much depends on the skill and experience of the interviewer.

Structured-Indirect

This method is often called the *performance of objective task* technique. Respondents are asked to memorise and/or report information about a topic, for example they are exposed to a range of advertisements and asked to recall what they remembered about them. The technique assumes, based on research on selective information processing, that respondents are more likely to recall information which is consistent with their own attitudes, and thus the amount and type of information recalled is used to draw inferences regarding respondents' underlying attitudes.The method is an attempt to gain the data collection and processing advantages of a structured approach without asking respondents directly about behaviour and attitudes which they may be unwilling or unable to discuss. However, many researchers doubt whether it is valid to extend the research findings on which it is based to the measurement of factual information as a reliable indicator of attitudes and beliefs.

Unstructured-Indirect

These data collection methods are known as *projective* techniques. They are designed to obtain data indirectly about beliefs and feelings which respondents may be unwilling or unable to communicate by asking them to interpret the behaviour of others. The most commonly used techniques are the Thematic Apperception Test (TAT), role playing, cartoon completion, word association and sentence completion.

The Thematic Apperception Test uses one or more pictures or cartoons depicting a scenario concerning the product or topic being investigated. The situation is ambiguous with no hint as to whether its interpretation should be positive or negative toward the product or topic. The respondent is asked to describe what has happened or will happen, and can thus indirectly project personal attitudes into their interpretation of the situation.

Role playing presents the respondent with a situation in which they are asked to describe the feelings or reaction of a third person. Their response is believed to reveal their own attitudes. A variant of the technique is to ask respondents to characterise a person based on the products they have bought – their description is thought to reveal their attitudes toward the products.

The cartoon completion technique asks respondents to complete a cartoon showing people in a situation relevant to the product or topic, by completing a caption to respond to a remark made by one of the characters, e.g. 'We have just bought a satellite dish', 'Our neighbour is thinking of buying a time-share', etc.

The word association technique uses a list of carefully selected words which are presented in turn to respondents, who are asked to give the thoughts that come to them when they hear the word, or to give as many single associated words as possible in response to each word. The test is analysed by the frequency of responses, the amount of hesitation in responding, and the number of respondents unable to respond to particular words in a certain time. Non-response is assumed to indicate a high level of emotional involvement, and hesitation a lesser level. Sentence completion is similar – the respondent is asked to finish an incomplete sentence with the first phrase that comes to mind, and these are analysed.

Projective techniques are used in exploratory research, to discover hypotheses to be tested using more direct techniques. Their advantage is in eliciting feelings and attitudes which respondents might not reveal when questioned directly. Their disadvantages lie in their complexity, which means that they need highly-skilled interviewers and interpreters. The cost per interview is therefore high, which leads to the use of small samples.

Communication Media

The three main media of communication are the personal interview, the telephone interview and the mail interview. Structured communication techniques may use any of these, while unstructured techniques typically need personal interviews. Table 2.1 analyses the advantages and disadvantages of each method.

Table 2.1 Comparison of communication media

	Personal	Telephone	Mail	E-mail/Internet
Versatility	High – can use visual cues, explain complex questions, probe answers	Medium – can explain or probe, but not use visual cues	Low	Low
Cost	Most expensive	More expensive than mail unless interview is very short	Less expensive	Potential for low costs, especially if Internet connections easily available and can be shared
Time	Depends on size of sample, number of interviewers, and ease of contacting respondents	Usually faster than other methods	Depends on how many follow-up mailings required to achieve acceptable response	Fast
Sample control	Easiest to control – can select exactly who is to be interviewed, e.g. from electoral register or mailing list	Relies on less efficient sampling methods (simple random or systematic). Sample bias may result due to unlisted phone numbers.	Can control selected sample for mailing, but no control over return of questionnaire or whether selected person is actually the one to complete it	Can only select from that part of the population with access to e-mail/Internet
Quantity of data obtainable	Most	Least	Medium	Medium

Table 2.1   Continued

	Personal	Telephone	Mail	E-mail/Internet
Quality of data	Good if well administered. Dependent on interviewers, thus proper training and control of interviewers required to minimise chances of bad interviewing techniques or cheating, which could bias results	As for personal interviews – data quality dependent on quality of interviewers	Found to be better quality on sensitive topics, but bias can result from misunderstood questions or inability to remember events	Very easy for respondents to return partly completed forms, either intentionally or by accident, thus biasing results
Non-response (respondents unavailable or refusing to participate)	Callbacks necessary to reduce proportion unavailable. Little can be done about refusals.	Good timing of calls, and callbacks, can reduce proportion not available. Easier for respondents to refuse as they are not face-to-face with interviewer.	Avoids problem of non-availability. Prepaid return envelopes, reminders and incentives (free gifts, entry to prize draw, etc.) can be used to lessen refusal rate.	Respondents may not read their mailboxes. If questionnaire received, promise of results being available on Internet may increase response.

Observation Methods

The other method of collecting data is by observation, which involves recognising and recording behaviour. Marketers frequently use informal observation, such as noting competitive prices or product availability. Techniques for formal observation are designed to minimise the large error potential in informal observation. Observation is useful in collecting data about behaviour which the respondent is unaware of or unwilling to discuss, and potential bias caused by the interviewing process is eliminated. However, attitudes and feelings cannot be observed, and it is also difficult to observe many personal activities such as those which take place within the home. For the observation method to be cost effective in terms of observer time, the behaviour to be observed must be reasonably predictable or occur frequently, and must be of short duration. Observation methods are therefore far less frequently used than communication methods.

There are several ways of classifying observation methods. The setting may be natural or contrived, e.g. watching people shopping normally as opposed to in a mock 'store' created for the purpose of the research. Observation may be disguised or undisguised, according to whether respondents are aware of being observed. In structured observation, observers are told exactly what they are to measure and how it is to be measured, while in unstructured observation observers monitor any behaviour that seems relevant to the research questions. Direct observation is the observation of behaviour as it actually occurs, while indirect observation looks at some record of past behaviour, for instance looking at the cans and packets in a family's waste bin to estimate their consumption of convenience foods.

Observation may be human or mechanical. Mechanical means include motion picture cameras, the Audiometer, which records when radio or TV sets are switched on and the station to which they are tuned, and the eye camera, which records eye movement to discover how respondents read a magazine or advertisement – in what sequence, and for how long, they look at specific parts. There are also devices which measure respondents' physical reactions to stimuli, such as the *psychogalvanometer*, which measures changes in perspiration rate, and the *pupilometer*, which measures changes in the diameter of the pupil of the eye.

Another technique which has been attempted is brain wave analysis – the electrical 'signals' emitted from the brain can be monitored to indicate the level and type of interest of respondents in the stimuli they are presented with. The left hemisphere of the brain deals with more sequential and rational activities, while the right hemisphere specialises in pictorial and emotional responses. Thus the level of brain waves emitted from each side of the brain can indicate the type of interest in the stimulus. However, brain wave monitoring needs to be done under laboratory conditions, which may affect responses. There are also other complex theoretical and methodological issues associated with the analysis, which require further research.

Experimentation

Experimentation – the testing and evaluation of different alternatives – is a frequent part of marketing activities. For instance, a product may be sold for a period at a higher or lower price than normal in order to monitor the effect on sales, or a charity may try out different wordings of appeals to discover which one attracts most donations. Here, we discuss the essential features of a controlled experiment, the usefulness of *ex post facto* studies which resemble experiments, and the errors which can occur in experimental research. We then look at some of the most common experimental designs, and at suitable environments for conducting experiments.

What is Experimentation?

Experimentation involves the manipulation of one or more variables, in such a way as to measure its effect on other variables. Variables being manipulated are known as *independent* variables, while those variables which reflect the impact of the independent variable are known as *dependent* variables. For instance, in the price manipulation example cited earlier, price is the independent variable and sales the dependent variable.

The *treatment group* is that part of the population which is exposed to manipulation of the independent variable – in the example, those stores where the price is changed. In order to measure the effects of manipulation, it is also necessary to have a part of the population where the independent variable is unchanged, i.e. in some stores price should be left at its original level. This group is known as the *control group*.

It can only be claimed that effects on the dependent variable are caused by manipulation of the independent variable, if effects of other variables are measured or controlled. The two most usual methods of achieving this are by randomisation – random assignment of population elements to treatment and control group; and by matching – assigning elements specifically to treatment or control groups in a way that achieves a balance on key dimensions. A well-designed experiment thus allows measurement of the causal relationship between an independent and a dependent variable, because it controls all other possible causal relationships relating to other variables.

Ex Post Facto *Studies*

Although frequently used in marketing research, these are not true experiments. They attempt to trace back over time from a present situation, in order to discover the causes of some aspect of that situation. For instance, in attempting to discover why one grocery store has consistently higher sales than another in a similar area, a researcher may discover a difference in management style, and deduce that a more democratic management style is a factor leading to success. However, this cannot be proved – many other factors may have been overlooked which have greater impact upon sales, and it is impossible to say how much, if any, of the difference in sales is due to management style. The shortcomings of this type of research are that the independent variable is not manipulated by the researcher, and that there is no preselection of population elements into treatment and control groups in order to control extraneous variables.

Ex post facto studies are frequently used because experimentation may be impractical or impossible, but they do not have the validity of controlled experiments, and are vulnerable to many of the errors we now discuss.

Common Experimental Errors

1. *Premeasurement* refers to changes in the dependent variable produced as a result of initial measurement. A firm wishing to test the effect of a change in packaging (the independent variable) on people's consumption of a certain

chocolate bar may interview respondents before and after the change. A respondent who has never before tried the chocolate bar may, after the first interview, decide to try it, and like it. By the time of the second interview, his or her consumption pattern may have totally changed – but this is due to the interest brought about by the original interview, rather than any effect of the packaging change.

2. *Interaction* error occurs when respondents' interest in, or sensitivity to, the independent variable is changed by the premeasurement. Marketing research may test attitudes to a product before and after a particular advertising campaign. If the same people are interviewed, the very fact that they have answered questions about the product may cause them to pay more attention to the campaign than they would have otherwise. Here the premeasurement and the independent variable (the advertising) jointly affect the dependent variable (attitude to product).

3. *Instrumentation* error refers to changes in the measuring instrument over time. These are most likely to be due to human involvement – interviewers or observers may become more skilled as the experiment progresses, or they may become bored and disinterested so that the quality of interviewing or observation diminishes.

4. *Maturation* refers to changes due solely to the passing of time, which may affect the dependent variable. This can be especially problematic in experiments that continue over a long period of time, for instance repeated questioning of young people on attitudes to a magazine. As these respondents grow older, their tastes and perceptions are likely to change rapidly.

5. *History* refers to events outside the control of the experimenter which occur between pre- and post-measurement, and affect the dependent variable. A store may attempt to measure the effect of a price reduction on sales of a particular brand of ice cream. However, if there is an unexpected heatwave during the experimental period, it will be difficult to separate the effects of the price reduction and the weather in accounting for increased sales.

6. *Selection* of treatment and control groups can cause errors if the groups are initially unequal with respect to the dependent variable, or in sensitivity to changes in the independent variable. Random assignment and matching, described earlier, are techniques which can minimise this problem.

7. *Mortality* refers to the loss of respondents from the different experimental groups. A long-running experiment is almost certain to lose some respondents between start and finish. If different types of respondents are lost from the treatment group and the control group, the groups may no longer be well matched, and conclusions may not be valid.

8. *Measurement timing* errors can occur when either pre- or post-measurements are made at an inappropriate time for measuring the effect of manipulating the independent variable. A typical situation is when post-measurements are taken too early, measuring the immediate rather than the long-term effect of a change.

9. *Reactive* errors occur when the experimental situation itself causes effects that alter the effects caused by the manipulation of the independent variable. Respondents 'shopping' in an experimental store may behave differently to their normal shopping behaviour. If they see prominently displayed products which they think are of interest in the experiment, they may buy them because they feel they ought to – or conversely, some people may resist buying them. Either way, results are affected. Reactive errors can only be controlled by the structure of the experimental setting.

10. *Surrogate situation* errors occur when the experimental situation is somehow different, in terms of environment, sample population or variable manipulation, to the actual situation which will occur. The experimental store cited above is an example of such a situation or a product which has been successfully test marketed may not sell as well as predicted because competitors respond to its introduction by increased advertising of, or price reductions on, competing products.

Experimental Design

All the types of error described above, apart from reactive, measurement timing and surrogate situation errors, can be controlled for by the experimental design. However, different designs are most efficient in the control of different types of error, so researchers need to select a design that controls for the most potentially serious and most likely errors in their particular situation. Experimental designs can be divided into basic designs which consider the impact of only one independent variable at a time, and statistical designs which may consider the impact of more than one.

Basic designs
After-only Here the independent variable is manipulated and then a post-measurement is made. For instance, a new product is displayed in stores and its sales are monitored. After-only designs do not control for errors of history, maturation, selection or mortality. Neither is it easy to interpret results, with no standard of comparison.

Before-after Here pre-measurements are made, followed by the manipulation of the independent variable, followed by post-measurements. For instance, sales of a product are monitored, the price is reduced and sales are monitored again in a similar fashion. If no errors exist, price can be said to be the cause of any change in sales. However, this design may also be affected by errors of pre-measurement, history, interaction, instrumentation or mortality.

The two above designs cannot control history effects because they lack a control group, and are thus often referred to as quasi-experimental designs.

Before-after with control   This is like the before-after design, except that the test population is divided into a treatment group and a control group. All sources of potential error apart from interaction and mortality should affect both groups equally, so their effects on the control group can be measured and these changes subtracted from the total changes in the treatment group, to measure changes due solely to manipulation of the independent variable. However, pre-measurement may cause interaction errors, and mortality errors may be caused by loss of group members if the experiment is a lengthy one.

Simulated before-after   This design controls pre-measurement and interaction errors by using two different, randomly selected groups of respondents for the pre- and post-measurements. However, the other potential errors in the before-after design can still occur.

After-only with control   Here, both treatment and control groups are selected, but only post-measurements are taken. The design eliminates interaction errors, and all other errors eliminated by the before-after with control design apart from selection error. It is thus suitable when selection error is unlikely to be a problem, for instance with large random samples.

Solomon four-group   This design, also known as the four-group six-study design, consists of two treatment groups and two control groups. One treatment group and one control group are subject to a before-after with control design, while an after-only with control design is used on the other treatment group and control group. This design controls for all sources of error controllable by design. (The effects of interaction and mortality, which cannot be controlled by the before-after with control design, can be estimated by comparison with the after-only groups.)

Statistical designs
Statistical designs allow the researcher to measure the effects of more than one independent variable, and also to control for specific extraneous variables. This is done by structuring a combination of several experiments of basic design to run simultaneously. Statistical designs are thus susceptible to the same errors that can occur in the basic designs used.

Randomised blocks design   This design is appropriate when it is thought that there is one major extraneous variable likely to influence results – for instance, reactions to car advertisements may differ according to the gender of the respondent. Treatment and control groups are stratified on the basis of this variable – for instance, if gender was the extraneous or blocking variable, the sample would first be divided into male and female subgroups, and individual respondents within these groups would then be allocated randomly to treatment or control groups. The randomised blocks design is generally more useful than a completely randomised design because in most marketing research studies there is at least one extraneous variable, e.g. gender, age, income, etc., which should be controlled for. However, if there is more than one such variable this design cannot be used – a Latin square or factorial design is needed.

Latin square designs   These allow the control of two non-interacting extraneous variables. They require that each of the two blocking variables and the independent variable be divided into an equal number of blocks or levels. For instance, we may wish to examine the impact of price reductions on sales of a confectionery product. We suspect that the impact will vary according to the region of the country and also to the type of store in which it is sold. We would then construct a Latin square design in the form of a table with the two blocking variables as the rows and columns. Here we will divide each variable into three blocks – North, Midlands and South for the regions, supermarkets, small stores and newsagents for the store types. The independent variable (price) must also be divided into three, so we will use three different reductions – 2p, 4p and 6p. These levels are randomly assigned to the cells of the table so that each level occurs once and once only in each row and each column.

Table 2.2 shows our design, known as a 3 × 3 Latin square as it has three rows and three columns.

A basic design experiment is then conducted in each cell, usually either a before-after or after-only design, with or without control. For instance, an after-only design with control, using groups of 10 stores, would entail 10 supermarkets in the North making a 4p reduction, 10 in the Midlands making a 2p reduction, 10 in the South making a 6p reduction, 10 small stores in the North making a 6p reduction, etc. For each of the 9 cells a control group of 10 stores would hold the original price. Thus the effect of each price reduction could be seen once in each type of store and once in each region. Levels of sales could be analysed to find out how reductions affected sales, and how the effect varied by region and store type.

Latin square designs are often used in marketing research, particularly in retailing. One drawback is that it is not always easy to subdivide blocking and independent variables into the same number of groups, and another is the requirement for the blocking and independent variables to be non-interacting. Also,

Table 2.2   3×3 Latin square design

Store type	Region		
	North	Midlands	South
Supermarket	4p	2p	6p
Small store	6p	4p	2p
Newsagent	2p	6p	4p

only two extraneous variables can be controlled. However, the technique can be extended to control for three such variables – this is known as the Graeco-Latin square design. Other modifications of the design have been created to deal with the situation where effects may carry over from one cell to another – such as, in our example, the 6p reduction in the newsagents leading to people buying the product there instead of, as previously, with their supermarket shopping.

Factorial design Factorial designs can measure the effect of two or more independent variables, and allow for the possiblity of interaction between the variables, i.e. that the effect of the variables taken together may be different from the sum of their effects taken separately. Interaction is measured by using factorial designs and analysis of variance (ANOVA) analytical procedures.

A factorial design with only two independent variables can be shown as a table, one variable being represented by the rows and the other by the columns. A cell is needed for each possible combination of independent variables, i.e. if there are 4 levels of one variable and 5 of the other, 20 cells are required. The same basic experiment is then carried out in each cell. Analysis of variance procedures can determine the effects of each variable and of their interaction.

If there are more than two independent variables, the number of cells required will increase rapidly, especially if each has several different levels. Thus factorial designs can become very complex and costly. It is often the case, however, that only some of the effects and interactions are of interest, and then a fractional factorial design can be used, consisting of only the relevant part of the full design.

Experimental Environments

Experimental environments can be classified according to how closely they mirror the normal situation in which the observed behaviour takes place. An experiment testing the effect of different product prices on sales in a normal store obviously has a much higher degree of realism than an attempt to measure such effects by showing respondents the same products in a laboratory setting and asking how much they would be willing to pay for them. Where human respondents are concerned, it is necessary to make a study as realistic as possible, in order to minimise reactive error.

Experiments with a high degree of artificiality are known as *laboratory* experiments, and those with a high degree of realism as *field* experiments. The next section looks at typical uses of these experimental types, and the advantages and disadvantages of each.

Laboratory experiments
These are often used in initial testing of new products and promotional material. They take place in an isolated setting, where independent variables can be manipulated under carefully controlled conditions. This means that researchers can

be sure that the experiment will produce similar results if replicated (*internal validity*). Effects of history are minimised as the experimenter is in control of the laboratory situation. Laboratory experiments generally use much less time and fewer resources, and they also have the advantage of keeping ideas secret from competitors. However, the great strength of internal validity is counterbalanced by the weakness of low *external validity*, or *generalisability*. Behaviour of respondents in a laboratory setting may not be replicated when they are in a more normal situation with many other influences and distractions. Thus, laboratory experiments are often used at a 'screening' stage of development, and the products or advertisements receiving a favourable reception go on to market testing. Laboratory experiments may also be subject to *reactive* errors, when respondents are influenced either by the experimental situation or the experimenter.

Respondents may deduce the purpose of the experiment and attempt to behave as expected, or may react to non-verbal cues by the experimenter. Reactive errors may be minimised by using control groups, and by using skilled experimenters and, as far as possible, standard and impersonal means of communication such as written instructions or tape recordings.

Field experiments

Field experiments in marketing research generally take place in the market-place. This means that the advantage of a high degree of realism is offset by a lack of control of extraneous variables, and sometimes even of the independent variable – for example, some retailers may be unwilling to cooperate in varying the price of a product, making random selection of stores impossible. Extraneous variables such as competitor activity or weather conditions may affect findings. Internal validity is thus lower than for laboratory experiments, but external validity is higher due to the more realistic environment. Marketers therefore tend to place greater reliance on their results.

One of the most common types of field experiment conducted in marketing research is test marketing. We now discuss the various ways in which this is carried out.

Test Marketing

Test marketing may be used to judge market acceptance of a new product, or to test alternative marketing mixes – different advertising strategies, different types of packaging, price changes, etc. In addition, the introduction of a new product to a test market may highlight problems with the product that were not evident until the product was actually bought or used in a realistic way. The three basic types of test marketing are *standard*, *controlled* and *simulated* market tests.

Standard market tests

Here a sample of market areas is selected – regions, towns, etc. – and the product is sold as normal, using either a standard marketing mix or varying the mix in specific and controlled ways. Test markets are selected carefully to be representative, both demographically and in terms of competition, of the wider market. They should be large enough to give meaningful results and (if being used for new product testing) should allow testing of the product in all conditions in which it is likely to be used. A new washing-up liquid, for instance, should be test marketed in both hard and soft water areas. If more than one version of the product, or more than one marketing mix, is to be tested, then test markets must also be sufficiently similar to allow valid comparisons between them. The length of time for which test markets should be run depends on initial consumer response, the purchase cycle for the product and the extent of competitive activity. It is generally recommended that tests of new products should run for 10–12 months to achieve correct market share forecasts.

Standard test marketing is an example of an after-only design experiment and thus is subject to the errors discussed for this design. In addition, test markets may be subject to greatly increased competitor activity, designed to produce unfavourable results for the test and thus stop the product reaching the wider market. Test marketing may also give competitors advance warning of products being developed, allowing them to produce competitive products which may even beat the original to the wider market. Another disadvantage of test marketing is its high cost.

Standard test markets are widely used as a successful standard test marketing experiment is a good predictor of new product, or new marketing mix, success. They also have the advantage of testing retailer support for the product.

Controlled market tests

A controlled market test differs from a standard market test in that the product is not distributed through normal channels, but by a market research firm on behalf of the company. This firm will pay a number of stores for the product to be placed with them – perhaps a small number of stores in several areas (*controlled-store test*) or a large percentage of stores in a few smaller areas (*minimarket test*)

The advantages of these tests are that they are somewhat less visible to competitors, and competitors have no access to sales data. They are also quicker and less costly than standard test markets. However, the small sample of stores makes results less reliable, makes it hard to test the effect of advertising as so few stores stock the product and there can be no estimate of retailer support as the participating retailers are being paid for cooperating in the test. These tests are therefore more often used as a final check before proceeding to standard test marketing than as the only precursor to national market launch.

Simulated test markets

As the name suggests, these fall into the category of laboratory experiments. A sample of respondents is selected, representative of the target market. They are not informed of the true purpose of the test. They are exposed to advertising for the new product, in a disguised format – for instance, they may see a televsion programme with several advertisements during the commercial breaks, only one of which is for the test product. Respondents then have the opportunity to purchase the product, either in a real or simulated shopping environment. After allowing a reasonable time for respondents to use the product, they are contacted again and asked for their evaluation of it. The percentage of the original sample who purchased the product is used to estimate the percentage of the target market who would try it, given knowledge of it and its availability to them. The after-use evaluations are used to estimate how many of the triers will continue to use the product. These estimates are combined with an estimate of usage rate in order to produce an estimated market share for the product.

Due to the artificial environment, simulated test markets are vulnerable to *surrogate situation* errors and *reactive* errors. These can be controlled to some extent by comparing behaviour in laboratory situations with that observed in the actual market-place – an experienced researcher may have discovered, for instance, that for every 20 people who buy a new snack food in a laboratory situation, only 14 will buy in the actual market. This finding can be used in future situations with similar products.

Simulated test markets are more frequently used to determine whether a product should go on to standard market testing than as the sole test before national marketing. Some companies have also used them to test competing products to determine how much of a threat they are to their own products and thus plan a more informed defensive marketing strategy.

SAMPLING

Once we have decided the method we will use to collect data, we must consider the question 'How will we collect this data?' The alternatives are to take a census or a sample. In a census we use all available elements of the population of interest, e.g. if we wanted to find out what consumers thought about a new brand of children's breakfast cereal, we would go to all households with children. For a sample, we would select, based on clearly defined criteria, a subset of these households from which it would be valid to draw inferences about the whole population.

Sampling offers major benefits over taking a census. It saves time and money as fewer interviews are carried out, and thus most market research studies use sampling. Before we discuss how a sample is selected, we must define some basic concepts.

Sampling Definitions

Element   An element is the unit about which information is required – an individual person, family, company, etc.

Population   A population, or universe, is the aggregate of all the elements defined prior to the selection of the sample.

Sampling unit   A sampling unit is the element or elements available for selection at some stage of the sampling process.

Sampling frame   A sampling frame is a list of all sampling units available for selection at a stage of the sampling process. Telephone directories, the electoral register and mailing lists are commonly used sample frames.

Study population   A study population is the aggregate of elements from which the sample is actually selected. This is likely to differ from the population defined at the start of the survey as some members of the original population may be omitted through incomplete sampling frames, e.g. people who have no telephone or have an ex-directory number (for the telephone directory as a sampling frame), or people who have recently moved house (for the electoral register as a sampling frame).

A couple of examples will illustrate the use of these terms:

1. The population for a consumer survey on a new brand of coffee, where we are mailing questionnaires to a random selection of respondents in Birmingham, where the coffee is being test-marketed, could be defined by:

    Element: coffee drinker age 18+
    Sampling units: coffee drinkers age 18+
    Area: Birmingham
    Time: 1–14 October 1997

    A possible sampling frame for this survey would be the electoral register.
    Here we can see that the element and the sampling unit are the same, as the sample is selected directly from the population (a single stage sample).

2. In a survey of how young people spend their leisure time, we may want to interview young people age 18–25 in households in towns with a population of under 100,000. Here the element would be 'adult age 18–25'. But we are required to go through three stages of sampling in order to find our respondents – first, to select appropriate towns, then, to select appropriate households, and finally, to select adults age 18–25. Thus the primary sampling unit would be towns with population under 100,000, the secondary sampling unit would be households, and the tertiary, and also final, sampling unit would be adults age 18–25. Similarly, the first sample frame would be a list of towns with population under 100,000, the second sample frame would be a list of households within these towns, and the third would be a list of adults age 18–25 within these households.

Sampling Procedures

We can now describe the general procedure for selecting a sample (see Figure 2.2).

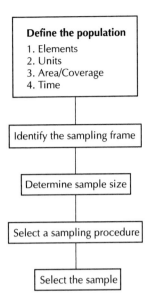

Figure 2.2   Selecting a sample

We continue with a discussion of specific sampling methods. First we must make a basic distinction between probability and non-probability samples. In probability sampling, sampling is done by mathematical decision rules so that each element of the population has a known chance of being chosen for the sample. This allows calculation of the sampling error – the likely extent to which results for the sample differ from those for the population as a whole. In non-probability sampling, the selection of sample elements is based partly on the judgement of the researcher or interviewer. There is thus no known chance of selection and no straightforward means of calculating sampling error. Table 2.3 categorises sampling procedures as probability or non-probability methods.

Table 2.3   Classification of sampling procedures

Non-probability procedures	Probability procedures
1. Convenience sample	1. Simple random sample
2. Judgement sample	2. Stratified random sample
3. Quota sample	3. Cluster sample
	(a) Systematic sample
	(b) Area sample

Non-probability Sampling Procedures

Convenience Sample

A convenience sample is selected on the basis of the convenience of the researcher. Examples would be calls for volunteers for product testing or a university researcher using students as research subjects. Sample elements are either self-selected or selected because they are easily available, and so it may be unclear what actual population the sample is drawn from, or how representative the sample is of the population. Thus sampling error cannot be measured and we cannot make any conclusive statements about results. The convenience sample should therefore most often be used at an exploratory stage of research as a basis for hypothesis generation.

Judgement Sample

A judgement (or purposive) sample is selected on the basis of expert judgement as to what particular sampling units would be most useful to research. For instance, in selecting stores in an area to test a new product, experts might select the 'best' for the purpose on criteria such as typical shopper profile or turnover of similar products. Again, sampling error is unmeasurable and conclusive statements cannot be made, but the method will give better results than convenience sampling as long as the expert judgement is valid.

Quota Sample

A quota sample seeks to replicate in the sample the distribution of the population, on the basis of defined control characteristics such as age, gender, social class, income, etc. For instance, if we know that 15% of the population are aged between 35 and 44, and our total sample is to be 1000, then 150 people aged between 35 and 44 should be interviewed. This can get much more complicated if we have several control characteristics and may cause problems for interviewers trying to find the last few respondents in their quota. In a quota sample we must attempt to include the most salient control characteristics related to the subject of interest and ensure that the proportions for each category are correct and up to date, which is not always easy. The selection of specific sample elements to fit the quota is left to the interviewer – this may introduce an unknown bias and thus it is again impossible to measure sampling error. However, quota samples are used in much consumer research, and with carefully selected control criteria are likely to produce the best results of non-probability methods. But they are likely to be less valid than probability sampling methods, which we shall now consider.

Probability Sampling Methods

Simple Random Sampling

The most simple method of probability sampling is known as *simple random sampling*. Here, the selection of sample elements is made by numbering each element in the population, then generating a list of random numbers and picking the elements corresponding to these numbers, up to the total number required for the sample. This means that each element in the population has an equal chance of being selected, and also, for a sample size of n, each possible combination of n elements has an equal chance of being selected. We shall now discuss the types of statistics that can be calculated from a simple random sample. First, we need to explain the notations and definitions used in probability sampling.

Conventional Symbols

Table 2.4 shows the symbols used in sampling. Generally, Greek letters are used for population parameters and English letters for sample statistics.

Dichotomous variable
A dichotomous or binomial variable may take only one of two values, for instance 'yes' or 'no', 'male' or 'female'.

Discrete variable
A discrete variable can take only a finite or a countable number of values. Thus, the number of students in a class, the marks they obtain in an examination and the price of a carpet are discrete variables.

Continuous variable
A continuous variable may take any value within an appropriate range, although it will be measured only to a suitable level of accuracy. Height and weight are continuous variables.

Table 2.4   Symbols used in sampling

		Population symbol	Sample symbol
Discrete and continuous measures	Size of population or sample	N	n
	Mean (or average)	μ	$\bar{x}$
	Variance	σ^2	s^2
Dichotomous measures	Proportion answering 'yes'	π	p
	Proportion answering 'no'	$(1 - \pi)$	$(1 - p)$ or q
	Variance of proportion	σ^2	s^2

Parameter

A parameter describes some measure of the defined population, for instance the average mark in an examination, obtained by adding all the marks and dividing by the number of people sitting the exam.

Statistic

A statistic describes some measure of the selected sample, and is used to estimate the population parameter. Thus, if in the above example a simple random sample of n exam papers was selected, the average mark obtained by adding these n marks and dividing by n would be a statistic.

Sampling fraction

The sampling fraction is the size of the sample divided by the size of the population.

Mean

The mean or average of a sample is the sum of the sample values divided by the sample size.

Degrees of freedom

The number of degrees of freedom of a sample indicates the number of values that are free to vary in a random sample of given size. This can also be expressed as 'sample size less number of statistics calculated'. If, for example, we have calculated the mean of a sample of n observations, only $n-1$ of those values would be free to vary – once we had set values for $n-1$ sample observations, only one possible value for the last observation would give the correct mean.

Variance

The variance is the sum of squared deviations about the mean divided by the available degrees of freedom. Thus the population variance is given by the formula

$$\sigma^2 = \frac{\sum_{i=1}^{N}(X_i - \mu)^2}{N}$$

and the sample variance by the formula

$$s^2 = \frac{\sum_{i=1}^{n}(x_i - \bar{x})^2}{n - 1}$$

Standard deviation

The standard deviation is the square root of the variance.

Sampling error

Statistics used to estimate population parameters are subject to sampling error – the likely difference between the sample statistic and the true parameter due to the fact that a sample rather than a census has been taken.

Example

An example will serve to illustrate the various concepts discussed. Table 2.5 shows the ages of the 50 students in an undergraduate statistics course.

The mean of this population is 22.22, the variance 33.41, and the standard deviation 5.78. These values can be calculated using the formulae given. Any good spreadsheet program or mathematical calculator should have a function to calculate these parameters and also sample statistics, directly. Now, let us select 10 random numbers in order to take a simple random sample. Say our numbers are 1, 9, 12, 13, 14, 25, 29, 31, 41, 47. This is a sample of 10 from 50 so our sampling fraction is 10/50 = 0.2. The ages of these students are 20, 20, 19, 19, 20, 18, 19, 21, 26, 37. The sample mean is 21.9, sample variance is 32.99, and standard deviation 5.74.

Table 2.5

Student number	Age	Student number	Age
1	20	26	19
2	19	27	19
3	19	28	20
4	18	29	19
5	20	30	19
6	18	31	21
7	21	32	20
8	19	33	23
9	20	34	22
10	18	35	18
11	22	36	18
12	19	37	20
13	19	38	19
14	20	39	19
15	22	40	20
16	21	41	26
17	18	42	35
18	18	43	42
19	21	44	27
20	20	45	30
21	20	46	32
22	22	47	37
23	21	48	27
24	18	49	40
25	18	50	28

Confidence Intervals

The mean of a simple random sample provides a good estimator of the mean of the whole population, but it is of course highly unlikely that it will be exactly equal to it due to sampling error. Thus we use an interval estimation of the population mean, i.e. the population mean lies in the interval 'sample mean plus or minus a sampling error', with a given probability. This is known as a *confidence interval*, and the probability that the true population mean lies within this interval is the level of confidence. We express confidence intervals as sample mean plus or minus a specified number of standard errors, where standard error $s_x = \frac{s}{\sqrt{n}}$. The table of areas under the normal curve will tell us the number of standard errors for different levels of confidence.

It is common to use a 95% confidence level whose confidence interval is sample mean plus or minus 1.96 standard errors. Thus for our example, the 95% confidence interval would be

$$21.9 \pm (1.96 \times \frac{5.74}{\sqrt{10}}) = 21.9 \pm 3.56 = 18.34 \text{ to } 25.46$$

This means that if we took 100 independent random samples of size 10 and calculated the 95% confidence level for each, we could expect the true population mean to lie within that confidence interval in 95 out of the 100 samples. We can also talk about the precision of our estimate of the mean at a 95% confidence level, precision being the width of the confidence interval. (In this example, you will see that the confidence interval is rather large – we will discuss ways of reducing it when we look at more complex sampling methods.)

Thus it is possible with simple random sampling to measure our sampling error and state clearly how accurate our statistics are, something that was impossible with the non-probability sampling methods discussed earlier. Although confidence intervals are sometimes quoted for results from non-probability samples, such calculation implicitly assumes that the sampling procedure yielded a simple random sample – an assumption likely to be invalid and certainly untestable.

Effect of Sample Size on Precision

A sampling error occurs when the mean $\bar{x}$ of any individual sample is used as an estimate of the population mean μ. For this reason we talk about the *standard error* rather than the standard deviation of the sample mean. The formula for the standard error of the sample mean is

$$s_{\bar{x}} = \frac{s}{\sqrt{n}} = \frac{\sqrt{\sum_{i=1}^{n}(x_i - \bar{x})^2/n - 1}}{\sqrt{n}}$$

We note that the standard deviation varies inversely as the square root of the sample size and so will decrease as the sample size increases, thus also lessening the width of the confidence interval around the mean and increasing the accuracy of our estimate. Increasing sample size thus improves our estimation of the population mean, although we must remember this is not a proportional relationship – estimation improves more as we go from small samples to large ones, than if we increase an already large sample. Marketers may often need to make a decision on the point at which the benefits of better estimation are outweighed by the costs of using a larger sample.

Effect of Population Size

So far we have not discussed the size of the total population. For most marketing research the total population of interest will be very large and thus we need not be concerned about corrections for population size. However, for finite populations our previous formula for the standard error of the sampling distribution of the mean needs to be corrected by the finite correction factor $\frac{N-n}{N-1}$, so that our formulae become

$$\sigma_{\bar{x}} = \frac{\sigma_x}{\sqrt{n}}\sqrt{\frac{N-n}{N-1}} \text{ and } s_{\bar{x}} = \frac{s_x}{\sqrt{n}}\sqrt{\frac{N-n}{N-1}}$$

For large values of N relative to n, the finite correction factor is approximately equal to 1. Thus the correction can be ignored as long as the sampling fraction is relatively small – a frequently used rule of thumb in marketing applications is to use a correction factor only if the sample includes more than 5% of the population. If we ignore the correction factor when we should have used it, we overstate the standard error and thus increase the size of our confidence interval.

Non-sampling Errors

We must remember that calculation of confidence intervals measures only sampling error. Other possible sources of error have been discussed earlier in the data collection section of this chapter. If such non-sampling errors occur in probability sampling procedures, an unknown element of bias is introduced and we cannot state our results with known accuracy. It is thus critical to control non-sampling errors.

Sample Size

We have seen that in simple random sampling we can calculate the confidence level of our estimate of the mean using the equation $\bar{x} \pm 1.96 \frac{s}{\sqrt{n}}$ at the 95% confidence level and the precision of the estimate by using part of this equation:

$$\text{Precision} = \pm 1.96 \frac{s}{\sqrt{n}}.$$

Now suppose we want to reach a given level of precision. If we have a value for s, we can solve this equation for the required sample size n. For instance, suppose that we wish to obtain an estimate, at the 95% confidence level, of the mean age, plus or minus 1 year, of a target segment for a new children's breakfast cereal. Assume we have estimated, from previous research, that the value for s is likely to be around 4. (For another approach when previous research is unavailable, see problem 'Woodsville Bus Company' at the end of this chapter). The required sample size can then be obtained by substituting in the equation:

$$\text{Precision} = \pm 1.96 s / \sqrt{n}$$

$$1 = 1.96 \times 4 / \sqrt{n}$$

$$\sqrt{n} = 7.84$$

thus $n = 61.4656$, i.e. a sample size of 62 will be required.

In this example we have expressed precision in the relevant units, years. We call this *absolute precision*. Precision may also be expressed as a percentage of the mean value calculated – here precision would vary according to the size of the mean and is called *relative precision*. Using $.b$ to denote the precision percentage expressed as a decimal, we can write our equation for a 95% confidence level as

$$.b\bar{x} = \pm 1.96 \frac{s}{\sqrt{n}}$$

This can be rearranged to make

$$.b\sqrt{n} = 1.96 \frac{s}{\bar{x}}$$

with $.b$ to denote the precision percentage expressed as a decimal. we can write our equation for a 95% confidence level as

$$.b\bar{x} = \pm 1.96 \frac{s}{\sqrt{n}}$$

This can be rearranged to make

$$.b\sqrt{n} = 1.96 \frac{s}{\bar{x}}$$

This rearrangement demonstrates that we do not need to know both mean $\bar{x}$ and standard deviation s, but only the ratio of the standard deviation to the mean, $\frac{s}{\bar{x}}$. This ratio is known as the coefficient of variation.

Another ratio often used in practice is the relative allowable error, defined as 0.5(precision)/mean. For instance, if a researcher will accept an error of 1 year either way on a mean age of 10 years, the precision will be ± 1 year = 2 years, and the relative allowable error is $1/10 = 0.1$.

An instrument called a nomograph has been developed so that researchers do not have to solve the equation whenever they wish to find an optimal sample size. Using coefficient of variation and relative allowable error, the optimal sample size for a specific confidence level can be simply read off a graph. (See Figure 2.3)

Difficulties with Calculation of Optimal Sample Size

We see above that to calculate required sample size we need a value of s for absolute precision and a value of $\frac{s}{\bar{x}}$ for relative precision. Although it is unlikely that we will be able to cite an exact value for s, researchers experienced in the problem area are likely to be able to obtain an approximate value for optimal sample size for required precision of each variable. To assure required precision for all variables we would have to select the largest of all these optimal sample sizes.

Optimal Sample Size for a Proportion

Our previous formulae have dealt with the measurement of optimal sample size for a continuous or discrete variable. Now let us look at the corresponding calculations for a dichotomous variable.

Suppose we want to find out what proportion of the population in a certain area have milk delivered to their door. We believe it to be slightly over half the population, so we assume $p = 0.6$, and we want 0.05 as the absolute precision at a 95% confidence level. Then our formula is

$$\text{Precision} = 1.96\sqrt{\frac{p(1-p)}{n}}$$

$$0.05 = 1.96\sqrt{\frac{(0.6)(0.4)}{n}} \quad \text{so} \quad \sqrt{\frac{0.24}{n}} = \frac{(0.05)}{1.96} \quad \text{and} \quad n = 369$$

giving a required sample size of 369.

In this case we need to know the overall proportion p in order to determine the required sample size. However, as in this example, p is likely to be the value we are trying to obtain by carrying out the study. As in the discrete or continuous variable case, experience in the problem area and consideration of the measurement scales used can give us reasonable estimates of p. A p of 0.5, however, will give us the

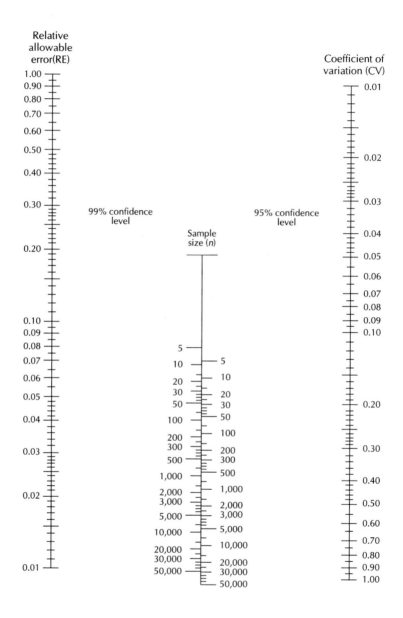

Figure 2.3 Nomograph for determining sample size for interval estimates of the mean using traditional methods of inference. (*Source: Nomograms for Marketing Research*, Audits and Surveys Inc., published in Tull and Hawkins (1984))

highest possible sample size to obtain a given level of precision and can be used as a benchmark.

We can see then that the formula for calculation of required sample size relies in most studies on an initial estimate of the variables of interest and thus functions as a guide to the researcher in determining optimal sample size rather than a hard and fast rule. A researcher can assume different possible values of $\bar{x}$, s, p, etc. and see what sample sizes are required.

There are several other factors which will affect the determination of sample size, such as the study objectives, cost, and time. We shall briefly look at these now.

Study objectives

Sample size is affected by the use to which the information is to be put. If precise informational inputs are not required, a small sample may be adequate – for instance, a company doing a survey to determine the level of interest in a new magazine might be happy to estimate to within 10 or 15%. However, in a poll of voting intentions, an estimate which was only 1 or 2% out could make the difference between correct and incorrect prediction of the result, so a much larger sample would be required.

Cost

Financial constraints may limit the number of interviews or mailings it is possible to carry out and thus force the sample size downwards. Conversely, if the study is well-financed, researchers must guard against choosing a larger than necessary sample size just because it can be afforded.

Time

The larger the sample, the longer the study will take. But a long survey time may mean that final results are less valid or less useful. Sample size may have to be limited so that results are produced in appropriate time.

Stratified Sampling

We now turn to more complex types of probability sampling, which are more frequently used in practice than simple random sampling. First we consider stratified sampling, the advantage of which is that it may result in a decrease in the standard error of an estimate for a given sample size.

Sample selection

The first step in sample selection is to divide the population into mutually exclusive and collectively exhaustive subgroups or strata – that is, each sampling unit will belong to one and only one stratum. Suitable strata could be chosen on the basis of gender, age (with mutually exclusive age groups covering the whole span of ages in the population) or some other suitable variable. Having subdivided the population, an independent random sample is selected from each stratum.

Stratified sampling will only be of use in reducing the standard error of an estimate of a variable if the designated strata are more homogeneous on the variable of interest than the population as a whole. For instance, let us return to our student population, and imagine we are carrying out a survey on student spending. This class in fact contains several part-time students, those numbered 41–50, who are considerably older than the rest of the class, and it would be reasonable to suppose that this group might have different spending patterns to younger students. Thus for this survey we could stratify the population into two groups, full-time and part-time students. These two strata are more homogeneous than the whole population on the variable of age, which we believe will affect the variables of interest in the survey.

Proportionate stratified sampling
If we draw samples from each stratum in proportion to the relative sizes of each stratum in the whole population, this is known as proportionate stratified sampling. Let us try this with the student sample. There are 40 full-time and 10 part-time students, so a proportionate stratified sample of 10 will include 8 full-time students and 2 part-time students. Conveniently, the sample previously selected is suitable. We shall call full-time students Stratum 1 and part-time students Stratum 2. Table 2.6 gives comparative results for each stratum.

The overall sample mean is now a weighted average of the within-strata means, with the weight for each stratum being the ratio of the population size of the stratum to the overall population size, i.e.

$$\bar{x} = \sum_{i=1}^{A} \left(\frac{N_i}{N}\right) \bar{x}_i$$

where N_i is the population size within stratum i, $\bar{x}_i$ is the mean of stratum i, and A is number of strata.

In our example this works out to 21.9, that is, exactly the same as the mean calculated without stratification. To calculate the standard error of this mean, we need to use the formula

Table 2.6

	Mean	Variance	Standard deviation
Without stratification	21.9	32.9	5.74
Stratum 1	19.5	0.86	0.93
Stratum 2	31.5	60.5	7.78

$$S_{\bar{x}} = \sum_{j=1}^{A} \frac{(W_j)s_{st.j}}{\sqrt{n_{st.j}}}$$

where A is number of strata
w_j is the weight for each stratum
$s_{st.j}$ is the standard error within stratum j
and $n_{st.j}$ is the size of sample from stratum j.

For our example this works out as

$$\frac{(0.8)(0.93)}{\sqrt{8}} + \frac{(0.2)(7.78)}{\sqrt{2}}$$

giving the final answer of 1.36.

Using the unstratified sample, the standard error of the mean was 5.74. The use of a stratified sample has reduced this to 1.36.

Confidence interval
The 95% confidence interval for the stratified sample is $21.9 \pm \frac{(1.96 \times 1.36)}{\sqrt{10}}$ $= 21.9 \pm 0.84 = 21.06$ to 22.74. The unstratified 95% confidence interval was 18.34 to 25.46. The absolute precision has thus been reduced from ± 3.56 to ± 0.84. Thus a stratified sampling procedure is much more efficient than an unstratified one. The reason for this is that we are only using within-stratum variability in calculating the overall standard error, and across-strata variability becomes irrelevant. By using stratified sampling we can increase the precision of our estimates without increasing sample size. Alternatively, we could use a smaller sample than that used in unstratified sampling to obtain the same precision.

Disproportionate stratified sampling
It is also possible to allocate the overall sample size to strata on a basis disproportionate with stratum sizes. The reason for this would be to allow for differences in variability of the variable of interest between strata (e.g. if age were the variable of interest, some strata may have a very small spread of ages and some may have much greater dispersion of ages.) For a fixed sample size, the overall standard error can be reduced by sampling more heavily in strata with higher variability. As an extreme case, suppose we had a stratum in our student population where the ages of all the students were 19. This stratum has no variability and thus a sample of 1 is sufficient to measure its mean accurately. Conversely, a stratum with high variability will require a larger sample size to produce an efficient estimate of the mean (because in order to calculate the standard error within a stratum we divide the within-stratum standard deviation by the square root of the stratum sample size).

The optimal allocation of a fixed sample size among strata is the one giving the least standard error for the overall estimate. Obviously, then, we need to know something about the variability in strata before we select the sample. In the case of retail store audits, for example, it has been found that large stores show more variability in sales than small stores, and thus they tend to be sampled at a disproportionately higher level.The formulae used to combine within-strata statistics to provide estimates for the whole sample are exactly the same as for proportionate stratified sampling.

Cluster sampling
So far, we have discussed probability sampling methods where each element for the sample is selected individually. In cluster sampling, a cluster of elements is selected at one time. Thus, for this method, the population must be divided into mutually exclusive and collectively exhaustive groups from which a random sample of groups are selected. Let us return to our student population and divide them into 10 groups of 5 as shown in Table 2.7.

There are two ways in which we can select a cluster sample of size 10. For the simpler way, one-stage cluster sampling, we would randomly select two of the above groups and use all the elements in each. For two-stage cluster sampling, we select groups and then select a random sample of elements from within the chosen groups, for instance our random selection of groups could be 1, 3, 4, 7, 9, after which we would randomly select two elements from each group.

The big difference between cluster sampling and simple random sampling is that in cluster sampling not all combinations of elements in the sample are equally likely. In fact, most combinations are impossible. Thus it is crucial to the success of cluster sampling that the groups are as close as possible in heterogeneity on the variable of interest to the heterogeneity of the whole population. In our example above, this criterion is clearly not satisfied as we know that groups 9 and 10 contain

Table 2.7

Group	Student numbers
1	1 2 3 4 5
2	6 7 8 9 10
3	11 12 13 14 15
4	16 17 18 19 20
5	21 22 23 24 25
6	26 27 28 29 30
7	31 32 33 34 35
8	36 37 38 39 40
9	41 42 43 44 45
10	46 47 48 49 50

part-time students who are older than the others. If group 9 or 10 (or both) are selected in our cluster sample, the sample mean will be too high. If neither group is selected, it will be too low. Either way, bias has occurred due to the use of cluster sampling.

Ideally, groups would be exactly as heterogeneous as the population – this ideal is never reached in practice, but the closer it can be approached, the less bias there will be in our estimates. Thus the criterion for forming groups for cluster sampling is exactly the opposite of that used in forming strata for stratified sampling.

The size of the standard error generated from a cluster sample, compared with that generated from a simple random sample depends on the relative heterogeneity of the groups and the population. If the groups are exactly as heterogeneous as the population, both methods will give the same standard error. If the groups are less heterogeneous than the population, cluster sampling will give a greater standard error than that obtained by simple random sampling. This comparison of standard errors generated by different sampling procedures is known as assessing the statistical efficiency of the procedures.

If, in practice, groups are always less heterogeneous than the population, so that cluster sampling is less statistically efficient than simple random sampling, why is cluster sampling used? Simply because cluster sampling procedures are often much cheaper than other procedures for a given sample size. For instance, a store audit which required interviewers to visit each sample store would be much cheaper if the selected stores were located in a few specific geographical areas rather than a random sample being picked which entailed interviewers travelling to every corner of the country. The combination of statistical efficiency with cost is known as overall or total efficiency. Cluster sampling is often the most overall efficient method in terms of standard error per pound spent.

We now go on to discuss briefly various methods of cluster sampling.

Systematic sampling   In systematic sampling, every kth element in the sampling frame is selected, starting from a random numbered element between 1 and k. If we wanted to select a sample of 10 from our student population, then $k = 50/10 = 5$. This ratio, number in population divided by required sample size, is known as the sampling interval. So first we would generate a random number between 1 and 5, say 4. Then the sample is obtained by starting with the fourth element and taking every fifth element thereafter, so our sample of 10 would be the elements 4, 9, 14, 19, 24, 29, 34, 39, 44, 49. Given a starting random number and sample size, sample selection is automatic, so the selected elements form a cluster sample. As we use all the elements in the cluster, systematic sampling is defined as a one-stage cluster sampling procedure. There are only k possible samples that can be selected, e.g. in our example only 5 samples of 10. If the population is large relative to the sample size, the sampling interval, and thus the number of possible samples, will increase. It can be shown that the mean of the sampling distribution of means generated by taking repeated systematic samples equals the population mean. Thus the mean from a systematic sample is an unbiased estimator of the population mean, so confidence intervals may be calculated as with simple random sampling. If we are sampling from a truly random sampling frame, the results from a systematic sample are likely to be almost identical to those from a simple random sample.

Systematic sampling is often used in practice because it is easier and cheaper to select a sample systematically than by simple random sampling, duplication of elements cannot occur and it is not always necessary to have a complete sample frame – for instance, an interviewer could select every tenth house without a full listing of houses. Systematic sampling may also be used to select elements within strata in stratified sampling.

Area sampling Area sampling was developed as a solution to the problems of incomplete and inaccurate sample frames. It means that geographic areas, or pieces of land, are selected for the sample, and then a further selection is made from the people who live in these areas. Area sampling usually involves more than one stage. Here is an example of a multistage area sample (4 stages):

Stage 1 – the UK is divided into counties and a sample of counties is chosen by one of the probability methods.

Stage 2 – the cities, towns and rural areas in the chosen counties are listed, thus stratifying each county into three strata. A probability sample is again selected within each stratum.

Stage 3 – Each location selected at Stage 2 is further subdivided, e.g. cities into districts, etc. All these are listed and another probability sample chosen.

Stage 4 – All households in the areas chosen at Stage 3 are listed and a final probability sample taken from these to decide on the final sample.

Multistage area sampling is much less statistically efficient than simple random sampling, because of the accumulation of standard errors (one for each stage of the sample). The formulae for calculation of standard error in a multistage area sample are too complex for discussion in this book. In practice, the final sample of a multistage area sample is often treated as if it had been directly selected from the population, e.g. in the case above the selected households would be treated as having been selected from a listing of all UK households. Thus the formulae for simple random sampling and stratified sampling are used, leading to an understatement of standard error.

The highest statistical efficiency when using multistage area sampling is achieved by choosing a large number of clusters (areas) and a small number of elements within each cluster. This is because elements within clusters (e.g. the people living in a specific district of the city) tend to be more homogeneous than the population as a whole, so even a small sample may yield a reasonably small sampling error. Clusters tend to be more heterogeneous (e.g. people living in different city districts may differ greatly in terms of age, income, beliefs, etc.), so a large number of clusters is necessary to reduce the sampling error.

However, more clusters mean more lists of elements to be made and higher interviewer travel costs. Thus consideration of overall efficiency may mean reducing the number of clusters and increasing the number of elements selected from each. Researchers must make a trade-off between statistical efficiency and cost, based on research objectives and budget, and the amount of acceptable error.

Probability area sampling   Often in area sampling, elements do not all have the same probability of being selected. There may be several reasons for this, some intentional and others not. For instance, a researcher wanting to do detailed analysis of some particular subgroup may deliberately oversample that subgroup in order to have a large enough sample for meaningful analysis. Or disproportionate stratified sampling may be done at some stage of area sampling in order to reduce sampling error. It could be found also that the cluster sizes used were incorrect (due to new building for example) or that a sample yields a different proportion of a particular subgroup to that found in the whole population. In such case, weighting of samples will be necessary to achieve unbiased estimates for the whole sample. Most good computer statistical analysis packages have a facility for doing this.

Finally, Table 2.8 shows a comparison of the various sampling methods we have considered on the basis of four criteria which are likely to be of prime importance to a researcher.

CONCLUSION

A market researcher needs to be able to select the data collection technique which is most likely to elicit the necessary information reliably, in the required time and within the available budget. This chapter has described and compared a wide range of data collection and sampling methods with examples of the most widely used probability sampling techniques. Appendix A of this book includes a summary of the formulae required for simple random sampling. Readers wanting further information or guidance on the choice or use of particular methods are referred to the marketing research texts listed at the end of this chapter. Also, Triola and Franklin's book includes worked examples for various types of samples from different population distributions.

Table 2.8 Summary of Sampling Methods

Considerations	Non-probability samples			Probability samples				
	Convenience	Judgement	Quota	Simple random	Stratified	Systematic	Area
1. Is there a sampling error?	No	No	No	Yes	Yes	Yes	Yes
2. Statistical efficiency	Cannot measure	Cannot measure	Cannot measure	Base level for comparison	High if stratification variables well chosen	Rather low	Low
3. Population list required?	No	No	No	Yes	Yes	Not always necessary	Only for selected clusters
4. Cost	Very low	Low	Medium	High	High	Medium	Medium to high

REFERENCES AND FURTHER READING

Aaker, D., Kumar, V. and Day, G. (1995) *Marketing Research*, 5th edition, New York: John Wiley and Sons.

Bagozzi, R.P. (1994) *Principles of Marketing Research*, Cambridge (Mass.): Basil Blackwell Ltd.

Churchill, G.A. (1994) *Marketing Research: Methodological Foundations*, 6th edition, London: The Dryden Press.

Green, P., Tull, D. and Albaum, G. (1988) *Research for Marketing Decisions*, 5th edition, Englewood Cliffs: Prentice-Hall.

Oxenfeldt, A.R. (1961) *Pricing for Marketing Executives*, Wadsworth.

Pessemier, E.A. (1960) 'An Experimental Model for Estimating Demand', *Journal of Business*, **33**, October.

Tagg, Stephen K. (1997) 'World Wide Web Surveys', *Academy of Marketing Conference Proceedings*, The Manchester Metropolitan University, pp.1663–8.

Triola, M.F. and Franklin, L.A. (1994) *Business Statistics*, Reading (Mass.) Addison Wesley.

Tull, D.S. and Hawkins, D.I. (1984) *Marketing Research: Measurement and Method*, 3rd edition, New York: Macmillan.

PROBLEM: DETERMINING SAMPLE SIZE

(a) The Director of Woodsville Bus Company wants to determine how often residents of Woodsville use the city's buses in one month. He wants to know how many people he should survey in order to achieve a 95% confidence interval with a margin of error of plus/minus 2 times per month. Unfortunately, there is no previous data available, so he cannot estimate the standard deviation of the sample or of the population. His assistant advises him that a good rule of thumb in this situation would be to assume that the range of the data covered approximately 4 standard deviations. He believes that no one uses the buses more than 80 times a month, and that therefore the range of the data would be from 0 to 80. What size of sample will be required?

(b) Spending constraints require the Director to limit his sample size to 200. A random sample survey of 200 residents is carried out and it is found that the mean number of times for using the buses is 21.3 with a standard deviation of 18.1. Using these results, find out the 95% confidence interval for the true mean.

PROBLEM: PROPORTIONATE STRATIFIED SAMPLE

Introductory Comments

For proportionate stratified sampling, the sample size of each stratum (n_i) is given by the proportion of the population that falls into that stratum (N_i/N). The formula for the standard deviation of the estimate of the mean can be written as:

$$s_{\bar{x}} = \sqrt{\sum \left(\frac{N_i}{N}\right)^2 \frac{s_i^2}{n_i}}$$

and since $n_i = \dfrac{N_i}{N}.n$

$$s_{\bar{x}} = \sqrt{\frac{\sum w_i s_i^2}{n}}$$

where: N_i = size of ith stratum
n_i = sample size in the ith stratum
N = size of the total target population
n = total sample size
w_i = weight of the estimate of the ith stratum
s_i = standard deviation in the ith stratum
$\bar{x}_i$ = mean in the ith stratum

Problem

Consider the situation in Table 2.9 where beer consumers were divided into four segments (strata) on the basis of demographics. A proportionate sample would be drawn with sample size in each stratum proportional to the size of the sample:

$$n_i = \frac{N_i}{N} \cdot n$$

Table 2.9 An example of proportionate stratified sampling

Stratum	Size of stratum	Average beer consumption	Standard deviation of beer consumption
1	8,000	20	4
2	6,000	10	4
3	4,000	15	5
4	2,000	6	2

Assuming different samples are drawn from each of k strata, the mean and standard deviation of a variable in the entire target population can then be estimated as follows:

$$\bar{x} = \sum_{i=1}^{k} w_i x_i$$

Where: k = number of strata

$$s_{\bar{x}} = \sqrt{\sum_{i=1}^{k} w_i^2 s_{\bar{x}}^2} = \sqrt{\sum_{i=1}^{k} w_i^2 \frac{s_i^2}{n_i}}$$

Questions

1. Calculate a proportionate sample of size 200 from the four strata.

2. Now assume a proportionate sample of 200 were drawn from the target population and the results in the table above were obtained.
    Estimate the overall average beer consumption.

3. Calculate the standard deviation.

3
Further statistical techniques

This chapter is divided into four main sections which look at parametric tests, non-parametric tests, equation modelling and finally factor analysis and cluster analysis.

Contents

Parametric tests
Non-parametric tests.
Equation modelling techniques
Other frequently used techniques.

Objectives

After reading this chapter you should:

- Know the difference between parametric and non-parametric statistical tests.
- Understand when to use all the statistical tests described in this chapter.
- Understand how to use all the statistical tests described in this chapter.
- Be able to undertake statistical tests of significance for the tests described in this chapter.
- Understand when to use equation modelling techniques such as LISREL and Logit/Probit models.

INTRODUCTION

This chapter describes a number of the more commonly used statistical tests and analysis. It is divided into four major parts, namely parametric tests, non-parametric tests, equation modelling methods and, finally, other techniques. A decision flow chart is used as an aid to the correct choice of the appropriate test and examples are used to illustrate how to use many of the statistical tests described. As is clearly explained, to correctly use these tests a clear understanding of the assumptions underlying the tests, as well as the type of measurement used, is required. There are two basic families of statistical techniques: *parametric statistics* which are based on data which is measured on an interval or ratio scale (for these tests normality is sometimes assumed). Variables which are measured on ordinal or nominal scales use *non-parametric statistics* (these tests are distribution free).

Choice of Statistical Test

The most appropriate statistical test to use can be determined by looking at the decision flow chart (Figure 3.1). Go to START and take any of the six branches (measures of association, test of randomness, models of relationship or tests of differences). The list of tests given here is not exhaustive and should be viewed only as a list of the most commonly used statistical tests. An excellent source of other statistical techniques is Kanji (1995).

Use of the Statistical Decision Flow Chart

In the flow chart (Figure 3.1), the question 'Are the samples related or independent?' is posed. The following text explains the difference between these two terms.

> Related samples use paired or matched observations for two samples X_i and Y_i which are dependent row by row. Related samples share relevant or common traits, for example the same people's view before and after an advertising campaign. Independent samples are not paired or matched observations for each sample X_i and Y_j. An example of independent samples would be people's views on an advertising campaign in London as against people's views on the same advertising campaign in Cardiff.

For each statistical test described in this chapter the assumptions upon which the test is based are clearly stated, the original reference for that test given and an example of using that test shown.

PARAMETRIC TESTS

Student *t* Test

The student *t* distribution was first reported by Gosset (1908) under the pseudonym of 'Student' which is why the distribution is often referred to as student's *t* distribution. Its statistical properties are listed below:

- It has a mean of zero.
- It is symmetrical about its mean.
- It generally has a variance greater than one, however the variance approaches one as the sample size increases.

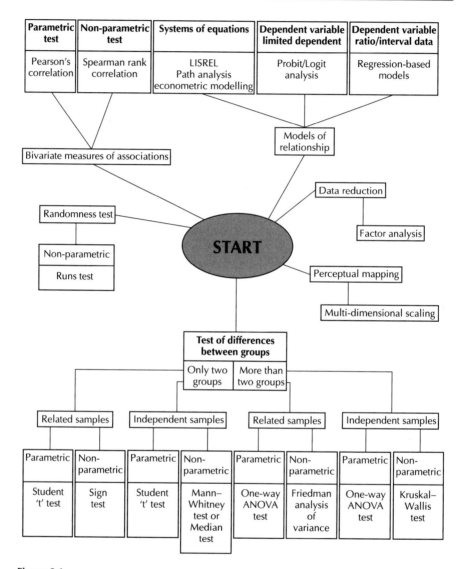

Figure 3.1

- The value t can take on values between plus and minus infinity.
- The t distribution is really a family of distributions, which varies according to n.
- In general the t distribution is less peaked and has higher tails than the normal distribution.
- The t distribution approaches the normal distribution as n increases.

One area where the student t test is often used is to see whether two samples differ with respect to their means. This test is used when n is smaller than 30 and the population variance is unknown. The assumptions of the test are that each sample is drawn from independent random samples and the underlying distribution of each population is normal. The formula for this test is as follows:

n_1 = number of observations in sample 1 s_1^2 = standard deviation of sample 1.
n_2 = number of observations in sample 2 s_2^2 = standard deviation of sample 2.

The pooled variance is:

$$s_p^2 = \frac{(n_1 - 1)s_1^2 + (n_2 - 1)s_2^2}{n_1 + n_2 - 2}$$

$$t = \frac{(\bar{x}_1 - \bar{x}_2) - 0}{\sqrt{\left(\frac{s_p^2}{n_1} + \frac{s_p^2}{n_2}\right)}}$$

which is distributed as student's t with n_1+n_2-2 degrees of freedom.

Example

The following data were based on a random sample of the time spent by families watching television per week in two regions of the UK. The marketing manager of a large company is interested to know whether the time spent watching television by families in one region is different to the other region.

	Region A	Region B
n	12	10
Mean	16.21 hours	14.99 hours
Variance (s^2)	8.53	7.82

$H_0 : \mu_a = \mu_b$	$H_1 : \mu_a \neq \mu_b$

The hypothesis to be tested is

$$s_p^2 = \frac{(12 - 1)^*8.53 + (10 - 1)^*7.82}{12 + 10 - 2}$$

$$= \frac{93.83 + 70.38}{20}$$

$$= 8.21$$

$$t = \frac{16.21 - 14.99}{\sqrt{0.6842 + 0.8210)}}$$

$$= \frac{1.22}{1.227}$$

$$= 0.9942$$

Therefore as the calculated value (0.9942) is less than the critical value from Students' t tables on page 305 (2.0860 at the 5% level with 20 degrees of freedom, 2-tailed test), we can conclude the difference in the amount of time spent watching television in the two regions is not statistically significant at the 5% level, i.e. we cannot reject the null hypothesis at this level.

Pearson's Product Moment Correlation Coefficient

This simple correlation coefficient is defined as:

$$r = \frac{\sum XY - \sum X \sum Y / n}{(\sum X^2 - (\sum X)^2 / n))^* (\sum Y^2 - (\sum Y)^2 / n))}$$

where $\sum XY$ = sum of cross products. $\sum X^2$ = sum of X squared.
$\sum Y^2$ = sum of Y squared. $\sum X$ = sum of X.
$\sum Y$ = sum of Y. n = number of observations.

This formula is used if the data sets are measured on parametric lines. The value of r can vary between -1 and $+1$, where the sign indicates the slope of the relationship between x and y and a value of one indicates perfect correlation.

One-Way Analysis of Variance

This method of analysis of variance is used to break down the total variance of a variable into additive components which may then be associated with various factors. These separate factors are then seen as the causes or sources of variation of the variable being analysed. The development and introduction of this technique is due to Fisher (1926, 1939) who initially applied it to the analysis of agricultural experiments. However, its use soon expanded into many other areas of research. An example of a three-sample data layout for a one-way analysis of variance is shown in Table 3.1.

Sum of squares among groups is given by

Table 3.1

		Samples	
	1	2	3
	x_{11}	x_{12}	x_{13}
	x_{21}	x_{22}	x_{23}
	x_{31}	x_{32}	x_{33}
	.	.	.
	.	.	.
	$x_{n1\,1}$	$x_{n2\,2}$	$x_{n3\,3}$
Total	T_1	T_2	T_3
Mean	x_1	x_2	x_3

$$SSG = \sum_{j=1}^{k} T_j^2 \left(\sum_{j=1}^{k} \sum_{i=1}^{n} x_{ij} \right)^2 / n$$

The total sum of squares by

$$SST = \sum \sum x_{ij}^2 - \frac{\left(\sum_{j=1}^{k} \sum_{i=1}^{n} x_{ij} \right)^2}{n}$$

The error sum of squares by

$$SSE = SST - SSA$$

where k is the number of observed sets of data
n is the total number of observations
T is the sum of all the observations
T_i is the sum of the ith column
T_j is the sum of the jth column
SSG is the sum of squares among the groups
SSE is the error sum of squares
SST is the total sum of squares

Table 3.2 ANOVA table for one-way analysis of variance

Source of variation	Sum of squares (SS)	Degrees of freedom square	Mean (MS)	Variance ratio (VR)
Among groups	SSG	$k-1$	$MSA = SSG/(k-1)$	$VR = MSA/MSE$
Error	SSE	$n-k$	$MSE = SSE/(n-k)$	
Total	$\overline{SST}$	$\overline{n-1}$		

Table 3.3

| Car | Brand of Petrol | | |
	Zoom	Go-Fast	Standard
1	4.63	3.68	4.50
2	4.36	3.96	4.38
3	4.22	4.09	4.50
4	4.77	4.22	4.64
5	4.91	3.95	4.77
6	4.77	4.09	4.76

Figures in the above table are the kilometres travelled per litre of fuel.

The one-way analysis of variance (Table 3.2) is used when the measurements are obtained from an experiment involving only one criterion. The example shown here is the kilometres per litre achieved for three different makes of petrol (Zoom, Go-Fast and Standard). Each brand of petrol was used with six different cars of the same weight, engine size and with only the driver in the car. Similar road conditions applied to all the tests. The results are shown in Table 3.3.

Therefore we are testing the hypothesis H_o; the means are the same against H_1; the means are different.

$$H_0 : \mu_{zoom} = \mu_{go\ fast} = \mu_{standard} \qquad H_1 : \mu_{zoom} \neq \mu_{go\ fast} \neq \mu_{standard}$$

The first step in calculating the ANOVA is the construction of Table 3.4.

Table 3.4

| | Car | Zoom | Go-Fast | Standard | | |
		Brand of petrol				
	1	4.63	3.68	4.50		
	2	4.36	3.96	4.38		
	3	4.22	4.09	4.50		
	4	4.77	4.22	4.64		
	5	4.91	3.95	4.77		
	6	4.77	4.09	4.76		
Sum		27.66	23.99	27.55	Grand total	79.2
Mean		4.610	3.998	4.592	Grand mean	4.40
						$n = 18$

Table 3.5

Source of variation	Sum of squares (SS)	Degrees of freedom square	Mean (MS)	Variance ratio (VR)
Among groups	1.45	2	$MSA = 0.725$	$VR = 16.860$
Error	0.65	15	$MSE = 0.043$	
Total	2.10	17		

$$SST = 4.63^2 + 4.36^2 + 4.22^2 + 4.77^2 + \ldots + 4.77^2 + 4.76^2 - (79.2)^2 / 18$$
$$= 350.58 - 6272.64 / 18$$
$$= 350.58 - 348.48$$
$$= \mathbf{2.10}$$

$$SSG = \frac{27.66^2}{6} + \frac{23.99^2}{6} + \frac{27.55^2}{6} - 79.2^2/18$$

$$= \frac{765.07}{6} + \frac{575.52}{6} + \frac{759.00}{6} - 6272.64/18$$

$$= 349.93 - 348.48$$
$$= \mathbf{1.45}$$

$$SSE = SST - SSG$$
$$= 2.10 - 1.45$$
$$= \mathbf{0.65}$$

The ANOVA table for this example is given in Table 3.5.

Finally, the decision is based on the critical value of 3.68 from F statistical tables on pages 306–11. This is found by setting α at 0.05 with degrees of freedom equal to 2 and 15; these degrees of freedom are taken from Table 3.5. Since 16.860 is greater than 3.68, H_0 is rejected and we can accept H_1 that the three types of petrol do give different km per litre.

NON-PARAMETRIC TESTS

Non-parametric Statistical Tests

There are three situations where non-parametric statistics are used. Firstly, where a parametric statistic cannot be used because the data does not meet the assumptions on which that test is based. Secondly, a parametric test may not be applicable if the data set consists of ranks, for example, a consumer may be asked to indicate how satisfied they are with the service in a restaurant on a ranking scale from 1 (not satisfied) to 5 (very satisfied). Thirdly, non-parametric procedures can be used if the question does not involve a parameter, e.g. is this a random data set?

Advantages and Disadvantages of Non-parametric Statistics

The major advantages of non-parametric statistics are fivefold, and can be summarised as follows. Firstly, in most cases the probability statements accompanying the test are exact. Secondly, the calculations required within the tests are usually fairly easy to perform. Thirdly, the assumptions required by the test are usually few and very easily met (distribution free). Fourthly, due to the three advantages above, non-parametric procedures have numerous applications. Finally, data measured on nominal or ordinal scales can be analysed by non-parametric tests. The only major disadvantage of non-parametric tests is that, if large samples are used, the calculations can become tedious if a computer is not used.

The One Sample Runs Test

The one sample runs test is a non-parametric statistical test, used to test the hypothesis that a sample is in fact random. The test is based on the number of runs within the sample where a run is defined as a sequence of like symbols preceded and followed by either a different symbol or no symbol at all. This statistical method uses a cut-off value with which to test the data. Against this could be the sample mean, median, mode or a user specified value. The formula for the one sample runs test is given by the following:

$$z = \frac{r - \left(\dfrac{2n_1 n_2}{n_1 + n_2} + 1\right)}{\sqrt{\dfrac{2n_1 n_2(2n_1 n_2 - n_1 - n_2)}{(n_1 + n_2)^2(n_1 + n_2 - 1)}}}$$

where n = total number of observations
n_1 = the number of observations less than the mean
$n_2 = n - n_1$
r = the number of runs, where a run is defined as a sequence of the same symbols preceded or followed by either a different symbol or no symbol at all.

Example

A firm manufacturing soap powder requires the mean weight of packages to be 476 grams. A sample of 21 consecutive packages filled by the same machine was removed from the production line with the following weights: 501.2, 490, 481.6, 484.4, 462, 470.4, 467.4, 467.6, 481.6, 487.2, 492.8, 490, 498.4, 470.4, 462.0,

464.8, 495.6, 492.8, 495.6, 498.4 and 481.6. Does this data indicate a lack of randomness in the over and under fills in the packs ?

In this case the value of n is equal to 21, $n_1 = 7$ and $n_2 = 14$. The number of runs is 9 as shown below:

1 501.2, 490.2, 481.6,
2 484.4,
3 462.0, 470.4,
4 467.4, 467.6, 481.6, 487.2, 492.8,
5 490.0, 498.4,
6 470.4,
7 462.0, 464.8, 495.6,
8 492.8, 495.6, 498.4,
9 481.4

$r = 9$

$$z = \frac{9 - \left(\dfrac{2^*7^*14}{7 + 14} + 1\right)}{\sqrt{\dfrac{2^*7^*14^*(2^*7^*14^* - 7 - 14)}{(7 + 14)^2(7 + 14 - 1)}}}$$

$$z = \frac{-1.3333}{1.9720}$$

$$z = -0.6761$$

Therefore as the calculated value of -0.6761 is less than the critical value of ± 1.96, we conclude that the mean weight of soap powder packed into packages appears to be random (see Figure 3.2).

The Median Test

If it seems likely that two populations are normally distributed and have equal variances, then the 't' test can be used. However, if these conditions are not met then the median test provides a non-parametric alternative. As the name suggests, this test is based upon the median as a measure of central tendency.

The test first combines the two samples to calculate the combined median. This value is then compared with all the observations in both samples and the results from this are then displayed in the form of a 2×2 contingency table (see Table 3.6). From this table the test statistic is calculated. This test statistic has a chi-squared distribution, and is calculated using the following formula:

$$\chi^2 = \frac{N((a)(d) - (b)(c))^2}{(a + c)(b + d)(a + b)(c + d)} \qquad N = n_1 + n_2$$

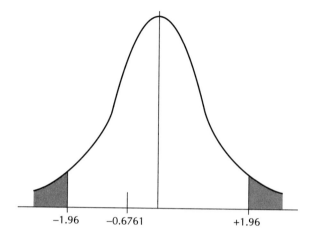

-1.96   -0.6761   +1.96

Figure 3.2

Table 3.6   2×2 contingency table

	Sample 1	Sample 2	Total
Above median	a	b	$a+b$
Below median	c	d	$c+d$
	$a+c=n_1$	$b+d=n_2$	$N=n_1+n_2$

Example

A marketing manager has collected data on the effects of advertising in two different regions. In region A, bill posters were put through the door of possible customers, in region B no advertising was used. The marketing manager wishes to know if they can conclude that sales in region A are higher than in region B. The number of products sold in the shops supplied in each region for last month are given below.

    Region A 409, 473, 482, 394, 410, 446, 443, 451, 487, 407, 408
    Region B 421, 478, 444, 485, 438, 382, 467, 480, 358, 447, 382, 446, 478
    The median is 445.

    The median is calculated for the whole data set (24 observations in this case) by putting them in ascending order and then finding the middle observation, which is $(24+1)/2 = 12.5$. Therefore the median is half-way between observation 12 and 13 which in this case is 445. If there is an odd number of total observations the median will lie on an actual number, therefore this observation will be removed from the analysis for the calculations.

In this case

$n_1=11$ $n_2=13$ $N=24$ $a=6$ $b=6$ $c=5$ $d=7$

These values can now be entered into the formula:

$$\chi^2 = \frac{24((6)(7) - (6)(5))^2}{(6+5)(6+7)(6+6)(5+7)}$$

$$\chi^2 = \frac{24(42-30)^2}{11*13*12*12}$$

$$= \frac{24*144}{20592}$$

$$= \mathbf{0.1678}$$

If this value exceeds the critical value obtained from χ^2 tables (page 304) with one degree of freedom, the null hypothesis is rejected. However, since the computed chi-squared value is not significant at the 0.05 level we can conclude that there may be no difference between the two regions.

The Sign Test (two sample)

The sign test is also a non-parametric statistical test which is used to test whether or not it seems likely that two data sets differ with respect to a central tendency (the median). This test is used if the two data sets are not the result of an independently drawn sample (whereas the median test is used if the data sets are the result of independently drawn samples). The test statistic can be calculated by first finding the difference between Y and X, where Y is the data on the first sample and X is the data on the second sample. If $X>Y$ the difference is recorded as a positive, and if $X<Y$ the difference is recorded as a negative. The resulting series of pluses and minuses is then used to calculate the test statistic. The test statistic follows the Standardised Normal Distribution if n is greater than 12.

The formula for the sign test is given by the following:

$$z = \frac{(k \pm 0.5) - 0.5n}{0.5\sqrt{n}}$$

where k is the number of occurrences of the less frequently occurring sign
0.5 is the continuity correction factor
$k+0.5$ is used if $k < n/2$
$k-0.5$ is used if $k > n/2$
if n is greater than 12 the normal approximation to the binomial distribution may be used.

Example

A manager wishes to know which of two sales people is more effective (i.e. sells more of the product 'Ultra Zoom'). The sales of 'Ultra Zoom' are shown below over a 12-day period for salespersons A and B.

Salesperson A   99, 81, 93, 86, 83, 97, 71, 86, 82, 95, 90, 87
Salesperson B   98, 84, 94, 84, 87, 86, 81, 92, 71, 89, 94, 89

therefore $k = 5$ (the number of occurrences of the less frequent sign – in this case positive signs in Table 3.7) and $n = 12$ and as $k < n/2$ we use $k + 0.5$.

$$z = \frac{(5 + 0.5) - 0.5 \cdot 12}{0.5\sqrt{12}}$$

$$z = \frac{-0.5}{1.7320}$$

$$z = -0.2886$$

Since the computed value of $z = -0.2886$ is less than the critical value of $z = -1.96$ from normal distribution tables (on page 303), the null hypothesis is not rejected at the 5% level, and it may be concluded that the two salespersons appear to have equal selling ability (see Figure 3.3).

Mann–Whitney Test

The Mann–Whitney test (1947), also known as the Wilcoxon test, is a non-parametric statistical test used to see whether two independent samples come from

Table 3.7

Salesperson A	Salesperson B	Sign $(X_i - Y_i)$
99	98	+
81	84	−
93	94	−
86	84	+
83	87	−
97	86	+
71	81	−
86	92	−
82	71	+
95	89	+
90	94	−
87	89	−

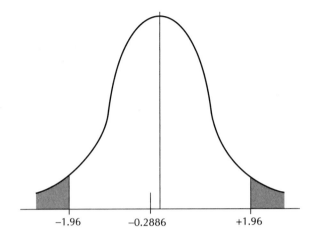

Figure 3.3

populations having the same distribution. This test is used instead of the t test if the test sample violates either of conditions 1 or 2 below.

1. The sample populations are normally distributed.
2. The sample populations have equal variances.

If both these conditions are found to be appropriate then the t test should be used as it has more power. However, if these conditions are violated then the Mann–Whitney test should be used. The only condition which has to be met for this test is that the samples are independent and random. The formula for the Mann–Whitney test is given by the following:

$$U = n_1 n_2 + n_1 \frac{(n_1 + 1)}{2} - R_1$$

where U = Mann-Whitney statistic
   n_1 = number of items in sample 1
   n_2 = number of items in sample 2
   R_1 = sum of the ranks in sample 1 (if ties in the rankings occur, simply average the rankings involved)

The mean is given by:

$$\mu_u = n_1 n_2 / 2$$

The standard deviation is given by:

$$\sigma_u = \sqrt{n_1 n_2 (n_1 + n_2 + 1)/12}$$

The test statistic is normally distributed and found by using the following formula:

$$z = \frac{U - \mu_u}{\sigma_u}$$

Example 4

The manager of a large department store employs two salespeople in the toy department and wishes to give a bonus to the best performer. The manager wishes to know if the two salespeople should be considered equally for the bonus. To test the hypothesis the weekly sales of the two people are shown in Table 3.8. Note that sales have been put in descending order and then ranked; person B has more observations because they have been employed longer.

$$H_0 : \mu_a = \mu_b \qquad\qquad\qquad H_1 : \mu_a \neq \mu_b$$

$$U = 15^*21 + \frac{15(15 + 1)}{2} - 211$$

$$U = 224$$

Table 3.8

Salesperson A		Salesperson B	
Sales	Rank	Sales	Rank
514	1	474	2
467	3	450	4
449	5	426	9
448	6	414	10
433	7	407	12
431	8	395	15
410	11	393	16
400	13	379	19
399	14	375	20
389	17	372	21
381	18	367	22
365	23	355	24
353	25	346	26
336	29	343	27
329	31	339	28
	$\sum$ 211	331	30
		320	32
$n_1 = 15$		303	33
		215	34
		213	35
		210	36
		$n_2 = 21$	

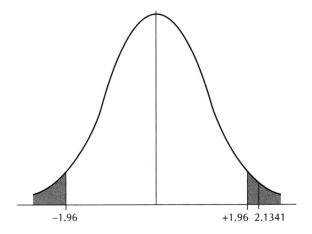

Figure 3.4

The mean is given by:

$$\mu_u = n_1 n_2 / 2 = 15{*}21/2 = \mathbf{157.5}$$

The standard deviation is given by:

$$\sigma_u = \sqrt{15{*}21(15 + 21 + 1)/12}$$
$$= 31.16$$

The test statistic is normally distributed and found by using the following formula:

$$z = \frac{U - \mu_u}{\sigma_u}$$
$$= \frac{224 - 157.5}{31.16}$$
$$= \mathbf{2.1341}$$

As the calculated value of 2.1341 is greater than the critical value of 1.96 (from normal distribution tables on page 303) we reject the null hypothesis of no difference between the two salespeople and accept the alternative hypothesis that there is a difference (see Figure 3.4).

The Kruskal–Wallis One-Way Analysis of Variance by Rank

This test (Kruskal and Wallis 1952) is a non-parametric statistical test which is used instead of the analysis of variance test when either of the assumptions 1 or 2 below are violated.

1. The sampled populations are normally distributed.

2.   The sampled populations have equal variances.

This test makes use of ranks rather than the original observations. It should be noted that the Kruskal–Wallis test is appropriate only if the samples are independent.

A large value of H tends to cast doubt on the assumption that the K samples used in the test are drawn from an identically distributed population. The critical value for the Kruskal–Wallis test is given by a chi-squared table. The formula for the Kruskal–Wallis test is given by the following:

$$H = \frac{12}{n(n+1)} \sum_{j=1}^{k} \frac{R_j^2}{n_j} - 3(n+1)$$

where H = Kruskal–Wallis test statistic
           k = the number of samples
           n_j = the number of observations in the jth sample
           n = $\sum n_j$, the total number of observations in all samples
           R_j = the sum of the ranks in the jth sample.

Example

A consumer was asked to rank 15 samples of ice-cream in order of preference. However, unknown to the consumer, the 15 samples consisted of 5 samples of each of 3 brands.

	Brands	
A	B	C
7	2	13
6	15	12
5	10	11
4	8	1
3	7	9

The null hypothesis is therefore that the three brands are equally preferred.

$$H = \frac{12}{n(n+1)} \sum_{j=1}^{k} \frac{R_j^2}{n_j} - 3(n+1)$$

	Brands	
A	B	C
7	2	13
6	15	12
5	10	11
4	8	1
3	7	9
Sum of ranks **25**	**42**	**46**

$$H = \frac{12}{15(15+1)}(25^2/5 + 42^2/5 + 46^2/5) - 3(15+1)$$

$$H = 0.05(125 + 352.8 + 423.2) - 48$$
$$H = 45.05 - 48$$
$$\mathbf{H = -2.95}$$

By referring to a Kruskal–Wallis test table (Siegel and Castellan 1988) with ($n_1 = 5$, $n_2 = 5$ and $n_3 = 5$) the probability of obtaining a value of -2.95 is 0.102. Therefore we cannot reject the null hypothesis that the three brands of ice-cream are equally preferred.

The Friedman Two-Way Analysis of Variance by Ranks

The Kruskal–Wallis test is used when data samples have been independently drawn from their respective populations. However, it is frequently necessary to analyse data which has not been drawn from independent samples. If only two samples are to be tested, the sign test can be used. However, if there are more than two samples the Friedman two-way analysis of variance test (1937) can be used.

This test is so called because it provides an analogue to the parametric two-way analysis of variance technique. The test starts by ranking the data in each column, with any tied observations being given the average of the rank to which they are tied. The test statistic is then calculated by measuring the extent to which the ranks in each column depart from randomness, focusing on the sum of the ranks in each column. The test statistic follows a chi-squared distribution, with $k-1$ degrees of freedom.

The formula for the Friedman test is given by the following:

$$\chi_r^2 = \frac{12}{nk(k+1)}\sum_{j=1}^{k} R_j^2 - 3n(k+1)$$

where n is the number of rows
       k is the number of columns
       R_j is the sum of the ranks in the jth column

Example

Five car owners were asked at random to rank three types of petrol in order of preference (a rank of one indicating first preference, etc.)

Car owner	Type of petrol		
	Zoom	Go Fast	Standard
1	1	2	3
2	2	1	3
3	1	2	3
4	1	2	3
5	1	3	2
Sum of ranks	6	10	14

$$\chi_r^2 = \frac{12}{nk(k+1)} \sum_{j=1}^{k} R_j^2 - 3n(k+1)$$

$$\chi_r^2 = \frac{12}{5^*3(3+1)} (6^2 + 10^2 + 14^2) - 3^*5(3+1)$$

$$= 0.20^*(36 + 100 + 196) - 60$$
$$= 66.4 - 60$$
$$= \mathbf{6.40}$$

If we refer to an exact chi-squared distribution ($n = 5$) the probability of obtaining a value of 6.40 when the null hypothesis is correct is less than 0.039. Therefore we may conclude that the three types of petrol are not equally preferred and accept the alternative hypothesis.

The Spearman Rank Correlation Coefficient

Several measures of correlation are available when the assumptions underlying the parametric correlation coefficient are violated. One of the most common is the Spearman rank correlation coefficient which as its name suggests, uses ranks. The test statistic focuses on the differences between X and Y. The range of values for the statistic are -1 and $+1$, where -1 indicates perfect negative correlation and $+1$ indicates perfect positive correlation. The resulting test statistic may be compared for significance with the appropriate critical value Spearman rank correlation tables on page 313.

The formula for the Spearman rank correlation test (1904) is given by the following:

$$r_s = 1 - \frac{6 \sum d_i^2}{n(n^2 - 1)}$$

where r_s = Spearman rank correlation coefficient.
          d = the difference in the ranks
          n = the number of paired observations

Example

A sample of 6 men and 6 women were asked to rank 6 different advertising ideas in order of eye-catching appeal. The results are shown in Table 3.9.

Table 3.9

Advertising idea	Men	Women
1	6	6
2	4	2
3	1	1
4	2	4
5	3	5
6	5	3

There we are testing the following hypothesis.

$$H_0 : r_s = 0 \qquad\qquad H_1 : r_s \pm 0$$

X	Y	d	d^2
6	6	0	0
4	2	2	4
1	1	0	0
2	4	-2	4
3	5	-2	4
5	3	2	4

$$\sum d^2 = 16$$

$$= 1 - \frac{6\sum d^2}{n(n^2 - 1)}$$

$$= 1 - \frac{6*16}{6(6^2 - 1)}$$

$$= 1 - 0.4571 = +\mathbf{0.5429}$$

Therefore, as the calculated value of (0.5429) is less than the critical value from Spearman rank tables on page 313 (0.7714), we can conclude that there appears to be no similarity in the way men and women rank the advertisements in terms of their eye-catching appeal. Great care should be exercised here due to the very small sample size.

EQUATION MODELLING TECHNIQUES

There are numerous equation modelling techniques, and three of the more commonly used methods are reviewed here (LISREL, Path Analysis and Logit/ Probit models). The most commonly used method of all is ordinary least squares regression analysis (reviewed in Chapter 4), however, as is explained later, this is not always the best method to use, particularly if a full system of equations is to be modelled simultaneously.

LISREL

LISREL (linear structural relations) was originally designed by Karl Jöreskeg and Dag Sörbom in the late 1960s and is the most general method available for estimating structural equations models. These models can be applied to analyse data derived from surveys, experiments, quasi-experimental designs and longitudinal studies. However, the major advantage of these type of model is that they can distinguish between latent concepts and observed indicators making them very applicable to numerous areas of social science.

In the early 1960s, the theory of using maximum likelihood estimation of structural coefficients was well known, however, even simple models proved to be prohibitively expensive in terms of the time required to solve them. Initial work focused on factor analysis and the ability to fix model coefficients and to express some factors as functions of other factors. This led to the development of confirmatory factor analysis. However, it soon became apparent that the basic LISREL model amounted to a general procedure for solving structural equation models (path analysis) in a manner that would preserve the distinction between concepts and indicators.

The LISREL model, in its most general form, consists of two parts: the *measurement model* and the *structural equation model*. The measurement model specifies how latent variables or hypothetical constructs are linked to observed variables. The structural equation model defines the causal relationships among the latent variables, describes the causal effects, and assigns the explained and unexplained variance. LISREL estimates the unknown coefficients within the model from the set of linear structural equations utilising an iterative search technique over the possible set of coefficients. The starting values for these coefficients are either estimated using a least squares method such as maximum likelihood or specified by the user. The power of LISREL is that it provides a very flexible methodology with the opportunity for an active interplay between theory, modelling and estimation.

There are many excellent books on LISREL, but the best starting point is probably the two books by Scott Long (1991a, 1991b), other books worth looking at are Bagozzi (1994) and Hayduk (1987). LISREL models can be very difficult to solve and very good knowledge of the underlying model and what types of restriction the model should have placed upon it are frequently required. Before estimating a LISREL model you should either consult a person who has already used this type of analysis and understands both the computer software and theoretical underpinning of the methodology, or read one of the recommend books on the subject.

An example of a typical LISREL model which was used to analyse satisfaction and full use of services associated with ATM usage is shown in Figure 3.5. The latent variables are in the centre, the exogenous variables on the left and the endogenous variables are on the right. The links between variables are shown by straight lines. This model was published in *The International Journal of Bank Marketing* (Goode, Chien and Moutinho 1996).

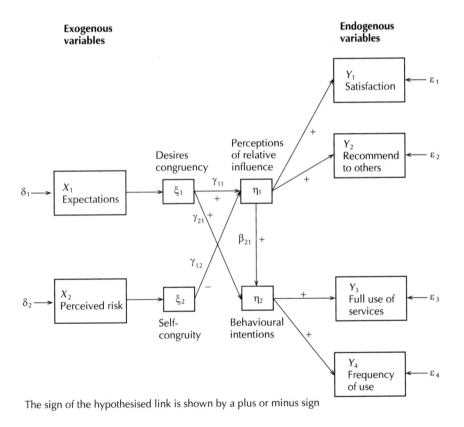

Figure 3.5 Path diagram for hypothetical model (SATIS)

Path Analysis

In a research study you may want to use an approach to structural equation modelling such as path analysis. Path analysis is a method for studying patterns of causation among a set of variables which was popularised in the sociological literature (Blalock 1971, Duncan 1975, Heise 1975).

If some of the variables under study are directly unobservable (or latent) and have at best moderate reliabilities you may decide to use multiple indicators and then assess the construct validity of the observable measures.

Though path diagrams are not essential for numerical analysis, they are useful for displaying graphically the pattern of causal relationships among sets of observable and unobservable variables. Path analysis provides a means for studying the direct and indirect effects of variables. The method is not intended to accomplish the impossible task of deducing causal relations from the values of the correlation coefficients. It is intended to combine the quantitative information given by the correlations with such qualitative information as may be at hand on causal relations to give quantitative information.

Path-analytic models assume that the relationships among the variables are linear and additive. A path coefficient indicates the direct effect of a variable as a cause of a variable taken as an effect. Path coefficients are equivalent to regression weights. Direct effects are indicated by path coefficients. Indirect effects refer to the situation where an independent variable affects a dependent variable through a third variable, which itself directly or indirectly affects the dependent variable. The indirect effect is given by the product of the respective path coefficients. A close approximation between the reproduced and original correlations can serve as evidence attesting to the validity of the proposed model. Essentially, we want the reproduced correlation to be close to the original correlations. When this is true, the hypothesised causal structure, under which the reproduced correlations were generated, fits or is consistent with the pattern of the intercorrelations among the variables. Thus, the ability of the hypothesised model to reproduce the correlation matrix R plays a crucial role in assessing the validity of the model (Dillon and Goldstein 1984).

Example – A Bank Marketing Research Study

Figure 3.6(a) and (b) presents path diagrams depicting the hypothesised relationships between four human resource management variables. In Figure 3.6(a) a single indicator of staff motivation (X_1), a single indicator of staff training (X_2), a single indicator of management training (X_3) and a single indicator of customer relationship management (Y_1) are shown. Four customer management variables are shown in Figure 3.6(b): a single indicator of generation of new business (X_4), a single indicator of customer relationships (X_5), a single indicator of quality of customer service (X_6) and a single indicator of profitability of the branch (Y_2). The

(a)

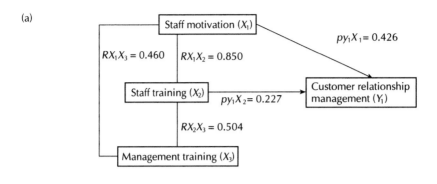

(b)

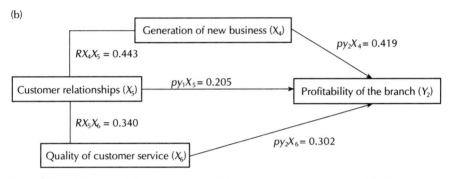

Figure 3.6 (a) Path analysis of the impact of human resource management factors on customer relationship management; (b) Path analysis of the impact of customer management factors on bank branch's profitability

implication is that the single indicators X_1, X_2, X_3, X_4, X_5, X_6, Y_1 and Y_2 are perfect indicators of their respective latent constructs. The system of equations corresponding to the hypothesised structures for the endogenous variables can be written as:

$$Y_1 = py_1x_1X_1 + py_1x_2X_2 + ey_1$$
$$Y_2 = py_2x_4X_4 + py_2X_5 + py_2x_6X_6 + ey_2$$

where all variables are expressed in deviation form. Values for the path coefficients were obtained directly from the correlation matrix and the use of the standardised regression weights.

The findings provided by the path analytical structures seem to indicate that an effective policy of customer relationship management is highly dependent on the motivation of staff within the branch. Although it can be noted that there is a lower direct causal effect between staff training and customer relationship management, the indirect effect between personnel training and the development of effective customer relations appears to be extremely salient (as measured by the correlation coefficient between staff training and staff motivation). Two other important observable indirect causations establish linkages between staff motivation and management training as well as between staff training and management training.

The measurement of causation between the three exogenous variables related to the impact of customer management policies on the overall profitability of the bank branch (endogenous variables Y_2) shows that the generation of new business for the branch has a strong direct causal effect on its profitability. Another important causal element is based on the provision of quality customer service, while a somewhat lower path coefficient is attached to the development of effective customer relationships.

The noticeable indirect causal effects are based on the detected correlation coefficients found between the generation of new business for the branch and the establishment of sustainable customer relationships, as well as between the perceived quality of customer service and the bank's orientation towards customer relations.

Path Analysis Calculations

$$PY_1X_1 = \frac{RY_1X_1 - RY_1X_2RX_1X_2}{1 - R^2X_1X_2} = \frac{0.620 - (0.590)(0.850)}{1 - (0.850)^2} = 0.426$$

$$PY_1X_2 = \frac{RY_1X_2 - RY_1X_1RX_1X_2}{1 - R^2X_1X_2} = \frac{0.590 - (0.620)(0.850)}{1 - (0.850)^2} = 0.227$$

$$PY_2X_4 = \frac{RY_2X_4 - RY_2X_5RX_4X_5}{1 - R^2X_4X_5} = \frac{0.510 - (0.391)(0.443)}{1 - (0.443)^2} = 0.419$$

$$PY_2X_5 = \frac{RY_2X_5 - RY_2X_4RX_4X_5}{1 - R^2X_4X_5} = \frac{0.391 - (0.510)(0.443)}{1 - (0.443)^2} = 0.205$$

$$PY_2X_6 = \frac{RY_2X_6 - RY_2X_5RX_5X_6}{1 - R^2X_5X_6} = \frac{0.440 - (0.391)(0.340)}{1 - (0.340)^2} = 0.302$$

Logit and Probit Models

Ordinary regression analysis or OLS is probably one of the most widely used statistical techniques in the social sciences. However, it is one of the most abused as well, and this is because there are a number of very important assumptions which underlie the OLS model. If these assumptions are not met the model will not produce reasonable estimates. Such a condition would arise when the dependent variable was a qualitative measure rather than a continuous, interval measure. These types of measures occur in situations like *voting, whether to enter into a contract or not, whether to purchase a product or not and the level of satisfaction derived from a particular product.* In all these situations and many others OLS should not be used, instead models of binary choice (0, 1) such as a Logit or Probit model should be adopted. A good introduction to Logit and Probit models is given by Pindyck and Rubinfeld (1991). It has been found that Logit and Probit models normally give very similar results so we will concentrate on the more commonly used Logit model.

The Logit model is based upon the cumulative logistic probability function and is given by:

$$P_i = F(Z_i) = F(\alpha + \beta X_i) = \frac{1}{1 + e^{-Zi}} = \frac{1}{1 + e^{-(\alpha + \beta X_i)}}$$

where e =   base of natural logarithms (2.718).
P_i =   the probability that a person will make a certain choice (which ranges between 0 and 1).
Z_i =   a theoretical continuous index which is determined by X_i.
X_i =   the set of explanatory variables in the equation.

This formula can be changed to the following:

$$\log \frac{P_i}{1 - P_i} = Z_i = \alpha + \beta X_i$$

This function can now be estimated using a regression method. The dependent variable in this equation is the logarithm of the odds that a certain choice will be made. The slope of the cumulative logistic distribution is highest at $P = 0.5$. This indicates that changes in the explanatory variables will have their largest effects on the probability of a particular choice at the middle point of the distribution.

Other probability choice models are available for more complex situations which are not zero, one choices. These include multi-choice Logit and Probit models for situations like the choice of a particular colour of car or the choice of a particular political party in a National election. Finally, ordered Logit and ordered Probit models exist for modelling situations of ordered choices, such as levels of satisfaction derived from a car or the level of satisfaction derived from using an ATM machine.

OTHER FREQUENTLY USED TECHNIQUES

Perceptual Mapping

A perceptual map is a graphical representation of consumer perceptions of competi   ands, or hypothetical 'ideal' brands, on key attributes. Perceptual maps ar used in the following circumstances:

1. Product positioning and repositioning – to identify current brand positions, close competitors, gaps in the market and 'ideal' brand positions.

2. Market segmentation – to segment the target market by brand choice criteria used, or attributes desired in an 'ideal' brand.

The three techniques now discussed are all relevant to perceptual mapping.

Multi-dimensional Scaling

Multi-dimensional scaling aims to produce a pictorial representation of the relationships between brands, product attributes and/or individuals in the target market. The perceptual maps thus produced for brands and product attributes can be used for product positioning, while those produced for consumers can be used to segment the market. Brand images may be elicited through either:

*   An aggregate approach, where relevant product attributes are identified and subsequently evaluated by respondents to build up a brand image, or

*   a disaggregate approach, rating competing brands on measures of how similar or dissimilar they are, and subsequently using analysis with multi-dimensional scaling techniques to break down these images into their constituent parts.

Types of Scaling

The majority of applications of multi-dimensional scaling in marketing involve three types of scaling:

1. Brand mapping using similarity data.

2. Dimension identification using brand attribute data.

3. Joint space analysis (identifying 'ideal' brand locations) using preference data.

Perceptual maps (brand maps) are usually derived from brand similarity judgements, that is, measures of how similar or dissimilar respondents believe each pair of brands to be using whatever criteria they choose. These measures are translated into a brand map using one of the several available computer algorithms. Brands are located on the map so that brands stated to be very similar to each other are close to each other, and those stated to be dissimilar are located far away from each other. The representation may be one, two, three or more dimensions, whatever adequately represents the data.

The next stage is for the researcher to interpret the dimensions of the map, that is, discover the criteria used by respondents in making similarity judgements. This task will be simplified if reasons for respondents' more extreme answers (high similarity or dissimilarity) were probed at the time of interview. Otherwise, respondents may be shown the maps and asked how they would interpret the dimensions, or researchers may do this themselves – this however runs the risk of imposing their own perceptions on the study. Another alternative is to use a property fitting algorithm. This entails qualitative research prior to brand mapping in order to evaluate all brands under consideration on all attributes. Each property is then examined in turn to see if it fits with the brand map, and those that fit well are used to describe the dimension.

Finally, joint space analysis identifies the 'ideal' locations on the brand map. There are two common ways of doing this. The first, known as 'unfolding' analysis, is to ask respondents to rank the brands in terms of preference, and the 'ideal' location is then plotted as a point closer to the second ranked brand then the third ranked, etc. The second method is to ask respondents to evaluate their 'ideal' brand by its coordinates in the perpetual space. For certain attributes an 'ideal' location will be mapped as a point, while for others a vector might be more appropriate – e.g. on a brand map of soft drinks, an ideal location on the attribute 'sweetness' is likely to be a point (the drink should be this sweet and no sweeter), while on a brand map for cars, the ideal location in the attribute 'fuel economy' is likely to be a vector (the car should be as economic as possible).

It is possible to construct perceptual maps at respondent levels – analysing data from each respondent separately, at segment level – aggregating data from respondents in specific market segments, or at the sample level – aggregating all data. Individual differences in perception (such as use of different evaluation criteria or different ratings of brands on the same criteria) or different 'ideal' locations can be used as bases for market segmentation.

Some Computer Algorithms for Multi-dimensional Scaling

There follows a brief summary of four of the more common algorithms used for multi-dimensional scaling.

The KYST algorithm uses similarity data from a group of respondents. It searches for a representation of the relationship between brands, in a predefined number of dimensions, such that distances between brands are as close as possible to the extent of stated similarity in the original data.

INDSCAL analyses similarity data at the individual respondent level. It assumes that respondents use the same evaluation criteria in making similarity or dissimilarity judgements, but that the importance of the criteria vary between respondents. The varying importances are used as a basis for segmentation.

PROFIT is an algorithm for fitting brand attributes data to a predetermined brand map by a regression procedure. Each attribute is fitted onto the map, so that the projections of each brand onto the attribute (i.e. their coordinates on the axis representing the attribute) are as close as possible to the original respondent evaluation score of the brand on that attribute.

The PREFMAP and PREFMAP2 algorithms construct a joint space of brands and individual respondents' 'ideal' brand locations based on preferences data. Market segmentation may then be based around 'ideal' brand locations.

Factor Analysis

Factor analysis is a data reduction technique which attempts to identify underlying relationships which may be present between a number of different variables. The aim is to explain the relationships within the data set in terms of the smallest number of independent summary variables, i.e. hidden basic variables are assumed to be some weighted combination of the observed variables. As a very simple example, we might have a sample which we can describe both by weight (w) and by height (h). If we wished to use only one variable to describe the sample, we could develop a 'size' rating (s) which takes into account both weight and height. An individual's size rating would be defined as

$$s = aw + bh$$

where a and b are the factor loadings of the original variables weight and height. Thus we can now describe each individual by only one measurement instead of two, but in the process we have sacrificed some precision – it is impossible to tell from a size rating the exact weight and height of that individual.

Typically we would have tens of variables which we wished to reduce to a few underlying factors in order to clarify understanding.

Principal Components Analysis

In marketing the most commonly used factor analysis technique is *principal components analysis*. This technique seeks to describe a set of associated variables in terms of a set of mutually uncorrelated linear combinations of the same variables. These combinations are chosen so that the first set describes as much of the total variance of the original data as possible, the next as much of the remaining variance as possible, and so on until no more factors can be extracted. In practice, a number of the large percentage of the original variance is explained by the first few factors extracted.

Interpretation of a principal components analysis is often simplified by a technique known as varimax rotation, which consists of rotating the individual variance scores within the space defined by principal component axes, so that each separate variable yields a factor loading close to one on one component and close to zero on all others. The analysis and varimax rotation would be carried out by a statistical computer package such as SPSS.

The general methodology would consist of:

- Deducing all variables relevant to the study, often through use of qualitative research.

- Asking respondents to evaluate each variable.

- Inputting respondent data into a suitable statistical computer package for analysis.

Computer output would be:

- A list of variables used in the analysis.

- A table detailing the percentage of total variance explained by each factor.

- A table of factor loadings of the variables on the principal component factors.

- A table of factor loadings of the variables on the varimax rotated principal component factors.

The final table would be used to arrive at a subjective interpretation of the factors. Each of the original variables will have a factor loading on each factor. Factor loading will be between one and zero, and the nearer to one that the loading is, the stronger the association between the factor and the variable. Each factor then has to be labelled by considering its weighted combination of variables.

Use in Perceptual Mapping

Marketing applications of factor analysis are generally used either to reduce large groups of descriptive variables into smaller, more manageable sets or to identify and label underlying factors (less easily articulated attitudes, beliefs, etc.) in behavioural analysis. Thus, in perceptual mapping, factor analysis could be used to reduce a large number of evaluative criteria to a more manageable number or to produce a set of attitudinal factors from evaluative criteria in order to carry out behavioural segmentation.

Cluster Analysis

Cluster analysis can be described as the process of sorting individuals into groups, where, on some suitable criterion, similarity between group members is high and similarity between members of different groups is low. The basic method is that individuals are scored on several dimensions and are grouped on the basis of the likeness of their scores. Cluster analysis can be useful in market segmentation and product positioning. For example, we could consider a bank that wished to carry out benefit segmentation of the banking market and surveyed 500 respondents, asking them to rate the importance of 20 criteria relating to their choice of bank.

Hierarchical Clustering

This is the most common method of forming clusters of respondents. Initially each respondent is taken to be a separate cluster (500 clusters in our example). The two most alike respondents are then combined to form a cluster, so there are 499 clusters. The process continues combining the next two most alike clusters (individual respondents or already formed groups) at each stage until the whole sample is reduced to one cluster. The researchers may then choose the level of clustering which groups the respondents in the most suitable way or gives a manageable and identifiable number of segments.

Distance and Similarity Measures

To decide how alike two individual respondents are, we may use a distance measure or a similarity measure. The Euclidean distance, a frequently used measure, is a measure of distance between two respondents, calculated over the full number of dimensions used in the study. (Euclidean geometry extends the simple process whereby we could graphically measure the distance between two respondents, each with two dimensions (i.e. an x and a y coordinate) into n-dimensional space.) The most commonly used similarity measure is the product moment correlation coefficient. This measures the similarity of respondent profiles rather than the distance between them. Being measured on a seven-point scale, a respondent whose scores on five criteria were $7, 6, 5, 7, 7$, would be classified as very similar to one whose scores were $6, 5, 4, 6, 6$, – the relative importance of the criteria is the same although the absolute ratings are not.

Once clusters have been formed there are several methods of deciding which clusters should be joined. Ward's (1963) method involves calculating the mean position or centroid of two clusters. The distance between the centroid and the original positions of the cluster elements is calculated using the error sum of squares measure and the two clusters for which this measure is lowest are joined. Nearest neighbour methods join the two most alike individuals (one from each cluster). Furthest neighbour methods define likeness as the likeness of the two most unlike individuals (one from each cluster). Centroid sorting methods calculate the mean position of the elements in a cluster and define the distance between centroids of clusters as the likeness measure. The average link method measures all combinations of pairs between two clusters.

A partitioning, or top down, method of clustering could also be used whereby elements are combined into a predetermined number of clusters and relocation attempted until no further improvement can be obtained. This method on its own offers no advantages over hierarchical clustering, but the two methods may be used in conjunction to cross-check clusters produced. Another variation, known as clumping or overlapping, allows elements to belong to more than one cluster. This can be valid, for instance in benefit segmentation of a market, where it is possible for an individual to have the characteristics of more than one segment.

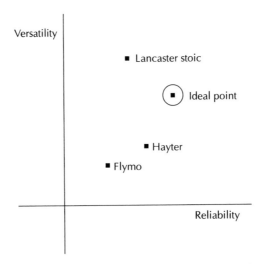

Figure 3.7   A simple market structure analysis of the lawnmower market (*Source:* O'Shaughnessy, p. 100)

Use of Perceptual Mapping

Cluster analysis can be used to segment respondents into a number of groups. These groups could be used as the basis for perceptual mapping at the segment level, aggregating responses in each group and thus developing a picture of the 'ideal' brand attributes for each segment.

Some examples of perceptual maps are shown in Figures 3.7, 3.8 and 3.9.

In Figure 3.8 the position of each centre on each dimension is measured by its relative position as the dimension vector is traced back through the centre of the circle. For example, S (Woburn Safari Park) scores highest on having a strong theme (vector 7), while A (American Adventure) is perceived as being the most noisy and rowdy (vector 5).

In Figure 3.9 the length of the vectors relate to the strength of association between the attribute and the ideal segment position. For instance, it is very important for segment A that a bank is best for the individual. It is of medium importance that the tellers should be friendly.

CONCLUSION AND SUMMARY

The book by Siegel and Castellan (1988) is considered to be the classic book on non-parametric tests and explains many non-parametric tests very well indeed. For any reader interested in computer programs that can be used to undertake some of the statistical tests covered in this chapter, the book by Cohen and Holliday (1982)

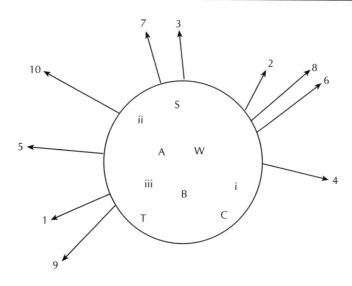

Leisure centres (stimuli)
A = American Adventure
T = Alton Towers
B = Belton House
C = Chatsworth House
W = Warwick Castle
S = Woburn Safari Park

Segments (points)
i = Mature couples
ii = Young families
iii = Wild young things

Dimensions (vectors)
1 = Big rides
2 = Educational
3 = Fun and games
4 = Sophisticated
5 = Noisy/rowdy
6 = Pre-teen
7 = Theme
8 = For the family
9 = Artificial/synthetic
10 = Good food

Figure 3.8 Perceptual map of the leisure centre market

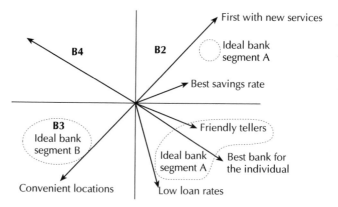

Figure 3.9 Perceptual map of five banks and ideal bank positions for three consumer segments (*Source*: Moutinho, p. 71)

contains numerous computer programs written in BASIC. Many other computer programs are available to undertake statistical analysis – the most flexible is SPSS (1992) which is available for both personal computers and mainframes. Other specialised packages include LIMDEP 6.0 (see Greene, 1990) for estimating limited dependent variable regressions (such as Logit or Probit) and LISREL 7.0 (see Jöreskog and Sörbom 1988, 1989) for estimating LISREL models.

REFERENCES AND FURTHER READING

Bagozzi R. (1994) *Advanced Methods of Marketing Research*, Cambridge (Mass.) Basil Blackwell Ltd.

Blalock, H.M. Jr. (1971) *Causal Models in the Social Sciences*, (ed.), Chicago: Aldine.

Crawford, I. M. and Lomas, R. A. (1980) 'Factor Analysis – A Tool for Data Reduction', *European Journal of Marketing*, **14**, (7), pp.414–21.

Cohen L. and Holliday M. (1982) *Statistics for Social Scientists, An Introductory Text with Computer Programmes in BASIC*, London: Harper and Row Publishers.

Dillon, W. R. and Goldstein, M. (1984) *Multivariate Analysis – Methods and Applications*, New York: John Wiley and Sons.

Duncan, O.D. (1975) *Introduction to Structural Equation Models*, New York: Academic Press.

Fisher, R.A. (1926) 'The Arrangement of Field Experiments', *Journal of Ministry of Agriculture*, **33**, pp.503–13.

Fisher, R. A. (1939) 'The Comparison of Samples with Possibly Unequal Variances', *Annals of Eugenics*, **9**, pp.174–80.

Friedman, M. (1937) 'The Use of Ranks to Avoid the Assumption of Normality Implicit in the Analysis of Variance', *Journal of the American Statistical Association*, **32**, pp.675–701.

Goode, M., Chien, C. and Moutinho, L. (1996) 'Structural Equation Modelling of Overall Satisfaction and Full Use of Services for ATMs', *International Journal of Bank Marketing*, **14**, (7), pp.4–11.

Gosset, W.S. [Student] (1908) 'The Probable Error of a Mean', *Biometrika*, **6**, pp.1–25.

Greene, W.H. (1990) *LIMDEP Econometric Software*, New York: Econometric Software, Inc.

Hayduk, L.A. (1987) *Structural Equation Modelling with LISREL: Essential and Advances*, London: John Hopkins Press Ltd.

Heise, D.R. (1975) *Causal Analysis*, New York: John Wiley and Sons.

Hooley, G.J. (1980) 'Multidimensional Scaling of Consumer Perceptions and Preferences', *European Journal of Marketing*, **14**, (7). pp.436–48.

Hooley, G.J. and Saunders, J. (1993) *Competitive Positioning – The Key to Market Success*, Hemel Hempstead, Prentice-Hall.

Jöreskog, K. G. and Sörbom, D. (1988) *Prelis User's Reference Guide*, Mooresville: Scientific Software, Inc.

Jöreskog, K.G. and Sörbom, D. (1989). *Lisrel 7 User's Reference Guide*, Mooresville: Scientific Software, Inc.

Kanji, G.K. (1995) *100 Statistical Tests*, London: Sage.

Kruskal W.H. and Wallis W. A. (1952) 'Use of Ranks in One-Criterion Variance Analysis', *Journal of the American Statistical Association*, **47**, pp.583–621.

Long, J.S. (1991a) 'Confirmatory Factor Analysis', Paper 33, *Quantitative Applications in the Social Sciences*, Sage University Paper, Sage.

Long, J. S. (1991b) 'Covariance Structure Models : An Introduction to LISREL', Paper 34, *Quantitative Applications in the Social Sciences*, Sage University Paper, Sage.

Mann, H. B. and Whitney D. R. (1947) 'On a Test of Whether One of Two Random Variables is Stochastically Larger than the Other', *Annals of Mathematical Statistics*, **18**, pp.50–60.

Moutinho, L. (1991) *Problems in Marketing: Analysis and Applications*, London: Paul Chapman Publishing Ltd.

O'Shaughnessy, J. (1984) *Competitive Marketing – A Strategic Approach*, Winchester (Mass.) Allen & Unwin Inc.

Pindyck R., and Rubinfeld D. (1991) *Econometric Models and Economic Forecasts*, 3rd edition, Singapore: McGraw-Hill.

Saunders, J. (1980) 'Cluster Analysis for Market Segmentation', *European Journal of Marketing*, **14**, (7), pp.422–35.

Siegel S. and Castellan N. J. (1988) *Nonparametric Statistics for the Behavioural Sciences*, 2nd edition, Singapore: McGraw Hill.

Silver, M. (1997) *Business Statistics*, 2nd edition, Maidenhead: McGraw Hill.

Spearman, C. (1904) 'The Proof and Measurement of Association Between Two Things', *American Journal of Psychology*, **15**, pp.72–101.

SPSS (Statistical Package for the Social Scientist) (1992) *SPSS, User Guide*, 5th edition, Chicago: SPSS.

Ward J.H. (1963) 'Hierarchical Grouping to Optimise an Objective Function', *Journal of American Statistical Association*, **58**, pp.236–44.

PROBLEM: THE KENDALL COEFFICIENT OF CONCORDANCE (W)

Introductory Comments

Let us consider a measure of the relation among several rankings of N objects or individuals. When we have K sets of rankings, we may determine the association among them by using the Kendall coefficient of concordance (W). Whereas R_s (Spearman) and R (Pearson) express the degree of association between two variables measured in, or transformed to, ranks, W expresses the degree of association among K such variables. Such a measure may be particularly useful in marketing studies of interjudge or interest reliability, and also has applications in studies of clusters of variables.

Rationale

As a solution to the problem of ascertaining the overall agreement among K sets of rankings, it might seem reasonable to find the R_s (or R) between all possible pairs of the rankings and then compute the average of these coefficients to determine the overall association. In following such a procedure, we would need to compute $\binom{K}{2}$ rank correlation coefficients. Unless K were very small, such a procedure would be extremely tedious. The computation of W is much simpler, and W bears a linear relation to the average R_s taken over all groups. If we denote the average value of the spearman rank correlation coefficients between the (K) possible pairs of rankings as R_{SAV}, then it has been shown that

$$R_{\text{SAV}} = \frac{KW - 1}{K - 1}$$

Another approach would be to imagine how our data would look if there were no agreement among the several sets of rankings, and then, to imagine how it would look if there were perfect agreement among the several sets. The coefficient of concordance would then be an index of the divergence of the actual agreement shown in the data from the maximum possible (perfect) agreement. Very roughly speaking, W is just such a coefficient.

Method

To compute W, we first find the sum of ranks, R_j, in each column of a $K \times N$ table. Then we sum the R_j and divide that sum by n to obtain the mean value of the R_j. Each of the R_j may then be expressed as a deviation from the mean value. The larger these deviations are, the greater is the degree of association among the K sets of ranks. Finally, s, the sum of squares of these deviations, is found. Knowing these values, we may compute the value of W:

$$W = \frac{s}{\frac{1}{12} K^2 (N^3 - N)}$$

where s = sum of squares of the observed deviations from the mean of R_j,

that is, s $= \sum \left(R_j - \frac{\sum R_j}{N} \right)^2$

K = number of sets of rankings, e.g. the number of judges.
N = number of entities (objects or individuals) ranked.

$\frac{1}{12} K^2 (N^3 - N)$ = maximum possible sum of the squared deviations, i.e. the sum s which would occur with perfect agreement among K rankings.

Problem

Suppose three ORION Company executives are asked to interview six applicants for a job position in the marketing department and rank them separately in their order of suitability for the job opening. The three independent sets of ranks given by executives X, Y, and Z to applicants a through f might be those shown in Table 3.10.

The bottom row of Table 3.10, labelled R_j, gives the sums of the ranks assigned to each applicant.

Now if the three executives had been in perfect agreement about the applicants, i.e. if they had each ranked the six applicants in the same order, then one applicant would have received three ranks of 1 and thus the sum of ranks, R_j, would be 1 + 1 + 1 = 3 = K. The applicant whom all executives designated as the runner-up would have

$$R_j = 2 + 2 + 2 = 6 = 2K$$

the least promising applicant would have

$$R_j = 6 + 6 + 6 = 18 = NK$$

Table 3.10   Rank assigned to six job applicants by three company executives

			Applicant			
	a	b	c	d	e	f
Executive X	1	6	3	2	5	4
Executive Y	1	5	6	4	2	3
Executive Z	6	3	2	5	4	1
R_j	8	14	11	11	11	8

In fact, with perfect agreement among the executives, the various sums of ranks, R_j, would be these: 3, 6, 9, 12, 15, 18, though not necessarily in that order. In general, when there is perfect agreement among K sets of rankings, we get, for the R_j, the series: $K, 2K, 3K, \ldots, NK$.

On the other hand, if there had been no agreement among the three executives, then the various R_j would be approximately equal.

From this example, it should be clear that the degree of agreement among the K judges is reflected by the degree of variance among the N sums of ranks. W, the coefficient of concordance, is a function of that degree of variance.

Questions

1. Calculate the Kendall coefficient of concordance (W).

2. Calculate the R_{SAV}.

3. Comment on the difference between the W and the R_{SAV} methods of expressing agreement among K rankings.

PROBLEM: HYPOTHESIS TESTS USING NOMINAL DATA TEST OF DISTRIBUTIONS BY CATEGORIES OF A SINGLE SAMPLE

Introductory Comments

Often a researcher needs to determine if the number of subjects, objects or responses that fall into some set of categories differs from chance (or some other hypothesised distribution). This could involve the partitioning of users into gender, geographic, or social-status categories. Conversely, it could involve the distribution of a particular sample, such as males, into heavy user, light user, or non-user categories.

The chi-square (χ^2) one-sample test is an appropriate way to answer the question: is there a significant difference? The χ^2 test requires the following steps:

1. Determine the number that would be in each category if the null hypothesis were correct (E_i). Check for small expected frequencies which can distort χ^2 results. No more than 20% of the categories should have expected frequencies less than 5, and none should have an expected frequency less than 1.

2. Calculate χ^2 as follows:

$$\chi^2 = \sum_{i=1}^{K} \frac{(O_i - E_i)^2}{E_i}$$

where O_i = observed number in ith category
        E_i = expected number in ith category
        K = number of categories

Problem

The advertising manager for PlikPlok, a new soft-drink beverage, wants to test three direct mail formats, each of which offers a £0.75 discount coupon for a purchase of a six-pack of PlikPlok, at the student union of a major university campus. Five hundred of each version were mailed to students selected at random. The coupons were redeemed as follows:

        Version A   135
        Version B   130
        Version C   155
            Total $\overline{420}$

Questions

1. Is there a significant difference?
2. Calculate χ^2.
3. What is the probability associated with the χ^2 value?

4

Demand analysis

Contents

Demand theory
Elasticity
Analysing, measuring and forecasting market demand

Objectives

After reading this chapter you should know:

- The major variables that affect demand.

- The main methods of estimating demand and their limitations.

DEMAND THEORY

No company can operate profitably unless there is a demand for its products or services, and the estimation of expected future demand is a key element in a company's planning. Here we discuss how the demand for a product can be analysed and modelled using demand functions – equations which use other relevant variables to predict demand. It is important to remember, however, that future demand is always uncertain, and that no equation can predict demand exactly. Unforeseen events may have an effect on demand – some may have such drastic effects as to make all predictions useless, such as the Gulf War's effect on the demand for foreign travel. Demand analysis needs therefore to be used with care, as a guide to expected demand given that market conditions remain similar. Marketers need to ensure that they also monitor the market and the environment for new or changing factors which may affect demand – competition, changing consumer tastes, innovations, external events, etc. A blend of quantitative analysis, market awareness and common sense is required.

The Demand Function

'Demand' is defined as the number of units of a particular product or service that customers are willing to purchase in a specified time period, under specified conditions. These conditions would include such factors as price, advertising and promotional expenditure on the product or service, availability and price of substitutes, income of expected customers, etc. The demand function is a statement of the relationship between the number of units demanded and the factors which affect this number – i.e. all the variables which may influence demand. For example, a demand function for package holidays abroad could be

$$Q = a_1P + a_2I + a_3Pop + a_4A + a_5T$$

This says that Q, the number of package holidays booked during a specified month, is a function of the average price of a package holiday (P), the average disposable income in £000s per annum (I), the size of the population (Pop), the amount of advertising expenditure (A), and the average UK temperature in degrees centigrade (T). The terms a_1, a_2, etc. are known as the parameters of the demand function. Later, we will look at methods of estimating these parameters – if they are not correctly specified, or not all variables affecting demand are included in the equation, demand will not be accurately predicted. Let us assume now that we have been able accurately to estimate these parameters and our equation is

$$Q = -50P + 100I + 0.01Pop + 0.1A - 200T.$$

This equation now indicates that demand for package holidays falls by 50 units for every £1 increase in the average holiday price, increases by 100 units with every £1 increase in average disposable income, increases by 0.01 units for every additional member of the population and by 0.1 units for every £1 spent on advertising, and decreases by 200 units for each degree rise in average UK temperature. Thus, if the average holiday price was £300, average disposable income £1000, population of the area 10,000,000, advertising expenditure £500,000 and average predicted temperature 15 °C, then we could estimate the demand as

$$(-50 \times 300) + (100 \times 1000) + (0.01 \times 10,000,000) + (0.1 \times 500,000) - (200 \times 15)$$

$$= (-15,000 + 100,000 + 100,000 + 50,000 - 3000)$$

$$= 232,000 \text{ units (holidays).}$$

Industry Demand and Firm Demand

Demand functions can be specified for a whole industry or for individual firms. The independent variables are likely to differ, perhaps most importantly in that a firm's demand function is likely to include variables relating to competitors, such as competitors' prices and advertising expenditures. Demand would be influenced positively by an increase in the firm's advertising expenditure, but negatively by an increase in competitor advertising.

Even for those variables common to both industry and firm demand functions, the parameters associated with them will be different. For instance, size of population would affect the demand for Thomsons' package holidays, and for all tour operators' holidays, but the parameter value in Thomsons' demand function would be smaller than that in the industry demand function.

The Demand Curve

The demand function specifies how demand is related to all the variables defining it. The demand curve is the part of the demand function which specifies the relationship between price charged and quantity demanded, given that all other independent variables are constant. A demand curve is normally shown as a graph.

For example, consider our demand function for package holidays:

$$Q = -50P + 100I + 0.01Pop + 0.1A - 200T$$

If we hold income, population, advertising expenditure and temperature constant at the values given in the example, we can express the price/demand relationship as

$$Q = -50P + 100,000 + 100,000 + 50,000 - 3000$$

$$= 247,000 - 50P$$

This demand curve is shown graphically in Figure 4.1. It is typical in that an increase in price causes a decrease in demand and vice versa. It is normal, as here, to plot demand on the horizontal axis and price on the vertical axis. If this curve is appropriate to the current situation, we can see that, at an average holiday price of £200, 237,000 holidays will be sold, whereas if the average price rises to £300, only 232,000 will be sold. Changes such as these are called movements along a demand curve.

Changes in one or more of the other independent variables in the demand function will lead to a change in the value of the constant in the demand curve equation and thus we could draw several demand curves, as in Figure 4.2, which will all be parallel to each other. If there is a change in one or more of the non-price variables in the demand function, then the price/demand relationship would be defined by a different demand curve. We would say a demand curve shift had occurred. For instance, a reduction in average disposable income from £1000 to £500 would reduce the constant term in our example by (100 x 500) = 50,000, and the appropriate demand curve would then be

$$Q = 197,000 - 50P.$$

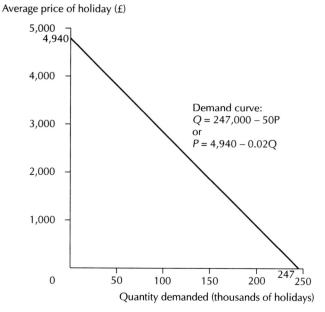

Figure 4.1   A hypothetical demand curve

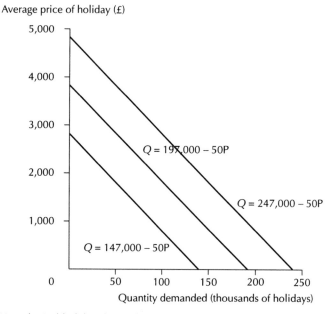

Figure 4.2   Hypothetical holiday demand curves

ELASTICITY

It is important for a company to know the sensitivity of demand to changes in the independent variables in its demand function. The measure of sensitivity used is known as elasticity, defined as the percentage change in demand attributable to a given percentage change in an independent variable. If Q is quantity demanded, X is an independent variable, and $\triangle$ denotes the amount of change in any variable, then the formula for elasticity is:

$$\text{Elasticity} = \frac{\text{Percentage change in } Q}{\text{Percentage change in } X}$$

$$= \frac{\triangle Q/Q}{\triangle X/X}$$

$$= \frac{\triangle Q}{\triangle X} \cdot \frac{X}{Q}$$

Elasticity of a demand function generally varies at different points on the function, and therefore elasticity may be measured either at a given point (point elasticity), or as the average elasticity over some range of the function (arc elasticity).

Price Elasticity of Demand

The most frequently used elasticity measure is price elasticity of demand which measures the sensitivity of quantity demanded to changes in price, all other variables in the demand function remaining constant. If we have a good estimate of price elasticity, we can forecast the increase or decrease in demand and thus the effect on total sales revenue which would follow a price change. Or we can work out the price reduction which would be necessary to increase sales to a specific target level.

For most products, price elasticity lies in the range of 0 to -10. If price elasticity is numerically greater than 1, demand is said to be elastic; while if it is less than one, demand is inelastic. Price elasticity exactly equal to 1 is called unitary elasticity. In this situation, the effect on revenues of a price change is exactly offset by a change in quantity demanded, thus total revenue ($P \times Q$) remains constant. If demand is elastic, the relative change in quantity is larger than that in price, so a price increase causes a larger percentage drop in demand, reducing total revenue. A price decrease, however, would cause a larger percentage increase in demand, hence increasing revenue. In the case of inelastic demand the situation is reversed, so a price increase will increase total revenue while a price decrease will reduce it.

The limits of price elasticity are 0 (completely inelastic) and $-\infty$ (completely elastic). In the completely inelastic situation, quantity demanded is totally

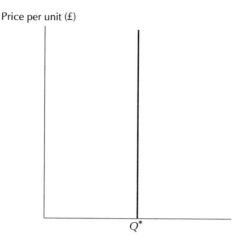

Price per unit (£)

Q^*

Quantity demanded per time period

Figure 4.3   Completely inelastic demand curve (elasticity = 0)

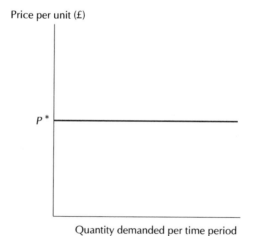

Price per unit (£)

P^*

Quantity demanded per time period

Figure 4.4   Perfectly elastic demand curve (elasticity = $-\infty$)

independent of price and thus remains constant whatever price changes are made (Figure 4.3). This would indicate that a firm could increase prices indefinitely and still sell the same number of units. Figure 4.4 shows the completely elastic demand curve. This indicates that a firm could sell an unlimited number of units at the price specified, but the slightest variation in price would lead to a total loss of demand. Obviously neither situation would apply in the real world, but it can be said that in monopolistic or less competitive industries, selling necessities (e.g. electricity), demand is relatively inelastic, while highly competitive industries have greater elasticity of demand.

Varying Elasticity and its Effect on Revenue

All linear demand curves, unless perfectly elastic or inelastic, vary in elasticity along their length. We have seen that the general formula for elasticity is

$$\frac{\triangle Q}{\triangle P} \cdot \frac{P}{Q}$$

where P represents price and Q quantity demanded. $\frac{\triangle Q}{\triangle P}$ represents the slope of the curve and is therefore constant and negative, but the ratio P/Q will vary from 0 on the horizontal axis to $+\infty$ on the vertical axis. Thus the price elasticity of the curve must range from 0 to $-\infty$, that is, from inelasticity through a point of unitary elasticity to elasticity.

Figure 4.5 shows elasticity at different points on a linear demand curve, and also the associated marginal revenue curve. Marginal revenue is defined as the addition to (or loss from, if negative) a firm's total revenue derived from selling one more unit of output, taking into account both the additional profit made from the sale and the additional cost of production. Marginal revenue can be seen to be positive where demand is elastic, zero at the point of unitary elasticity and negative where demand is inelastic. Figure 4.6 shows the associated total revenue curve, demonstrating the relationship stated previously – that total revenue increases with price reductions in the elastic range and decreases with price reductions in the inelastic range. Total revenue peaks at the point of unitary elasticity.

Determinants of Price Elasticity

The three main reasons for differing price elasticities between products are:

1. Necessity for consumers to have the product (high level of necessity implies inelasticity of demand).
2. Availability of substitutes (the more substitutes available, the more elastic the demand).
3. Proportion of buyer's income spent on the product (higher proportions spent imply more elasticity).

Thus demand for utilities such as electricity, gas or water is relatively inelastic, while products in highly competitive industries and major purchases such as cars or conservatories face more elastic demand.

Different segments within a market may also differ in terms of price sensitivity. For example, for rail travellers on business, price is relatively inelastic. Reliability of the train service, the availability of space in which to work and customer service aspects are likely to be more important than price. For leisure travellers, however, price will be more elastic – if prices are too high they may prefer to go by bus or perhaps not to make the trip at all.

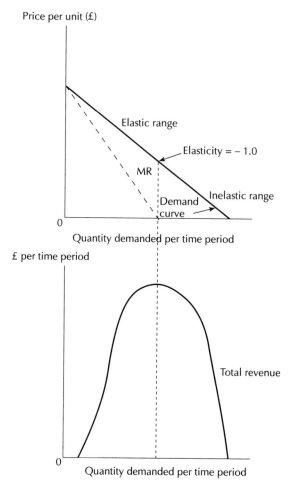

Figure 4.5 (top)   Demand and marginal revenue curves *and* **Figure 4.6**   Total revenue

Consumers also tend to be more price sensitive on expensive products and those which they buy more often. For these products, most consumers will have a good idea of the price they expect to pay, or of the prices of competing offerings, so they have a good frame of reference for price comparison. For less expensive items, bought infrequently, consumers are likely to be less price sensitive because they are not so sure of expected and competing prices.

Income Elasticity of Demand

For luxury items, income may be a more important factor than price in determining elasticity of demand. (Income may be measured on a per capita basis – personal or disposable income – or on an aggregate basis, e.g. gross national product.) The income elasticity of demand measures the sensitivity of quantity demanded to changes in income, holding other variables constant. Unlike the price/demand relationship, demand is likely to increase with an increase in income and vice versa. There are a limited number of products, called inferior goods, for which this does not hold – for instance, low-cost basic foods which consumers replace to some extent with more expensive products as their income increases. Products for which the typical demand/income relationship holds (increased income increases demand) are known as normal or superior goods.

Cross-Elasticity of Demand

Often, demand for a product is influenced by prices of other products. An increase in the price of broccoli, for instance, may cause an increase in demand for other green vegetables as consumers buy them in preference to the more expensive broccoli. This relationship holds for all products which can be regarded as substitutes for each other.

The opposite relationship would hold for products which complement each other – compact disc players and compact discs, video recorders and video tapes. Here, price increases in one product lead to a decrease in demand for the other. Where two goods are used together in this way, demand for them is known as joint demand.

$$\text{Cross elasticity is defined by } \frac{\triangle Q_Y}{\triangle P_X} \cdot \frac{P_X}{Q_Y}$$

where X and Y are two different products, and P and Q are price and quantity, as before. Cross elasticity is positive for substitutes, negative for complements and close to zero for unrelated goods.

Firms may use the concept of cross elasticity in forecasting how demand for their products may respond to changes in price of related goods. It may also be used to measure interrelationships between industries where price changes in one industry affect an industry producing substitute or complementary products.

Other Kinds of Elasticities

We have discussed the three most common demand elasticities – price, income, and cross-elasticity – but there are many more demand elasticities which could be relevant in particular industries. The basic formula for elasticity may be used to calculate any other elasticity in exactly the same way as those discussed.

Derived Demand

Sometimes the demand function for a product or service will contain as one of the independent variables the aggregate demand for some other product. For instance, the demand for car insurance will depend on the extent of car ownership and is thus derived from the demand for cars. Similarly, the demand of a car manufacturer for machinery used in car manufacture will be derived from the demand for that manufacturer's cars.

Acceleration principle

This principle states that when the demand for a final product (e.g. cars) increases, the demand for the relevant producer's goods (e.g. manufacturing robots) will increase at a faster rate. For example, a plant may be producing 1 million cars a year by, using 20 of a particular specialised robot. With steady production, they replace 2 robots per year in rotation. If demand increases by 20% (assuming the plant is operating to capacity), an additional 4 new robots will be needed, giving a total requirement of 6. Thus, derived demand for robots has increased by 200% for a 20% increase in final demand. However, if the opposite situation occurs and demand for cars decreases, derived demand will also decrease at a faster rate (the acceleration principle working in reverse). The acceleration principle explains the much greater cyclical fluctuations which occur in capital goods industries as opposed to consumer goods industries.

Time Characteristics of Demand

Time may be included in the demand function as an independent variable, relating to consumer trends or adoption of a product or it may be taken into account implicitly if variables are lagged – e.g. last month's advertising may affect this month's demand. Other time characteristics may be divided into short-run and long-run effects.

Short-run effects

Time may affect demand through seasonal influences such as climatic variations or special festivals. We expect demand for suncream to be highest in the summer and demand for Easter eggs to peak just before Easter. Short periods of slow-down in economic activity, e.g. high interest rates, will influence demand for different goods to varying extents. Demand for expensive durables such as cars is more variable than for non-durables such as food, as purchases of durables can usually be postponed if necessary. Thus, there are greater cyclical fluctuations in industries producing durables.

Long-run effects

These relate to changes which take place over a long period, such as changes in population or consumer tastes. It is possible for demand to be inelastic in the short run while being elastic in the long run. For instance, an increase in gas prices would be unlikely to have much effect on demand in the short term. However, in the long term, many consumers installing central heating would choose other, cheaper methods; purchases of gas fires and gas cookers would decrease, and the ultimate, long-run impact on demand might be much more substantial.

ANALYSING, MEASURING AND FORECASTING MARKET DEMAND

Market Analysis

We now turn to ways in which a firm can analyse market demand for its products. First we shall define three concepts: market potential, sales potential and sales forecast.

Market potential is the capacity of a market to assimilate a product or product line of an industry, that is, the amount of product that the market can purchase in the period for which plans are being made. For example, we may say that, based on economic forecasts and consumer trends, the washing machine manufacturing industry has a market potential of selling 5 million units in the UK next year.

Sales potential is the maximum share of market potential that an individual firm within the industry can expect to obtain. Continuing the above example, we might say that, based on current market share, production capacity, marketing strategy, etc., Hoover could expect to obtain a 20% market share next year. Hoover's sales potential would thus be 1 million units.

Sales forecast is a prediction of sales (either by value or by volume) for a product or product line that the firm expects in a future period under a given marketing plan. Hoover might, for instance, forecast sales of 60,000 units (value £15 million) of a specific model of washing machine. The sales forecast is based on the allocation of resources specified in the marketing plan, likely actions by competitors, other environmental variables and the total industry forecast.

Figure 4.7 shows how market potentials, sales potentials and sales forecasts are used in formulating market strategy. Industry market potential is based on economic, social and other environmental variables – indicators that may be useful include gross national product (GNP), employment rates, extent of home ownership, retail price index, interest rates, etc. Cultural and environmental trends, and changing buyer preferences, will also need to be considered. The measurement of market potential gives an upper limit to possible industry sales. Sales potential of the firm is based on previous sales performance and trends, and the predicted effect of changes in market competition or other changes likely to affect sales. The sales forecast, finally, estimates sales under a specific marketing plan. An unsatisfactory sales forecast may lead to revision of the marketing plan.

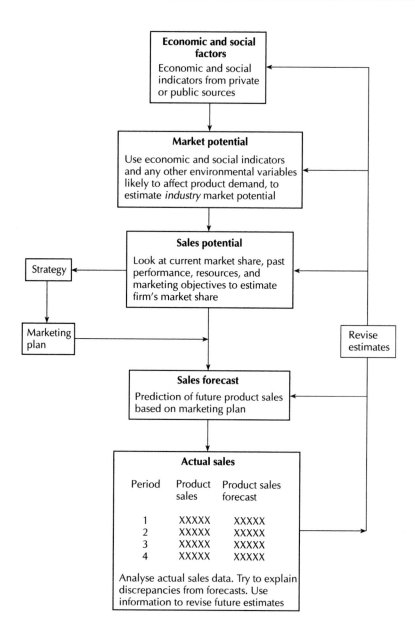

Figure 4.7   Developing and revising market potential, sales potential and sales forecasts

Data Sources

External

The measurement of market potentials is based on an analysis of the underlying economic, social and environmental factors affecting demand for a product. There are many governmental and non-governmental organisations which can supply useful secondary data, for instance:

OPCS (The Office of Population Censuses and Surveys) carries out a full UK census every 10 years which provides information on population, employment, etc.

British Social Attitudes, published annually by Social and Community Planning Research, is an in-depth survey of social attitudes to such matters as the environment, religion, gender issues, etc.

Euromonitor publish annually *International and European Marketing Data and Statistics*, covering demographic and economic trends, with information on the labour force, trade, consumer expenditure, retailing, housing, literacy, etc.

The Economist Intelligence Unit produces two journals: *Retail Business* carries out market surveys of four retail sectors every month, while the quarterly *Retail Trade Review* gives statistical analysis and forecasts for the retail trade, covering each sector once a year.

Mintel produces market reports on fast moving consumer goods and services, both for the UK and internationally.

Key Note Publications publish a series of Key Note reports for specific product sectors, examining market trends.

In addition, many of the major banks carry out their own economic surveys, the results of which are generally made publicly available. In particular, the National Westminster Bank publishes a series of *Industry Briefs*, which describe the salient features and recent trends in specific industries.

Internal

A good marketing information system which collects and analyses data from different areas of the firm (accounting, finance, sales, planning, production, etc.) can supply much useful information on the firm's market, current sales trends, competition, resources, etc. It is of course essential that such information is organised by some method or procedure that will provide an estimate for management. The next section considers such methods.

Market Measurement and Forecasting

Here we look at major measurement methods, and discuss their advantages, disadvantages, and the situations in which they might be appropriate.

Judgmental Forecasting

This method usually uses a panel of executives or industry experts, rather than a single estimator. Panel members are given information on past sales and are asked for an estimate of future sales, given their knowledge of the current marketing environment. They may also be asked to state how certain they feel about their estimate – this information would then be used to weight their replies.

Sales-force Estimates

In some companies the sales personnel, who are in direct contact with customers, are considered to be in the best position to estimate likely short-term sales. Their estimates, however, are often revised at a higher level.

Consumer Interviews

This involves questioning current or prospective customers on projected purchases of the firm's products under different conditions relating to price, income, competing products, advertising, etc. By aggregating the data collected on all relevant variables, the firm can estimate its demand function. However, respondents often find it difficult or impossible to state accurately how they would react in a hypothetical situation and therefore the information gained is likely to be of doubtful quality.

On the other hand, consumer survey techniques may be very useful in gathering other useful types of demand-related information, for instance awareness of advertising campaigns or of product prices.

Experimentation

Experimentation is most often used to investigate price elasticity of demand. In all analysis of historical data, it is impossible to isolate effects of price changes from effects of other uncontrolled factors. In an experimental situation, however, it is possible to vary price while either holding all other marketing and economic variables constant, or controlling their effects by using treatment and control groups upon which factors other than price act in exactly the same way. Pricing experiments may take place in the field or in a laboratory simulation.

Field experimentation

These experiments are carried out under 'real' conditions, by monitoring shoppers' purchases of the product under consideration with prices being varied in different stores, groups of stores or areas, or in different time periods. The major advantage of field experiments is that they take place under actual market conditions. They can be controlled to a certain extent for effects of factors other than price, but there are some factors outside the testing firm's control – most importantly, competitor actions. Competitors may change their prices or increase advertising, either as part of their overall strategy or deliberately to contaminate the market test. Field experimentation is also likely to be costly, and there may be a trade off between cost and sample size, leading to an inadequate and/or unrepresentative sample. Retailers may not be cooperative in raising or lowering prices as required, and price changes outside the range expected by customers may lead to lost sales.

Laboratory experimentation

Here the buying situation is replicated under laboratory conditions, to allow greater control of non-price variables. The influence of price on purchase can be measured, as long as 'purchasers' are making the same kinds of choices as they would in the actual market place.

An early laboratory technique was the barter experiment (Oxenfeldt 1961). Here respondents are asked several questions on unrelated subjects, and the questioner then rewards them for their cooperation by asking them to choose a gift from among several items. Choices would reflect which item is most valued. An alternative form of the experiment is to ask respondents to choose between the test product and a sum of money (the actual amount varying between respondents). A demand schedule could be derived by looking at the numbers preferring the product to the money at each amount offered. This method, however, does not take into account the option which customers generally have in the market place of buying a competing product if they do not feel the test product offers good value for money.

We now present a more advanced technique, that of Pessemier, one of the pioneers of these types of laboratory simulations.

Pessemier's Laboratory Experimentation Technique

A more sophisticated method than that described above was developed by Edgar Pessemier in 1959 (Pessemier 1960). His respondents were students at Washington State University and he sent them on a series of simulated shopping trips for a selection of frequently purchased items. For each product, the students had a selection of brands from which to choose and enough money was supplied for them to buy the highest priced brand in each category, if they so wished. At the end of the experiment, for each group of respondents, one of the shopping lists compiled by that group was picked at random and each member of the group received the products on the list plus any change from the money supplied. Pessemier believed that, because respondents had a chance of receiving both the products and the change, this would influence them to make realistic choices similar to those they would make on a true shopping trip.

Having established before the experiment the respondents' preferred brands, Pessemier was able to run a series of experiments, adjusting the price of the respondent's preferred brand upwards by successive increments while prices of other brands remained constant, or adjusting the prices of competing brands downwards while the price of the preferred brand remained constant. Respondents had to decide, on each simulated shopping trip, whether they would continue to buy their preferred brand, or switch because of increased price differentials. Thus a demand curve could be experimentally derived for each brand.

The advantages of Pessemier's method are the ability to control for variation in variables other than price, and that a vast amount of data can be obtained in a reasonably short time and at a reasonable cost. However, as with all experimental methods, no account can be taken of competitor reactions, nor of time lag effects of price changes (consumers may purchase several of an item when it is on sale at a price regarded as low, and thus not buy at all for some time, whatever the price is). Also, there may be a tendency for respondents to behave more rationally than normal in such an experiment – as they know prices are changing and they may have fewer distractions than when they are usually shopping, they may pay more attention to prices than they would under the normal conditions of a shopping trip.

Surveys of Purchase Intentions

This is an approach most commonly used in industrial markets where the costs of contacting buyers are low (because there are relatively few buyers, and/or most buyers are known to the manufacturer) and buyers are willing and able to state their purchase intentions. Manufacturers contact product users about their purchase plans for the future and use information provided in developing their own forecasts. For example, many car companies now ask in customer surveys when the respondent intends to replace their car and the makes they would consider buying at that time. Sometimes useful information as to future purchase intentions can be gleaned from general-purpose surveys and although such information is not usually concrete enough to actually forecast demand, it can often be used as a guide in forecasting.

Statistical Analysis of Historical Data

Statistical analysis may be applied to data derived either from experimentation or from past sales. It is important to remember, in analysing historical sales data, that there were no controls on the market environment in which these sales took place and therefore many factors in addition to price may have varied and thus have affected sales. The time series method of forecasting is a simple extrapolation of past sales patterns into the future, usually using graphical methods. Regression methods seek to derive an equation for demand in terms of price and other relevant variables. Sometimes a simple regression of price and quantity sold is used, but this assumes that other factors such as competitors' prices, advertising, etc. have remained constant. If, as is likely, there have been changes in some of these variables, this method may give inaccurate forecasts. Multiple regression methods are designed to account for some of the variations in non-price factors. We will now consider the steps involved in performing regression analysis.

Regression Analysis – the Variables

First we need to specify the independent variables that are expected to influence demand (the dependent variable). These will always include price and will generally include such factors as competitors' prices, advertising expenditures, consumer population size, buyer incomes, etc., as well as others specific to the type of product. Then we need to obtain accurate estimates of the selected variables for the period under consideration.

The Regression Equation

The regression equation specifies the manner in which the independent variables are hypothesised to interact to give the level of demand. The most commonly used specification is a linear relationship of the form

$$Q = a + bP + cA + dB + eC + \ldots$$

where Q = quantity demanded, P is price, and A, B, C, etc. are other independent variables influencing demand, while a, b, c, etc. are parameters. This type of function produces a straight line demand curve.

Linear functions are often used because many demand relationships have been shown to fit reasonably well to such a model and because there is a convenient statistical technique, the method of least squares, for estimating the parameters of the equation.

The second most commonly used specification of demand relationship is the power function

$$Q = aP^b A^c B^d \ldots$$

This type of relationship assumes that the marginal effects of each independent variable on demand are not constant, but depend on both the value of the variable and the values of all other variables in the demand function. This is in many cases a more realistic assumption than the constant marginal relation assumed by a linear model. The parameters of a power function may also be estimated by the least squares method, by first transforming the equation into a linear relationship by using logarithms – the general equation above is equivalent to

$$\log Q = \log a + (b^* \log P) + (c^* \log A) + (d^* \log B) + \ldots$$

A multiplicative demand function such as this also has constant elasticities over the complete range of values, and these elasticities are given by the parameters b, c, d, etc. which are estimated by regression analysis. The elasticity of linear demand curves, on the other hand, changes over their range.

The form of the demand function – linear, multiplicative, or some other form – should be chosen to reflect the true relationships between the variables under consideration. If this is not immediately evident, it may be necessary to test several

forms of equation and choose the one which best fits the data. Then it is necessary
to estimate the parameters – this is known as 'fitting'.

Estimating the Regression Parameters

Parameters are normally estimated by using the least squares method. This can be
described graphically as fitting a straight line to the data in such a way as to
minimise the sum of the squares of the deviations of each data point from the fitted
line. A simple two variable example can be used to illustrate the procedure – let us
assume that a company hypothesises that there is a linear relationship between sales
(S) of a certain product and marketing expenditure (ME) on that product, and that
they have collected the relevant data for the past eight years, as shown in Table 4.1.
The regression equation would then take the form

$$S = a + bME$$

The data are shown graphically in Figure 4.8 with the line of best fit drawn in. Note
that the parameter a is the intercept of the regression line on the y-axis (sales) and
the parameter b is the gradient of the line. The line has been drawn in such a way as
to minimise the sum of the squares of the vertical deviations of each point from the
regression line, i.e. (denoting vertical deviations by v) to minimise

$$\sum_{i=1}^{n} v^2 = \sum_{i=1}^{n} (y_i - \hat{y}_i)^2$$

where y_i is the ith observed value of sales and $\hat{y}_i$ is the ith predicted value of sales
   The equation for the gradient of this line is given by

$$b = \frac{\sum (x - \bar{x})(y - \bar{y})}{\sum (x - \bar{x})^2} \text{ or } b = \frac{\sum xy - \frac{(\sum x)(\sum y)}{n}}{\sum x^2 - \frac{(\sum x)^2}{n}}$$

where $\bar{x}$, $\bar{y}$ are the means of the observed x values and the observed y values
respectively, and Σ in each case implies $\sum_{i=1}^{n}$.
   The intercept a can then be found from the equation

$$a = \bar{y} - b\bar{x}$$

Table 4.1 Sales and marketing expenditure

	1987	1988	1989	1990	1991	1992	1993	1994
Sales (thousands)	29	35	33	36	37	37	40	39
Marketing expenditure (£ thousands)	420	450	480	550	600	580	600	620

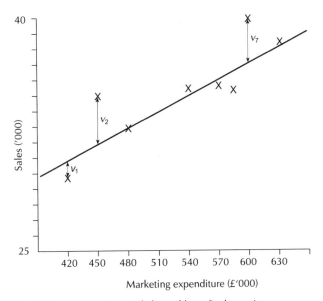

Figure 4.8 A simple linear regression with line of best fit drawn in

In our example we find that the sales/marketing expenditure regression relationship is estimated to be:

$$S = 13.85 + 0.04ME$$

Now, how do we interpret the coefficients we have calculated? Firstly, we must remember that, typically, these parameters are calculated using data which extends over a very limited range. The intercept, in this case the point where marketing expenditure is zero, is generally well outside the range of observed data, and therefore we cannot say that the intercept parameter, a, is the level of sales that would be achieved with zero marketing expenditure. a, in fact, generally has no economic meaning.

The gradient, b, gives an estimate of the change in sales associated with a one unit change in marketing expenditure – in this case, a £1000 increase in marketing expenditure is likely to lead to an increase in sales of 0.04 thousand, i.e. 40 units. Again, we must be careful in extending these estimates outside the observed data ranges.

The example shown here is a simple regression with only one independent variable. In practice, there are more likely to be several independent variables affecting sales and we would have a multiple regression equation of the form

$$S = a + bME + cA + dB + eC + \ldots$$

where A, B, C are other factors affecting sales. The principle of estimating parameters is the same, although the calculations would obviously become more complicated. However, although we have shown the procedure for deriving estimates of parameters, in practice it will seldom be necessary to perform these calculations as almost every spreadsheet program contains a regression program which will calculate regression parameters, and associated statistics, from given data sets with any reasonable number of independent variables. Provided that certain assumptions are satisfied, we can use regression analysis to make valid inferences such as those above on the effect of increasing market expenditure. These assumptions are:

1. The relationship between the variables has been expressed in the correct form, e.g. linear, multiplicative, etc.
2. The data points are scattered uniformly around the regression line.
3. Errors are independent, i.e. the deviation of any one point from the fitted line is not related in any way to the deviation of any other point.
4. Errors are normally distributed, with a mean of zero.

Regression Statistics

We now consider three statistics, output by most spreadsheet regression programs, which can aid us in determining the accuracy of a regression model.

Coefficient of determination

This statistic, typically denoted by R^2, indicates how well the regression model explains changes in the value of the dependent variable. It is the proportion of the total variation in the dependent variable that can be explained by the full set of independent variables used in the regression analysis and can thus take values between 0 and 1. Higher values of R^2 mean that the observed data points will be closer to the fitted regression line with smaller vertical deviations.

Let us briefly examine how R^2 is calculated. The total variation in a dependent variable, y, is measured by summing the squares of the deviations from the variable's mean:

$$\text{Total variation} = \sum (y - \bar{y})^2$$

Regression analysis breaks the total variation down into that part which can be explained by changes in the independent variables and that part which cannot be so explained. The regression equation derived from the data can be used to calculate the explained variation – denoting the value of y predicted by the regression equation $y = a + bx$ as $\hat{y}$, we have

$$\text{Total explained variation} = \sum (\hat{y} - \bar{y})^2$$

$$R_2 \text{ is thus } \frac{\sum (\hat{y} - \bar{y})^2}{\sum (y - \bar{y})^2}$$

The unexplained variation is a measurement of the deviations of the actual y values from the predicted values, i.e.

$$\text{Unexplained variation} = \sum (y - \hat{y})^2$$

Thus if all points lie exactly on the regression line, there would be no unexplained variation, and R^2 would equal 1. This is very unlikely to occur in practice and R^2 values of 0.8 or above are generally acceptable in demand estimation, though for some types of goods it may be necessary to be satisfied with lower values. However, very low values, say 0.3 or less, would indicate that the regression model used is not adequate to explain demand – possibly one or more important variables have been omitted.

Standard error of the estimate
This statistic provides a means for estimating a confidence interval for predicting values of the dependent variables – the regression equation gives us an estimate, the standard error indicates how accurate that estimate is likely to be. Assuming a normal distribution, we can say that there is a 68% probability that future observations of the dependent variable will be within the range of plus or minus one standard error of the estimate, a 95% probability that they will be within two standard errors of the estimate and a 99% probability that they will be within three standard errors. Smaller standard errors therefore mean greater accuracy of predictions.

We should note that the standard error increases as observations deviate from the mean, and therefore predictions are likely to be most accurate close to the mean, and least accurate at the upper and lower bounds of the observed data range.

Standard error of the coefficient
This statistic indicates the confidence with which we can rely on the estimated values of the regression parameters. The smaller the standard error of the coefficients, the greater confidence we can have that the regression equation has accurately estimated the marginal relationships between independent and dependent variables.

Multicollinearity
Multicollinearity means the existence of relationships between the 'independent' variables in a regression equation. If one or more of these supposedly independent variables are in fact correlated, regression analysis will be unable accurately to separate out the effects of each of the variables on the dependent variable. The existence of such a problem can be deduced by comparison of regression statistics – it would be indicated by a high R^2, showing that the model as a whole explains most of the variation in the dependent variable, accompanied by relatively large standard errors for the coefficients for the independent variables – i.e. the model is unable to estimate accurately the effects of each independent variable on its own. A

possible solution to this problem is to remove all but one of the correlated 'independent' variables from the regression equation before estimating the parameters. While the coefficient of the remaining variable will strictly relate to the effects of all the correlated variables rather then those of the single remaining variable, the equation will still be satisfactory for predictive purposes as long as the relationships between the correlated variables do not change.

Spurious correlations

It is also possible for two figures to give the appearance of being highly correlated when they are in fact unrelated. This may be pure chance or it may be because they each correlate separately with another, underlying variable. Many variables, for instance, such as personal computer ownership, number of meals eaten out or number of households with two cars can be shown to have increased in recent years – however, these variables are all likely to be related to an underlying trend of increasing disposable income among the relevant section of the population. The marketer must therefore exercise common sense to ensure that spurious correlations are not taken to be true

CONCLUSIONS

We have now discussed several methods of estimating demand, most of which seek to derive a demand curve indicating the short-range or medium-range response of the market to different price levels. Such techniques can be used to indicate the relative profitability of various price and output levels and can therefore aid marketers in making better pricing decisions than they would if they did not heed demand considerations. Nevertheless, demand is not the only factor that must be taken into account in pricing. Most importantly, estimated costs of production must be considered in conjunction with demand estimation. Also, changes to the price of a product may cause variation in sales of other products produced by the same company, and in such a case overall profitability must be considered. The effects of price changes over time should also be estimated – in the longer run competitor reactions, or stocking up by consumers, may affect future demand. Finally, the same demand curve may not apply to all segments of the buying population – demand elasticity may vary with social class, income, area, etc., and so several demand curves may need to be estimated for one product.

REFERENCES AND FURTHER READING

Draper, N.R. and Smith, H. (1981) *Applied Regression Analysis*, New York: John Wiley and Sons.

Glahe, F.R. and Lee, D.R. (1989) *Microeconomics – Theory and Applications*, 2nd edition, London: The Dryden Press.

Landsburg, S.E. (1991) *Price Theory and Applications*, 2nd edition, London: The Dryden Press.

Laric, M.V. and Stiff, R. (1988) *Marketing Management Analysis using Spreadsheets*, Englewood Cliffs: Prentice-Hall.

Makridakis, S. (1990) *Forecasting, Planning and Strategy for the 21st Century*, New York: Free Press.

Nicholson, W. (1995) *Microeconomic Theory – Principles and Extensions*, 6th edition, London: The Dryden Press.

Oxenfeldt, A.R. (1961) *Pricing for Marketing Executives*, Wadsworth.

Pessemier, E.A. (1960) 'An Experimental Model for Estimating Demand', *Journal of Business* **33**, October.

CASE: VECTOR COMPUTERS

Miriam Walker, the marketing manager at Vector Computers in Ayrshire, Scotland, was aware that when demand is elastic it is frequently assumed that organisations can increase profits by lowering the price. Although revenue is sure to increase, the profitability of this action depends on the ratio of fixed to variable costs.

The sales, costs and profit are given below for Vector, a computer manufacturer who is currently selling 100,000 small business computers per year at a factory price of £3000 each. If unit costs are £2700 and fixed costs are £54 million, then this manufacturer will generate a total profit of £30 million for the year.

Sales, costs and profit of VECTOR (millions)

Sales (£3000×100,000)		£ 300
Variable Costs (£2160 x 100,000)	£216	
Fixed Costs	£ 54	
Total Costs		£ 270
Profit		£ 30
Average cost per unit		£2700

Question

1. If the price of the computers is reduced £120 (−4%) and price elasticity is realistically estimated at −1.5, calculate expected sales. Comment on the achieved results.

CASE: DYSON VACUUM CLEANERS

In the process of making price adjustments the marketing manager of Dyson Vacuum Cleaners has learned the shape of the demand curve for battery-powered vacuum cleaners. The basic relationship was negative and the quantity purchased, Q, increases as the price, P, declines. This relationship can be expressed as:

$$Q = 4000 - 40 P$$

Fixed costs for tooling and overheads were estimated at £15,000 and variable costs for the vacuum cleaner were £20 per unit, then the total cost, C, will be

$$C = £15,000 + £20 Q$$

where, assuming that supply equals demand, the number of units produced is also Q. Because costs are subtracted from revenue (or turnover) to get profits, it is handy to have an equation that expresses total revenue, R, as a function of price. This can be obtained by noting that revenue is equal to price times quantity. Because the first equation above expresses quantity in terms of price, a revenue function can be obtained as follows:

$$R = PQ$$
$$= P(4000 - 40P)$$
$$= 4000P - 40P^2$$

Now that John Carter, the company's marketing manager, had equations for demand, costs, and revenue, it was a simple matter to express profits, K, in terms of price.

Question

1. Taking into account the equations for demand, costs, and revenue, express profits in terms of price for the Dyson vacuum cleaner.

5
Forecasting

This chapter is divided into three main sections which look at judgemental approaches, statistical methods and other methods of forecasting.

Contents

Judgemental approaches
Statistical methods
Other methods often used in forecasting

Objectives

After reading this chapter you should be able to:

- Understand the purpose of forecasting.
- Know the difference between quantitative and qualitative forecasting.
- Understand the different approaches to forecasting covered in this chapter.
- Use all the statistical approaches described to forecast with any data set.
- Undertake analysis of forecasting errors.
- Understand how to assess the forecasting power of a model and to choose between the different approaches.

A critical aspect of the management of any organisation is effective planning for the future. Indeed, the long run success of any firm is closely related to how well management is able to foresee the future and develop appropriate strategies. Therefore, in order to plan for the future and make effective decisions, forecasts are very important (examples include demand, costs, cash flow, economy activity, etc.).

There are basically two broad approaches to forecasting. Firstly, *judgemental methods* which include expert opinion, market surveys and the Delphi method. All

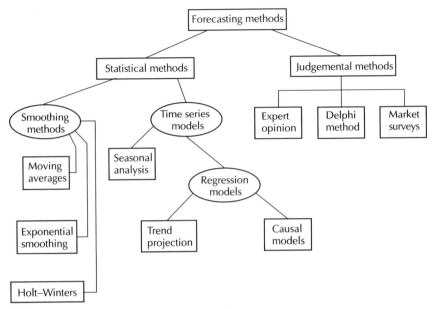

Figure 5.1   Statistical and judgemental approaches

these methods are based on people's ideas or opinions of situations. The second major area is *statistical methods*, which includes causal methods, smoothing methods, trend projection and seasonal analysis. All these statistical methods utilise historical data and statistical models to predict the future based on past historical trends or patterns.

JUDGEMENTAL APPROACHES

The three commonly used judgemental forecasting approaches are:

1. Expert opinions.
2. Market surveys.
3. Delphi technique.

Expert Opinions

This approach simply consists of gathering judgemental information and opinions from key personnel based on their experience and knowledge of a particular situation. The key personnel could be either from within a company or from leading experts in their field. These methods are both very flexible and quick, and are often used to determine long-run demand trends or growth areas.

Market Surveys

These methods utilise questionnaires, telephone contacts or personal interviews as a means to gather data. These methods are often used in strategic marketing planning – i.e., obtaining new product information or opinions on existing products, etc. Although these surveys are very flexible, the cost can be very high and can be subject to sample and response bias. The sample frame for respondents needs to be very carefully selected, so as to minimise sample bias.

Delphi Method

This approach uses a panel of experts who do not meet and is normally used for long-run forecasting, predicting technological change or future market demand for a new product. The individuals normally fax or telephone their responses which greatly increases the speed of generating the forecast. The method is based on an iterative approach which involves two or three rounds of iterations. In the first round all individuals are asked a series of questions and the results are then gathered together, these aggregate results are then given back to each member of the panel for the second round and they are asked if they wish to change their forecast. This process continues until either no individual changes their forecast or a level of general agreement exists.

This method has been used to forecast:

- demand for a new book by an unknown author.
- demand in the construction industry.
- growth of gross national product.

STATISTICAL METHODS

There are numerous statistical approaches available for forecasting from the univariate simple smoothing methods to complex multivariate regression models and univariate Box–Jenkins approach.

Smoothing methods include moving averages, exponential smoothing and Holt–Winters triple parameter smoothing. The major advantage of all the smoothing techniques is that they only use data on the variable to be forecast; however, this advantage needs to be balanced against the problem of not being able to forecast very far into the future.

Moving Averages

This method is based on the principle of filtering the peaks and troughs out of the data set by using a window of period n to average the data set. This method has

Table 5.1

	Demand (Y_t)	Third period moving average	FORECAST (F_t)	Error
Jan	342			
Feb	313			
Mar	356			
Apr	360	(342 + 313 + 356)/3	337	+ 23
May	377	(313 + 356 + 360)/3	343	+ 34
Jun	350	(356 + 360 + 377)/3	364	− 14
Jul	380	(360 + 377 + 350)/3	362	+ 17
Aug	410	(377 + 350 + 380)/3	369	+ 41
Sep	421	(350 + 380 + 410)/3	380	+ 41
Oct	418	(380 + 410 + 421)/3	403	+ 14
Nov	417	(410 + 421 + 418)/3	416	+ 0
Dec	430	(421 + 418 + 417)/3	418	+ 11
		(418 + 417 + 430)/3	421	

been used to forecast share prices, demand patterns and commodity prices. A simple example of the demand for computer printers by a mail-order company, using a third period moving average is shown in Table 5.1.

Each forecast value is calculated by taking the average of the previous three values and as can be seen from Figure 5.2 the forecast series has much lower variance than the original series. If the data set is fairly stable, without large regular swings up or down, i.e. seasonal fluctuations, the moving average method will normally fit the original data set fairly well. However, if the data exhibits strong trends the moving average will also lag behind the original data set (see Figure 5.2). The period of the moving average can take any value, however it is normal for the period to be an odd value (3rd, 5th, 7th, 9th etc.) the higher the period the more smooth the forecast series with be. The choice of which period value should be used is up to the individual user, however sometimes a criterion like the minimisation of forecast errors is set (see the use of MAD or MSE on pages 129–30).

Exponential Smoothing

This is the second most frequently used smoothing technique and is based on the principle of taking a weighted average of past values to forecast the future. The weighting factor, called α, can take any value between 0 and 1. This method is commonly used in business to forecast demand and cost patterns. The exponential smoothing formula is

$$F_{t+1} = \alpha Y_t + (1 - \alpha)F_t$$

where $0 \leq \alpha \leq 1$

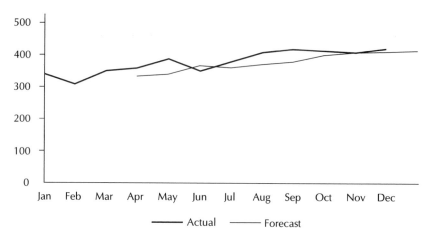

Figure 5.2   Moving averages

With this method the weights decline exponentially the further into the past you go, if alpha is greater than 0 and less than 1, hence its name. Two special cases exist if α is equal to 0 or 1.

If α takes the value of 1 the formula simplifies to

$$F_{t+1} = Y_t$$

which is a *simple naive* forecast, where the forecast for the next period is simply the same as the value of Y_t for this period.

If α takes the value of 0 the formula simplifies to

$$F_{t+1} = F_t$$

this is a simple forecast of no change, as the future forecasts will always be the same as the first F_t value.

Both these extremes are rarely used in practice, however it is important for users to understand what is meant by these two extremes.

Before the exponential formula can be used, two basic problems need to be addressed; first, what value should α take and second, how is the first value of F_t generated? The first question can be addressed by initially taking a value of 0.33 for α, a more precise value can be found later, however for business subjects 0.33 has been found to work fairly well. The value of α can be changed by running a simulation exercise to minimise the sum of average errors (see MAD or MSE on pages 129–30). The second problem of generating the first value of F_t is normally addressed by setting the first value of F_t to Y_{t-1} as shown in Table 5.2. The forecast for the next period is then calculated by using the last value of Y_t multiplied by plus F_t multiplied by 1 minus α.

Table 5.2

	Demand (Y_t)	$\alpha = 0.33$	Forecast (F_t)	Error
Jan	342			
Feb	313	342	342	−29
Mar	356	0.33*313 + (1-0.33)*342	332	+23
Apr	360	0.33*356 + (1-0.33)*332	340	+19
May	377	0.33*360 + (1-0.33)*340	346	+30
Jun	350	0.33*377 + (1-0.33)*346	356	−6
Jul	380	0.33*350 + (1-0.33)*356	354	+25
Aug	410	0.33*380 + (1-0.33)*354	362	+47
Sep	421	0.33*410 + (1-0.33)*362	378	+42
Oct	418	0.33*421 + (1-0.33)*378	392	+25
Nov	417	0.33*418 + (1-0.33)*392	400	+16
Dec	430	0.33*417 + (1-0.33)*400	406	+23
		0.33*430 + (1-0.33)*406	414	

Figures 5.3 and 5.4 show firstly the result of setting α to 0.33 and secondly the effects of varying α between 0 and 1 in steps of 0.2. The choice of which value α should take is normally decided by minimising the average of the errors (see MAD or MSE on pages 129–30).

The first value of F_t can also be found by a backward substitution method, which expands the initial formula back to Y_{t-10}. This is shown in Appendix C and is not recommended unless your mathematics and algebra manipulation are fairly strong.

There is also a self-correcting version of the exponential formula which corrects for past errors, as follows:

$$F_{t+1} = F_t + \alpha(Y_t - F_t)$$

Both moving averages and exponential smoothing take no account of seasonal patterns which are quite common in management data sets. Therefore we turn to classical decomposition.

Classical Decomposition

This method is based on the idea that any data series is composed of four major components, namely a cyclical factor (C_t), a seasonal factor (S_t), a trend component (T_t) and an irregular component (I_t). Figure 5.5 shows how one data set can be divided into these four components.

The cyclical factor refers to any recurrent upward or downward patterns in the data set that occur over time and are probably due to the general economic conditions such as booms or recessions. These cyclical factors normally have a cycle of greater than one year and can be seen by data points above and below the

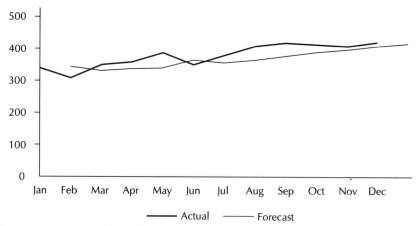

Figure 5.3   Exponential smoothing ($\alpha = 0.33$)

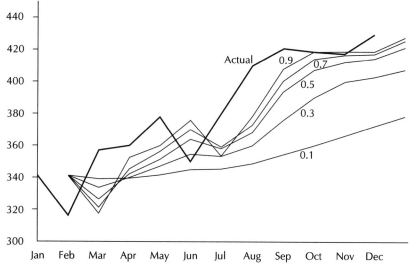

Figure 5.4   Exponential smoothing ($\alpha = 0.1$ to 0.9 in steps of 0.2)

trend line. Determining the cyclical component is often very difficult and knowledge of the level of economic, industrial or company activity is required. Industrial production indexes are often used to track the cyclical pattern of a data set.

The seasonal factor refers to periodic fluctuations of constant length that could be caused by seasonal influences such as the weather, month of the year, holidays etc. For example, the sales of ice-creams will normally be higher in hot weather than in cold weather.

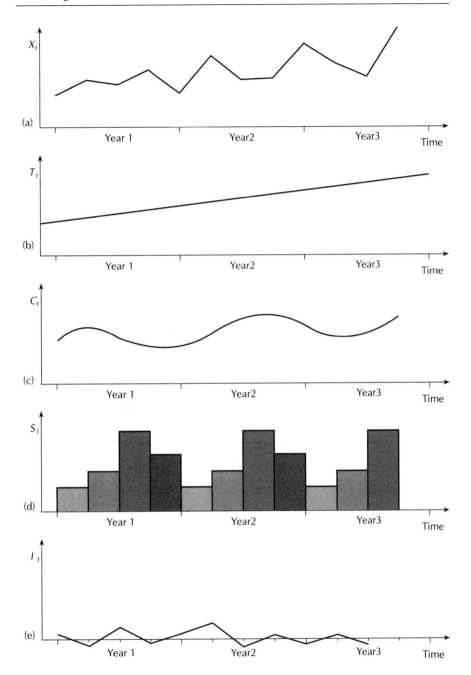

Figure 5.5   Decomposition (a) actual; (b) trend; (c) cyclical; (d) seasonal; (e) irregular

The trend factor describes the long-run movement of the data set over time; this could be upwards, downwards or no change. Moving averages or regression analysis is often used to calculate the trend component of a data set.

The irregular factor is the residual after the other three factors have been removed from the data set and is caused by short-term random events which follow no discernible pattern. It is therefore unpredictable and it is because of this random error that forecasts are never 100% accurate.

It is normally assumed that these four factors (C, T, S and I) act in an independent manner and that factors which caused them to change in the past will also cause them to change in the future.

There are two basic models used in seasonal analysis; the multiplicative model, $X_t = C_t^* S_t^* T_t^* I_t$ (where the individual components are multiplied together to form the series X_t) and the additive model, $X_t = C_t + S_t + T_t + I_t$ (where the individual components are added together to form the series X_t). The problem is how to separate these four components. Two main methods exist to undertake seasonal analysis, namely simple classical decomposition as shown in Table 5.3 and the complex Census X-II method developed by the Bureau of the Census of the US Department of Commerce (see Salzman 1968). Census X-II is available in the SPSS (1992) computer package under the TREND section. The Census X-II method is normally used in official government statistics for unemployment data and inflation data etc. If these components (C_t, S_t, T_t and I_t) can be separated, more accurate forecasts can be developed. Some data sets will exhibit very strong seasonal fluctuations, such as the high demand for foreign holidays in August or the low demand for central heating systems in the summer.

Table 5.3 shows the demand for CD players from a large department store over the last four years. X_t are actual sales of CD players. The first value (i.e. Q2) of the fourth quarter centred moving average is calculated by the average of the first four quarters of sales, i.e. (617+541+757+801)/4 = 679. The second value of the fourth quarter centred moving average (i.e. Q3) will be the average of (541+757+801+ 725)/4 = 706 and so on until the end of the data set. The values of T,C are found by averaging the two preceding values of the fourth quarter centred moving average (i.e. 679+706)/2 = 692.5) The final column SI is found by dividing actual sales X_t by the T,C column. The initial seasonal indices (SI) are then found by averaging all the Q1 SI values, Q2 SI values, Q3 SI values and Q4 SI values, as follows.

Q1 (0.973+0.954+0.963)/3 = 0.963
Q2 (0.861+0.900+0.863)/3 = 0.874
Q3 (1.094+1.064+1.031)/3 = 1.063
Q4 (1.111+1.133+1.064)/3 = 1.103

These values should sum to 4 for quarterly data; if they do not, the seasonal indices have to be reweighted by calculating a scalar factor equal to 4 divided by the sum of the seasonal indices and then multiplying each index by this value. In this case

Table 5.3

Year	Quarter	X_t	Fourth quarter centred moving average	T, C	$SI = X_t/TC$
1993	Q1	617	—	—	—
	Q2	541	679.00	—	—
	Q3	757	706.00	692.50	1.0931
	Q4	801	735.75	720.88	1.1112
1994	Q1	725	754.25	745.25	0.9728
	Q2	660	779.00	766.88	0.8606
	Q3	833	787.00	783.00	1.0639
	Q4	898	797.75	792.38	1.1333
1995	Q1	757	789.75	793.75	0.9537
	Q2	703	773.50	781.63	0.8994
	Q3	801	779.00	776.25	1.0319
	Q4	833	787.25	783.13	1.0637
1996	Q1	779	830.50	808.88	0.9631
	Q2	736	873.75	852.13	0.8637
	Q3	974	—		
	Q4	1006	—		

they sum to 4.003, so the scalar factor is (4/4.003 = 0.99925). The reweighted seasonal indices are as follows:

0.963*0.99925 = 0.9622
0.874*0.99925 = 0.8733
1.063*0.99925 = 1.0622
1.103*0.99925 = 1.1022

These seasonal indices can be applied to trend forecasts to reallocate the predicted values (see regression analysis on page 101). However, if we have forecast values for the next four quarters of 1995 we simply have to multiply the forecast value by the seasonal factor as shown in Table 5.4.

If no seasonal pattern is present in the data set all the seasonal indices would take the value 1. However, if there are strong seasonal patterns, one or more of the indices will be above 1, causing one or more of the seasonal indices to be below 1. In Table 5.3, sales in Q3 and Q4 appear to be stronger than sales in Q1 and Q2. Another way of looking at seasonal indices is to divide each seasonal factor by 4 and then multiply by 100, this will convert the indices into a percentage as shown in Table 5.5.

This information will tell the company where the peaks in demand are and where to use discounts, price reduction or advertising to stimulate sales. For this company there appears to be some seasonal fluctuation but this is not very strong. This method of calculating expected percentage sales becomes even more useful if monthly data are used instead of quarterly data.

Table 5.4

		Forecast trend projection	Seasonal factors	Adjusted forecast
1995	Q1	833	0.9622	802
	Q2	846	0.8733	739
	Q3	860	1.0622	913
	Q4	874	1.1022	963

Table 5.5

		Expected percentage of sales
Q1	(0.9622/4)*100	24.1%
Q2	(0.8733/4)*100	21.8%
Q3	(1.0622/4)*100	26.6%
Q4	(1.1022/4)*100	27.6%

Holt–Winters Triple Parameter Exponential Smoothing

Holt–Winters is a very powerful technique and is based on the work of Brown's double-parameter method. There are a number of seriously restricting assumptions that must be met if Holt–Winters triple parameter method is to be used.

• There must be at least two years of data which is either monthly or quarterly.

• The data set must remain the same in terms of the product or the service.

The second assumption is normally the most restrictive given that most products have short life cycles of less than two years (see Goldratt and Fox 1986).

The Holt–Winters method is fairly flexible in its use and has been used to forecast the total value of an inventory, future cash flows and the aggregate demand for electricity or gas. The method is based around four equations which model:

the exponentially smoothed series (ES_t).

$$ES_t = \frac{\alpha X_t}{I_{t-L}} + (1 - \alpha)(ES_{t-1} + b_{t-1})$$

the seasonality component (I_t)

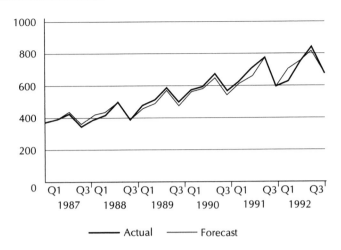

Figure 5.6   Holt–Winters forecasting ability

$$I_t = \frac{\beta X_t}{ES_t} + (1 - \beta)I_{t-1}$$

the trend component (b_t).

$$b_t = v(ES_t - ES_{t-1}) + (v - 1)b_{t-1}$$

the forecast equation (F_{t+m}).

$$F_{t+m} = (ES_t + b_t^* m)I_{t-L+m}$$

These four equations have three smoothing parameters (α, β and v) which can all vary between 0 and 1 in a similar manner to the exponential smoothing method described earlier. The choice of what values these parameters should take now becomes a much more complex problem than for exponential smoothing, however it has been recommended by Holt and Winters that a good starting point is $\alpha = 0.2$, $\beta = 0.6$ and $v = 0.2$. Once the model is running the value of the three parameters can be varied using a simulation process to minimise forecast errors (see MAD or MSE on pages 129–30).

Due to lags in the equations an initialisation is required. Initial estimates of the four seasonal indexes if quarterly data is used, or twelve if monthly data is used, and the first value of ES_t and b_t, are given in Table 5.6 which gives the cash flow for a wine importing company. This is shown graphically in Figure 5.6.

The first step, when applying the method, is to calculate the trend of the data set using the mean of the first and last year of the data set.

First year mean of sales is:

$$(362+385+432+341)/4 \quad \begin{aligned} &= 1520/4 \\ &= 380 \end{aligned}$$

Table 5.6

Year	Quarter	Period	X_t	ES_t	X_t/ES_t	Initial seasonal factors	Revised initial seasonal factors
		-3				0.9664	0.9846
		-2				0.9974	1.0162
		-1				1.1112	1.1321
		0		339.2		0.8510	0.8670
1991	Q1	1	362	355.5	1.0182		
	Q2	2	385	371.8	1.0354		
	Q3	3	432	388.1	1.1130		
	Q4	4	341	404.4	0.8431		
1992	Q1	5	382	420.7	0.9078		
	Q2	6	409	437.0	0.9357		
	Q3	7	498	453.4	1.0984		
	Q4	8	387	469.7	0.8239		
1993	Q1	9	473	486.0	0.9732		
	Q2	10	513	502.3	1.0212		
	Q3	11	582	518.6	1.1221		
	Q4	12	474	534.9	0.8860		

Last year mean of sales is:

$$(473+513+582+474)/4 \quad = 2042/4$$
$$= 510.5$$

These values are then used to calculate the initial trend value for the equation b_0,

$$(510.5-380)/8 \quad\quad = 16.3125$$

This value can now be used to calculate the first value of ES_0, using the following equation.

$$ES_0 \quad = (X_1+X_2+X_3+X_4)/4-2.5 * b_0$$

(Note: the value of 2.5 in the above equation is a constant and X_1 to X_4 are the first four values of sales. If monthly data is used the constant becomes 6.5.)

$$ES_0 \quad = \frac{(362 + 385 + 432 + 341)}{4} -2.5*16.3125$$

$$ES_0 \quad = 380-40.78125$$

$$ES_0 \quad = 339.219$$

This value for ES_0 is used for the first value for ES_t in Tables 5.6 and 5.9. Utilising these values of ES_0 and b_0 the initial trend line can be written as:

$$\hat{ES_t} = ES_0 + b_0 * t$$
$$= 339.2 + 16.31 * t$$

If we then used the time trend (in the column titled period) all the values of ES_t in Table 5.6 can be calculated, e.g.

Value for period 1 = 339.2 + 16.31 * 1 = 355.531
Value for period 2 = 339.2 + 16.31 * 2 = 371.844
Value for period 3 = 339.2 + 16.31 * 3 = 388.130

and so on until the end of the data set.

The next column $X_t/\hat{ES_t}$ is simply calculated by dividing the column X_t by the new column ES_t. The initial seasonals are then calculated by averaging all the estimates for each of the Q1 values, Q2 values, Q3 values and finally Q4 values. This is shown Table 5.7.

Finally the average values for the seasonals calculated for Q1, Q2, Q3 and Q4 are forced to add up to 4. The summation of the initial four seasonals adds up to (0.9664+0.9974+1.1112+0.8510) = 3.926. Therefore as 4/3.926 is equal to 1.0188, if we multiply all the seasonals by 1.0188 they will now add up to 4 (see Table 5.8). In this case the scalar factor (1.0188) to force the seasonals to add up to four is very close to one, however this is not always the case. If monthly data is used the seasonals should add up to twelve.

The calculated values for the seasonal indices I_t, b_t and the initial value of ES_t are shown in bold type in Table 5.9 and are used to calculate the forecast values F_t. The values of α, β and v have been set to Holt–Winters recommendations ($\alpha = 0.2, \beta = 0.1, v = 0.05$).

Overall the Holt–Winters model predicts the series very well, producing a very respectable mean squared error of 290.03 (see pages 129–30 for an explanation of

Table 5.7

Year		X_t/ES_t		
1991	Q1	1.0182	Quarter 1	= (1.0182 + 0.9078 + 0.9732)/3
	Q2	1.0354		= 0.9664
	Q3	1.1130	Quarter 2	= (1.0354 + 0.9357 + 1.0212)/3
	Q4	0.8431		= 0.9974
1992	Q1	0.9078	Quarter 3	= (1.1130 + 1.0984 + 1.1221)/3
	Q2	0.9357		= 1.1112
	Q3	1.0984	Quarter 4	= (0.8431 + 0.8239 + 0.8860)/3
	Q4	0.8239		= 0.8510
1993	Q1	0.9732		
	Q2	1.0212		
	Q3	1.1221		
	Q4	0.8860		

Table 5.8 Re-weighting the seasonals so they add up to 4.

Q1	0.9964* 1.0188	=	0.9846
Q2	0.9974* 1.0188	=	1.0162
Q3	1.1112* 1.0188	=	1.1320
Q4	0.8510* 1.0188	=	0.8670

Table 5.9

Year	Q	Period (X_t)	ES_t	I_t	b_t	F_t
		−3		0.9846		
		−2		1.0162		
		−1		1.1321		
		0	339.2	0.8670	16.3	
1991	Q1	1	362	357.9	0.9873	16.4	
	Q2	2	385	375.2	1.0172	16.4	380.4
	Q3	3	432	389.2	1.1298	16.3	443.3
	Q4	4	341	403.4	0.8648	16.2	351.9
1992	Q1	5	382	413.1	0.9810	15.9	414.3
	Q2	6	409	423.6	1.0120	15.6	436.4
	Q3	7	498	439.5	1.1301	15.6	496.2
	Q4	8	387	453.6	0.8636	15.5	393.6
1993	Q1	9	473	471.7	0.9832	15.6	460.2
	Q2	10	513	491.2	1.0152	15.8	493.1
	Q3	11	582	508.6	1.1315	15.9	573.0
	Q4	12	474	547.1	0.8668	16.1	453.0
							536.3

MSE and errors). For a fuller explanation of this and other smoothing techniques (double parameter, adaptive-response-rate smoothing, etc.) see Jarret (1987).

Regression Models

This model is based on the classical regression technique which estimates linear relationships between two or more variables. Here we concentrate on the simple two-variable case. This model will estimate the two parameters α and β which define the straight line relationship (see Figure 5.7). These parameters are estimated to minimise the sum of squared errors. The formula for a linear regression equation is shown as:

$$Y_t = \alpha + \beta X_t + \epsilon_t$$

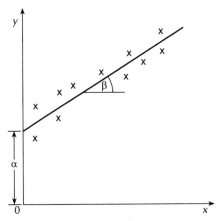

Figure 5.7   Regression, estimated line for α and β

Where Y_t is the dependent variable
          X_t is the independent variable
          α is the intercept coefficient
          β is the slope coefficient
          ϵ_t is the error term

It is important to note that the regression model is based on the seven assumptions of classical least squares (or ordinary least squares – OLS) listed below.

1. Each of the explanatory variables is non-stochastic with values fixed for repeated samples.
2. The expected or average value of the random errors is zero.
3. The variance of the random error is constant for each X value. If the variance either increases or decreases then *heteroskedasticity* could be a problem.
4. Each random error, e_i, is independent of the other. If they are related *serial correlation* or *autocorrelation* could be present.
5. The error terms, e_i for each explanatory variable X are normally distributed.
6. The number of observations exceeds the number of parameters being estimated, i.e. $n > k$. If this assumption is broken the model will not work. (Note: n is the number of observations and k is the number of estimated parameters).
7. No exact linear relationship exists between any two or more explanatory variables. If a fairly close relationship exists *multicollinearity* could be a problem.

If all these assumptions are met the estimated parameters (α and β) are said to be BLUE (Best Linear Unbiased Estimator). If one or more of the assumptions are violated there could be problems in forecasting into the future. For more information on this see Thomas (1985 p. 27.)

The parameters α and β are estimated using the following equations:

$$\beta = \frac{\sum XY - \sum X \sum Y / n}{\sum^2 - (\sum X)^2 / n}$$

$$\alpha = \sum Y / n - \beta \sum X / n$$

Table 5.10 provides data to illustrate the application of these formulae using the quarterly cash flow for a wine company for Y_t (measured in hundreds of pounds). The X_t variable is the level of advertising undertaken by the company in national newspapers and magazines (measured in hundreds of pounds).

$$\beta = \frac{18633 - 48.7 * 4566 / 12}{200.53 - 48.7 * 48.7 / 12} = \frac{102.65}{2.889} = \underline{35.5}$$

$$\alpha = 4566 / 12 - 35.5^* (48.7 / 12) = 236.4$$

Therefore the estimated equation is

$$Y_t = 236.4. + 35.5 X_t$$

The interpretation of this regression equation is that for every additional unit of advertising expenditure the cash flow of the company will rise by 35.5 units (this is the slope term). The intercept term (236.4) is the predicted level of cash flow if advertising expenditure fell to zero. Great care should be exercised in this

Table 5.10

Cash flow (Y)	Advertising expenditure (X)	(X^2)	$(X*Y)$
360	3.4	11.56	1224
350	3.0	9.00	1050
400	4.2	17.64	1680
400	4.5	20.25	1800
425	4.8	23.04	2040
350	4.1	16.81	1435
392	4.6	21.16	1803
377	4.0	16.00	1508
380	4.1	16.81	1558
369	3.7	13.69	1365
375	3.9	15.21	1462
388	4.4	19.36	1707
Sums 4566	48.7	200.53	18633

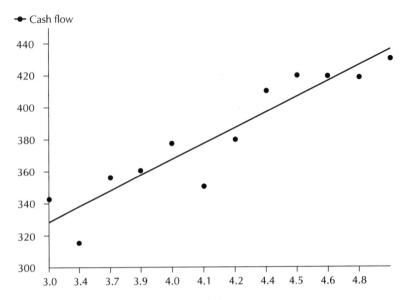

Figure 5.8 Regression for wine company cash flow

interpretation, particularly the intercept as the X_t variable does not include a cash flow for no advertising expenditure.

Figure 5.8 shows how well the estimated regression line fits the data. The regression line will not fit the estimated line perfectly and there will be errors between the actual data and the estimated line. If these errors follow a pattern such as shown in Figure 5.9, autocorrelation could be present which is a violation of the fourth assumption of OLS on page 124.

The presence of autocorrelation can be tested for by using the Durbin and Watson statistic (1951) which varies between 0 and 4 (see Pindyck and Rubinfeld (1991) Chapter 6 for an excellent description of the problems and consequences of autocorrelation). The Durbin and Watson statistic is given by the following formula:

$$\text{DW statistic} = \frac{\sum(\epsilon_t - \epsilon_{t-1})^2}{\sum \epsilon_t^2}$$

where ϵ_t is the vertical distance between each of the actual data points and the estimated line.

If the Durbin and Watson statistic is close to

0, positive autocorrelation could be present or
4, negative autocorrelation could be present or if
2, no autocorrelation appears to be present

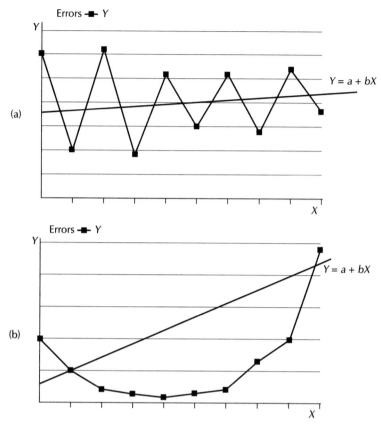

Figure 5.9   Regression error structures for (a) $+, +$ and (b) $-, +$ autocorrelation

Statistical test tables are available to test whether autocorrelation is present (see Pindyck and Rubinfeld, page 568). The presence of autocorrelation will lead the estimates to be inefficient and the sampling errors to be biased, however the estimated coefficients are unbiased (β_i's). Autocorrelation may be caused by the wrong functional form being used to estimate the equation, (i.e. the relationship is curved instead of being linear) or by important variables being omitted from the equation. If positive autocorrelation is present, the forecasted value will probably underestimate the true value. If negative autocorrelation is present, the forecasted value could under or over estimate the true value. There are a number of methods which may be used to help solve the problem of autocorrelation:

- Change the functional form (see section on trend extrapolation on pages 134–5).

- Include important variables which were omitted from the original equation.

- Use either the Cochrane–Orcutt or the Hildreth–Lu procedure (see Pindyck and Rubenfeld, pages 141 and 143).

Errors in Forecasting

Any forecast method is highly unlikely to forecast the future perfectly, and normally errors of a positive or negative value will be present. This being the case a method to assess the power of the chosen model is required, or to choose the optimal value for a smoothing factor (some methods allow the user to choose different values for factors like exponential smoothing or Holt–Winters triple parameter smoothing). Numerous methods are available to analyse forecast errors for example:

- Mean absolute deviation (MAD).

- Mean squared deviation (MSE).

- Tracking signal.

- Theil 'U' statistic.

Mean Absolute Deviation

The MAD method is the absolute (negative values are treated as positive) sum of all the forecast errors divided by the number of forecast values. The formula for MAD is shown below with a worked example (Table 5.11) from the exponential smoothing model (this was shown earlier in the chapter).

$$\text{MAD} = \frac{\sum |Y_t - F_t|}{n}$$

The smaller the value of MAD the better the forecast model is at predicting the data set, therefore in choosing between different models a user should choose the model with the lowest MAD value.

The MAD value for the above model is 285/11=25.909, however if we change the value of alpha for the above data set the value of MAD may fall. The best way of finding the optimal value of alpha is by simulation and this can be achieved by using a spreadsheet. Figure 5.10 shows how MAD falls as α is changed and that the best forecast is obtained when the value of MAD is at its lowest.

Mean Squared Error

Another method for analysis of forecast errors is MSE, but this method gives higher weight to larger errors than the MAD calculation because the errors are squared in the MSE calculation. The formula for MSE is as follows:

$$\text{MSE} = \frac{\sum (Y_t - F_t)^2}{n}$$

Taking the same example as before, the calculated MSE is given in Table 5.12

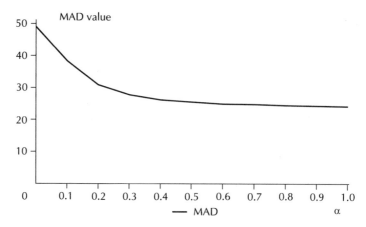

Figure 5.10 Mean absolute deviation v. α

The MSE value for this model is 8675/11=788.63 and if we change the value of α for this data set the value of MSE may fall. Again the best way of finding the optimal value of α is by simulation and this can be achieved by using a spreadsheet. Figure 5.11 shows how MSE falls as α is changed.

If the MSE value is squared rooted the root mean squared error (RMSE) is found which is in the same units of measurement as the original data set. In the above example the squared root of 788.63 is 28.08 (RMSE). It should be noted that MSE and RSME will give a greater weight to extreme values of errors. Whether MAD or MSE (RSME) is used depends on whether this is a desirable property.

Tracking Signal

Although MSE and MAD are often used to find the best forecast method, the values of both MAD and MSE will vary with the type of data being used. Therefore, if we have used only one model, we do not know whether it is acceptable or not as there are no limits on whether any individual MAD or MSE is good or bad. This problem is solved by reference to another method based on MAD, called tracking signal. If the value of the tracking signal is between -3 and $+3$, the forecast model is said to be acceptable. The formula for tracking signal is as follows:

$$\text{Tracking signal} = \frac{\sum(Yt - Ft)}{\text{MAD}}$$

For the above data set the tracking signal value is 215/25.909 = 8.298 and as this lies outside the limit -3 to $+3$ it would be unwise to use this model to forecast. The major advantage of a tracking signal is that it is not dependent on the magnitude of the data and if the tracking signal value is outside the limits -3 to $+3$ the forecast model should not be used to forecast.

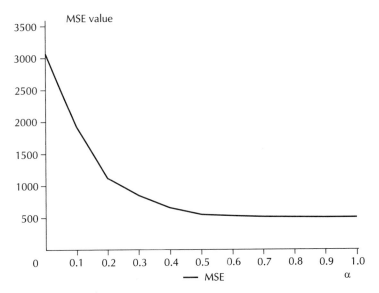

Figure 5.11 Mean squared error v. α

Table 5.11

	Demand (Y_t)	Forecast (F_t)	Error (Y_t-F_t)	Absolute Error
Jan	342			
Feb	313	342	-29	29
Mar	356	332	$+23$	23
Apr	360	340	$+19$	19
May	377	346	$+30$	30
Jun	350	356	-6	6
Jul	380	354	$+25$	25
Aug	410	362	$+47$	47
Sep	421	378	$+42$	42
Oct	418	392	$+25$	25
Nov	417	400	$+16$	16
Dec	430	406	$+23$	23
		414		
				sum = 285

Theil 'U' or Inequality Statistic

The Theil (1961) 'U' statistic is a more advanced way of analysing forecasting errors. This statistic will range between 0 and 1. If U is equal to 0 the forecast is said to be perfect and will fit the actual data without error. If U is equal to 1 the

Table 5.12

	Demand Y_t	Forecast F_t	Error $Y_t - F_t$	Error squared
Jan	342			
Feb	313	342	−29	841
Mar	356	332	+23	529
Apr	360	340	+19	361
May	377	346	+30	900
Jun	350	356	−6	36
Jul	380	354	+25	625
Aug	410	362	+47	2209
Sep	421	378	+42	1764
Oct	418	392	+25	625
Nov	417	400	+16	256
Dec	430	406	+23	529
		414		
				sum = 8675

predictive power of the model is said to be as bad as possible. The formula for the Theil 'U' statistic is:

$$U = \frac{\sqrt{1/T \sum (Y_t^s - Y_t^a)^2}}{\sqrt{1/T \sum (Y_t^s)^2} + \sqrt{1/T \sum (Y_t^a)^2}}$$

Where T is the number of periods forecasted or simulated over
         Y^s are the simulated or forecasted values
         Y^a are the actual values

Theil recommends that 'U' should be below 0.3.

This statistic can be decomposed into three components namely the bias (U^M), variance (U^S) and co-variance (U^C) statistics, where $U^M + U^S + U^C = 1$.

$$U^M = \frac{(\bar{Y}^s - \bar{Y}^a)^2}{(1/T)(\sum (Y_t^s - Y_t^a))^2}$$

$$U^S = \frac{(\sigma_s - \sigma_a)^2}{(1/T(\sum (Y_t^s - Y_t^a))^2}$$

$$U^C = \frac{2(1\rho)\sigma_s \sigma_a}{(1/T)(\sum (Y_t^s - Y_t^a))^2}$$

Where σ_s is the standard deviation of the simulated series

σ_a is the standard deviation of the actual series.

ρ is the correlation coefficient between Y^a and Y^s.

The bias is an indication of systematic error since it analyses the extent to which the average values of the forecast and actual series deviate from each other. It is preferable for the bias value to be close to 0, whereas a value greater than 0.2 would be worrying. The variance U^S is an indication of the model's ability to reproduce the peaks and troughs of the data set. If U^S is large the forecast series would be fairly flat and the actual series would fluctuate greatly, leading to large forecast errors. Therefore U^S should also be close to 0. Finally, the covariance measure U^C shows unsystematic errors, but as it is not reasonable to expect the model to be perfect, high values are of U^C are not worrying. The ideal values are for $U^M = U^S = 0$ and $U^C = 1$.

Confidence Intervals for Predicted Values

Another way of looking at predicted values (i.e. forecasts) is by calculating confidence intervals utilising either the 95% or 99% level. The larger the standard error the larger the confidence intervals will be; therefore, if the confidence intervals are very narrow we would tend to have more faith in the forecast. Wide confidence intervals would suggest that the forecast has a much higher probability of not being close to the point forecast. Confidence intervals can be calculated for all forecasting methods and it is standard in computer packages designed for forecasting techniques to print out these intervals as part of the normal output.

OTHER METHODS OFTEN USED IN FORECASTING

Methods of Environmental Forecasting

The key to organisational survival and growth is the company's ability to adapt its strategies to a rapidly changing environment. This puts a large burden on management to anticipate future events correctly because the damage can be enormous if a mistake is made. That is why a growing number of companies carry out macro-environmental forecasting.

How do companies develop macro-environmental forecasts? Large companies have planning departments that develop long-run forecasts of key environmental factors affecting their markets. General Electric (GE), for example, has a forecasting staff who study world-wide forces that affect its operations. GE makes its forecasts available to other GE divisions and also sells certain forecasts to other companies.

Smaller companies can buy forecasts from several types of suppliers. Marketing research firms can develop all forecasts by interviewing customers, distributors and

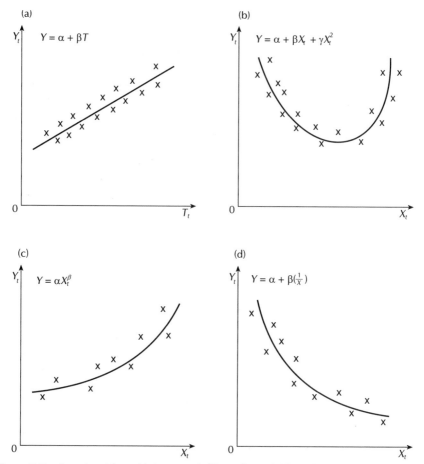

Figure 5.12   Functional form (a) time trend; (b) quadratic; (c) log; (d) reciprocal

other knowledgeable parties. Specialised forecasting firms produce long-range forecasts for particular macro-environmental components, such as the economy, the population, natural resources or technology. Finally, there are futurist research firms that produce speculative scenarios. Among the latter are the Hudson Institute, the Futures Group, and the Institute For the Future.

The major methodology for producing macro-environmental forecasts is trend extrapolation.

Trend Extrapolation

Researchers fit best-fitting curves (linear, quadratic or S-shaped growth curves) through past times series to use for extrapolation (see Figure 5.12). This method can be very unreliable in that new developments can completely alter the future direction of the variable's path. These changes in direction could be due to product life cycle effects, macro-economic effects (recession, boom, interest rate changes or exchange rate changes) or even the effects of a competitor's actions. Examples of different functional forms are:

$$Y_t = \alpha + \beta X_t^2 + \gamma X_t \text{ (quadratic } - \text{ Figure 5.12(b))}$$

$$Y_t = aX_t^b t \text{ which transforms into } \ln Y_t = \ln a + b \ln X_t(\log - \text{Figure 5.12(c))}$$

$$Y_t = \alpha + \beta(1/X_t)(\text{reciprocal} - \text{Figure 5.12(d))}$$

Leading Indicators

The leading indicators approach to forecasting is based on the view that economies experience business cycles (expansion followed by contraction) which create effects that influence other variables after a time lag. If these leading indicators can be found, they can predict the future path of other closely linked variables, particularly the turning points which other methods find difficult to predict. Leading indicators can either be composite variables which take a weighted average of a number of variables or single economic variables, such as:

- The number of business failures.

- The number of new houses started.

- The level of the stock price index.

- The level of demand for new consumer durables.

- The wholesale price index.

An excellent collection of papers on this subject is presented in *Leading Economic Indicators* edited by Lahiri and Moore (1991). However, some of the work in this book is of a highly technical nature. *Economic Trends* published by the Office for National Statistics also produces an article on its leading indicators in each November issue, which provides an up-to-date source of information on indicators for the UK. These types of variables can then be used to correlate trends and patterns with the variable under analysis in the hope of identifying leading indicators that can be used for forecasting.

Econometric Modelling

Researchers build large sets of equations that describe the underlying system. The coefficients in the equation are fitted statistically. Econometric models can contain more than 300 equations and have been used to model and forecast changes in the economy. Some of the famous models of the economy in the UK include the Treasury model, the National Institute model, the Liverpool model and the Cambridge model. These models are not only used to forecast the economy, but can also be used to undertake simulations of economic policy changes such as a reduction in income tax of 1%. Building these types of models requires a very high level of mathematical and statistical expertise and it is not recommended to students who many be new to this field (see Holden, Peel and Thompson (1982) for an excellent introduction to this area).

Cross-impact Analysis

Researchers identify a set of key trends (those high in importance and/or probability). The question is then put: 'If event A occurs, what will be its impact on other trends?'. The results are then used to build sets of 'domino chains', with one event triggering others.

SUMMARY

Forecasting is a very large subject, and the following further reading and references will expand on the approaches covered in this chapter. Some forecasters utilise both qualitative and quantitative methods to produce forecasts. This allows exogenous factors to be included in a forecast which may not have been present in a historical data set (examples of this may be changes in laws or trading with brand new markets and or products). These factors could cause discontinuities in a data set and lead to either under- or over-forecasting errors if only a statistical approach were adopted. Finally, one golden rule in forecasting is 'never forecast more than one-tenth out of sample', i.e. if you have ten observations you can make a one-step-ahead forecast.

REFERENCES AND FURTHER READING

Chatfield, C. (1988) 'What is the Best Method of Forecasting?', Journal of Applied Statistics 15 (1), pp. 17–36.
Durbin, J. and Watson, G.S. (1951) 'Testing for Serial Correlation in Least Squares Regression II', Biometrika 38, pp. 173–5.
Goldratt, E.M. and Fox R.E. (1986) The Race, New York: North River Press.
Holden, K., Peel D.A. and Thompson J.L. (1982) Modelling the UK Economy: An Introduction, Oxford: Martin Robertson.
Jarret, J. (1987) Business Forecasting Methods, Oxford and New York: Basil Blackwell Ltd.

Lahiri, K. and Moore, G.H. (1991) *Leading Economic Indicators: New Approaches and Forecasting Records*, Cambridge: Cambridge University Press.

Makridakis S. and Wheelwright, S.C. (1983) *Forecasting Methods for Management*, 3rd edition, New York: John Wiley and Sons.

Makridakis, S. *et al* (1984) *The Forecasting Accuracy of Major Time Series*, New York: John Wiley and Sons.

Pindyck, R.S. and Rubinfeld, D.L. (1991) *Econometric Models and Economic Forecasts*, 3rd edition, Singapore: McGraw-Hill International.

Salzman, L. (1968) *Computerized Economic Analysis*, New York: McGraw Hill International.

Schultz, R.Z. (1984) 'The Implementation of Forecasting Models', *Journal of Forecasting* **3**, pp. 3–23.

Silver, M. (1992) *Business Statistics*, London: McGraw-Hill International.

SPSS (Statistical Package for the Social Scientist) (1992) *SPSS, User Guide*, 5th edition, Chicago: SPSS.

Theil, H. (1961) *Economic Forecasts and Policy*, Amsterdam: North Holland.

Thomas, R.L. (1985) *Introductory Econometrics: Theory and Applications*, London and New York: Longman.

Thomas, R.J. (1993) 'Method and Situational Factors in Sales Forecast Accuracy', *Journal of Forecasting* **12**, (1), pp. 69–77.

Winters, P.R. (1960) 'Forecasting Sales by Exponentially Weighted Moving Averages', *Management Science* **6** (April), pp. 324–42.

PROBLEM: EXPONENTIAL SMOOTHING

Introductory Comments

An important feature of exponential smoothing is its ability to emphasise recent data and systematically discount old information. A simple exponentially smoothed forecast can be derived using the formula:

$$F_{T+1} = \alpha Y_T + (1 - \alpha)F_T$$

where
F_{T+1} = smoothed sales for the forecast of period $T+1$
α = the smoothing constant
F_T = smoothed sales for period T

The formula contains a portion (α) of current sales with a discounted value of the smoothed average calculated for the previous period to give a forecast for the next period.

The main decision made with exponential forecasting is the selection of an appropriate value for the smoothing constant (α). Smoothing factors can range in value from 0 to 1, with low values providing stability and high values allowing a more rapid response to sales changes. Using a smoothing constant of 1.0 gives the same forecasts that are obtained with the naive method. Forecasts produced with a low smoothing constant, such as 0.2, lag when there is a trend in the data, and forecasts generated with a high value, such as 0.8, will be likely to overestimate sales at turning points.

Problem

An example of how exponential smoothing forecasts can be derived by using seasonally adjusted data is shown in Table 5.13.

Questions

1. Calculate the sales forecasts (F_{T+1}) for periods 2, 3, 4, 5 and 6, using the formula $F_{T+1} = \alpha Y_T + (1 - \alpha)F_T$ and $F_{T+1} \times I_{T+1}$ where I_{T+1} represents the following seasonal indices respectively: 1.16 (period 3), 0.97 (period 4), 0.73 (period 5), and 1.13 (period 6). Take α as 0.2.
2. Also calculate the MAPE (mean absolute percentage error) for periods 3 to 6 inclusive, using the following formula:

$$\text{MAPE} = \frac{\sum_{i=1}^{m}(\text{forecast} - \text{actual}) / \text{actual}}{m} x100\%$$

where m = the number of forecasts to be made

PROBLEM: FORECASTING – SEASONAL INDEX, CENTRED MOVING AVERAGE AND REGRESSION

Introductory Comments

Isolating Seasonal Fluctuations

Seasonal fluctuations are generally large enough to be taken into account in monthly and quarterly sales forecasts (the same general principles apply to daily and weekly forecasts). This is typically done by computing a seasonal index number and using it to adjust the values obtained by forecasting trend alone.

In its simplest form, a seasonal index number for a period is the value for that period divided by the average value for all periods for a year. The resulting ratio is usually multiplied by 100, so that 100 represents an average value, an index number of less than 100 a lower than average value, and one of more than 100 a higher than average value. The many methods of computing seasonal indexes differ with respect to the number of past periods of data required, technical considerations with respect to the 'centring' of the period for which the index number is to be calculated, whether trend and cyclical influences in the data are removed before the calculation is made and other considerations.

Centred Moving Average

A relatively simple method of calculating a seasonal index number is the centred moving average method. Using the centred moving average method you would go through the following steps:

Table 5.13 Forecasting with exponential smoothing ($\alpha = 0.2$)

	Time period					
	1	2	3	4	5	6
Actual sales	49	77	90	79	57	98
Seasonally adjusted	67	68	78	81	78	87
Smoothed sales (F_T)		67.2	69.4	71.7	73.0	75.8

1. Decide how many years of data are to be included in the calculation. Although an index number can be calculated using only one year's data, data for at least two years are necessary to determine seasonal variation with reasonable accuracy. If seasonal effects seem to fluctuate very much, a longer period may be required.
2. Calculate a weighted average of monthly sales for the desired number of months in which the 'target month' is the middle month.
3. Calculate an index number for the 'target month' last year by dividing the weighted average monthly sales into the sales for the 'target month' last year and multiply by 100.
4. Repeat step 3 for the other months.
5. If more than one year's data has been used, average all the 'same month' indices obtained in steps 3 and 4. This is the unadjusted seasonal index.
6. Add the unadjusted monthly indices for each month of the year and divide by 12. If the average obtained is not equal to 100, divide each unadjusted monthly index number by the average and multiply by 100 to obtain an adjusted monthly index number.

Regression

The use of least squares regression for determining seasonal indexes requires at least three years of data and involves six steps:

1. Calculate the slope of the regression line formed by the data.
2. Detrend each observation by using the formula

$$DY_T = Y_T - bT$$

where:

DY_T = the detrended value for the period
Y_T = the value for the period before detrending
b = the slope of the regression line

3. Average the detrended values for each specific period (day, week, month or quarter).
4. Average the detrended values for all periods.
5. Compare the unadjusted seasonal index by dividing each period's average detrended values (step 3) by the overall average detrended period value (step 4) and multiplying the resulting values by 100.
6. Add the unadjusted index numbers for each period and divide by the number of periods in the year (12 for monthly data). If the average obtained is not equal to 100, divide each unadjusted index number by the average and multiply by 100. This gives an adjusted index number for each period.

Good descriptions of other methods of calculating seasonal index numbers are available elsewhere and should be consulted before a choice of methods is made in an actual forecasting situation.

Seasonal indexes are used both for deseasonalising time series and for seasonalising data that do not contain seasonal effects. To deseasonalise data, one divides by the appropriate seasonal index (and multiplies by 100), and to seasonalise data, one multiplies by the index (and divides by 100).

Problem

In early 1997, Alba Breweries wanted to calculate a seasonal index number for malt beverage shipments for the month of June. In this case, the average was calculated using data for the months December 1995 to December 1996 (see Table 5.14).

Questions

1. Calculate the weighted average.
2. Calculate an index number for June 1996.
3. Repeat the calculation for the January to December months.
4. Check whether indices need adjusting and, if so, adjust so that they sum to 1200 (i.e. their average is 100).
5. For the malt beverage monthly shipments data, calculate the regression slope and the estimated regression line against time. Multiply the estimated regression points by the adjusted seasonal indices to provide a seasonally adjusted data set.

Table 5.14   Alba Breweries shipments

Month	Thousand barrels
December 1995	13,122
January 1996	12,863
February	12,894
March	14,590
April	16,058
May	16,967
June	17,736
July	17,625
August	17,530
September	15,850
October	14,430
November	13,462
December	12,975

PART 2

Financial Analysis, Operations and Control Systems

6
Financial techniques

Contents

Pricing models
Investment appraisal techniques

Objectives

After reading this chapter you should know:
- The different techniques which may be used in setting prices.
- In what situations the different techniques could be used.
- How potential investments may be appraised and compared.

PRICING MODELS

Introduction

Setting the price for a product is a complex and challenging task. In addition to production and marketing costs, managers must also consider how they wish to position the product, the positioning and pricing of competing products, and customer perceptions of quality and value. Too high a price may not be competitive, while too low a price may make customers think that the product is of inferior quality. In this chapter we discuss various techniques which can be used to aid pricing decisions.

Break Even Analysis

Break even analysis is useful in analysing relationships between costs, sales revenues and profit. It is used to calculate the number of units which will need to be sold at a particular price, or the price at which the product must be sold, given an estimated level of sales, for the company to break even – that is, to cover its total costs, which are the sum of its fixed and variable costs. Fixed costs are those which are the same whatever the production level (e.g. business rates for factory premises), while variable costs are those which vary according to amount produced (e.g. cost of materials). Figure 6.1 shows total costs and total production levels for a product at a set price – where total costs and total revenues are exactly equal is the break even point. If fewer units than this were sold, the company would incur losses; if more were sold, they would make a profit. The formula for the break even point in units is:

$$\text{BEP} = \frac{\text{Total fixed costs}}{\text{Selling price per unit} - \text{variable cost per unit}}$$

The bottom line of this formula, the difference between unit selling price and unit variable cost is called the contribution per unit. Break even point is also often expressed in terms of money rather than units sold – it is then the break even point in units times the selling price. Thus, if total fixed costs were £100,000, variable cost per unit was £10, and the unit selling price was £15, the break even point in units would be:

$$\frac{£100,000}{(£15 - £10)} = \frac{£100,000}{£5} = 20,000 \text{ units}$$

In monetary terms this would give a break even point of 20,000×£15 = £300,000. Figure 6.2(a) shows this graphically.

It may also be useful to know what market share is represented by the break even volume of sales. In this example, if the total market were estimated at 400,000 units, the market share required to break even would be:

$$\frac{20,000}{400,000} = 5\%$$

Fixed costs must be correctly apportioned in calculating break even or misleading figures will be obtained. Capital expenditure on items, such as machinery, which will last for several years, should be allocated proportionally over the life of the equipment – if the full cost were allocated in the first year, break even point could be very high. Also, in determining break even for a particular proposal to produce, only fixed costs which vary as a result of acceptance of the proposal are relevant – previously incurred costs, such as those of prior research, are referred to as sunk costs and should not be included in the break even calculation.

In initial price setting, break even points are normally calculated for several different possible prices and compared with estimates of demand at those prices. This enables the elimination of undesirable prices, where demand is below break even, and indicates the preferable price range. If management have a specific profit level they wish to achieve, the break even formula can be amended to include this and work out the necessary level of sales. For instance, using the previous example, if a profit of £50,000 is required, this is added to the fixed costs:

$$\text{BEP} = \frac{100,000 + 50,000}{15 - 10} = \frac{150,000}{5} = 30,000 \text{ units}$$

Or if a 20% profit on sales is required, then £1 (20%) out of the £5 contribution on each unit must go towards profits, leaving only £4 to cover fixed costs. Thus:

$$\text{BEP} = \frac{100,000}{4} = 25,000 \text{ units}$$

Another use of break even is when a price change is being considered. In our example, the firm may wish to reduce the selling price to £14, perhaps to compete more effectively with a new product entering the market. The contribution per unit is thus reduced to £4.00. Let us assume they are currently selling 30,000 units per year, thus making a total profit contribution of £50,000. If the firm wishes to maintain this profit level, they will need to sell 150,000/4 = 37,500 units, an increase in sales of 7,500 units or 25%.

Using Break Even Points in Profit Analysis

Figure 6.1 shows a typical break even graph. The shaded region, to the right and above the break even point, is known as the profit path – it is the region where total revenue exceeds total costs, and the company makes a profit. The size and shape of this region can obviously be influenced by variation in the selling price of the product, and by variations in both fixed and variable production costs. The actual amount of profit made, given a particular profit path, will then depend on the volume of output.

Consider our previous example. Suppose, due to inefficiency in the manufacturing process, our variable costs per unit rise by 5%, i.e. to £10.50, and our fixed costs also increase by 5% to £105,000. The new break even point (assuming the same selling price of £15) will be

$$\text{BEP} = \frac{105,000}{4.5} = 23,333 \text{ units } (£349,995)$$

However, if we were able to make the production process more efficient and reduce both fixed and variable costs by 5%, our break even point would be:

$$\text{BEP} = \frac{95,000}{5.5} = 17,272 \text{ units } (£259,080)$$

Figure 6.2 shows that these relatively minor variations in production efficiency lead to major changes in the size and structure of the profit path wedge. Many firms have seen profits eroded due to the cumulative effect of small changes in the variables affecting the profit path. Individually, these changes may seem

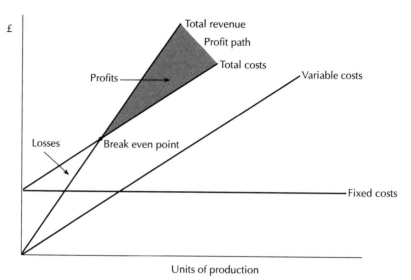

Figure 6.1   Break even graph

insignificant, but together, over time, they can create devastating changes in profits. It is therefore essential that management regularly assess the effects of changes in costs and selling prices, examining their effect on the product's break even point and profit path, and taking corrective action where necessary.

Modified Break Even

Using Break Even Points to Compare Competitors

Almost every industry nowadays is highly competitive, and new technology, together with competitive pressures, means that successful companies are continually seeking new and more profitable ways of doing things, from more efficient production methods to innovative methods of marketing and distribution. In practically every industry, there is a great difference in the profit paths of successful and less successful companies. Meaningful comparisons with companies in the same industry, and with similar companies in other industries, should be an ongoing management process.

However, many companies only make very superficial comparisons, such as looking at overall balance sheets, or feel unable to make comparisons with other companies in their industry because of widely differing sizes of companies. Indeed, direct comparisons of static ratios between companies of different sizes may be unsatisfactory. However, break even analysis lets us look at the comparative variable costs, in terms of the contribution per unit or per pound of sales. These can be directly compared – if, for instance, Company A's variable costs are £0.74 per

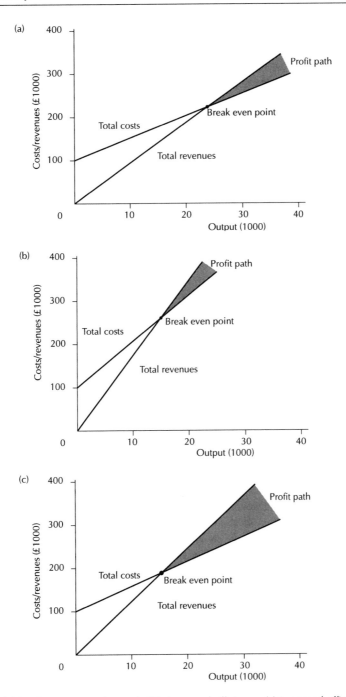

Figure 6.2 (a) Break even example graph; (b) decreased efficiency; (c) increased efficiency

pound of sales, and Company B's variable costs are £0.79 per pound of sales, then Company A receives £0.05 extra contribution per pound of sales and Company B's higher costs cannot be competitive. Company B will have a higher break even point (unless fixed costs are very low), will have less opportunity to make profits, and will be more vulnerable to reductions in selling price.

Some companies may say that they are unable to get sufficiently detailed figures from their competitors to carry out break even analysis. However, with some searching it is often possible to obtain sufficient data to estimate break even points and contributions reasonably accurately. The primary source of information would be the competitors' annual financial statements, and after that, other reports issued by the company. Obviously the data obtained will not be as detailed as that for one's own company, but studies have shown that estimates of fixed and variable costs made from published data have been surprisingly accurate.

Using Break Even Points in Setting Selling Prices

Although selling prices are not necessarily determined directly by selling costs, in the long run the selling price must cover costs and, in addition, include a profit element. Thus the study of cost/selling price relationships as measured by their joint effects on the profit path and break even point is an essential part of product management.

Effects of Selling Price Changes on the Break Even Point

How much extra business is needed to offset a 10% reduction in selling price? What will the break even point be after such a reduction, and what will be the contribution per unit sold? Conversely, what would be the effect of a 10% price rise? If this were likely to lead to the loss of 25% of the market, would it be a profitable move?

These are the sort of questions which can be answered by break even analysis. Let us look at them in the context of our example, keeping fixed and variable costs constant at their original values. Table 6.1 shows the effects on break even, and profits/losses at various sales volumes, for small selling price increases and decreases.

The change in selling price, and thus in contribution per unit, has made a great difference to the sales required to break even. To offset a 10% price decrease, which reduces the contribution per unit from £5 to £3.50, we would need to sell an extra 8571 units – an increase of almost 43%. Or, if we increased the price by 10%, we would only require sales of 15,385 to break even.

This type of analysis can be used to show the effects of any proposed price changes and can be extended, if necessary, to include the effects of changes in production costs. It provides a methodical means of presenting the various possibilities in such a way that they can be clearly compared and evaluated.

Table 6.1   Effects of selling price changes

	\+10%	\+5%	no change	−5%	−10%
			Selling price		
Contribution per unit (£)	6.50	5.75	5.00	4.25	3.50
Break even (units)	15385	17391	20000	23529	28571
Break even (£)	253846	273913	300000	335294	385714
			Profit or loss (£)		
Annual sales (units)					
18000	43154	9587	(30000)	(78794)	(142714)
20000	76154	41087	0	(50294)	(115714)
22000	109154	72587	30000	(21794)	(88714)
24000	142154	104087	60000	6706	(61714)

The Effects of Volume Increases

Does increased sales volume automatically lead to higher profits? Obviously, it would if all fixed and variable costs relating to the product remained constant at the increased volume of production. However, this is very rarely the case. More volume will often lead to higher fixed costs, for instance because extra production machines are required, higher labour costs due to hiring more workers or paying overtime to existing staff, increased promotion and advertising to sell the extra volume, overworked capacity and general inefficiencies. Therefore, any proposed sizeable increase in volume should be very carefully considered, with management looking at questions such as:

- Do we have sufficient capacity to produce added volume without increasing fixed costs?
- Do we have enough working capital to handle extra sales?
- Will we be able to sell the added volume effectively without increasing costs?
- Where will the extra sales come from?

Breakeven analysis can help in answering these important questions and aid management in making the most appropriate decision. One method of determining the volume at which profits will be maximised, assuming constant production costs and constant demand, is called marginal analysis.

Marginal Analysis

The basic idea of marginal analysis is that, since profits are the difference between revenues and costs, it is profitable to produce an extra unit if, and only if, its

Table 6.2   Costs, revenues and profit for Product X

Output (units)	FC (£)	TVC (£)	TC (£)	MC (£)	Price (£)	TR (£)	MR (£)	TP (£)
0	20	0	20	–	15	0	–	−20
1	20	4	24	4	14	14	14	−10
2	20	8	28	4	13	26	12	−2
3	20	12	32	4	12	36	10	4
4	20	16	36	4	11	44	8	8
5	20	20	40	4	10	50	6	10
6	20	24	44	4	9	54	4	10
7	20	28	48	4	8	56	2	8
8	20	32	52	4	7	56	0	4
9	20	36	56	4	6	54	−2	−2

production and sales produces extra revenue higher than the extra cost it generates. The expense added by the extra unit of output to total costs is known as the marginal cost and the revenue it generates as the marginal revenue. So the optimum output for profit maximisation is that at which marginal costs exactly equal marginal revenues.

Let us illustrate this with a simple example. Table 6.2 shows the costs, revenues and profits associated with production at various outputs of a hypothetical product, Product X.

We can see from the last column that profits will be highest at an output of either five or six units. To see why this is so, compare the marginal costs and marginal revenue columns. As output increases up to five units, for each extra unit of output, marginal costs are less than marginal revenues gained. It is thus profitable to produce the extra unit and total profit rises. For an increase in output from five to six units, marginal costs exactly equal marginal revenues, and profits will be the same at either output. If production is increased, however, beyond six units, marginal costs exceed marginal revenues for each extra unit. Total profits therefore decrease, so the optimum output level is either five or six units.

The table also shows that when total revenue is maximised (output of seven or eight units), the marginal revenue is between two and zero. Production of more than eight units causes total revenue to decrease, i.e. marginal revenue becomes negative. Figure 6.3 shows these relationships graphically. We have now found the optimum production level to be five or six units. At what price should these units be sold? From the demand curve we find that we can sell five units at £10 or six units at £9. So the price should be set at either £9 or £10.

The marginal relationships can also be derived through the use of simple calculus. Marginal revenue (MR) can be regarded as the rate of change of total revenue (TR) with respect to quantity sold (Q), and thus may be calculated by differentiating the formula for total revenue with respect to Q. Similarly, marginal

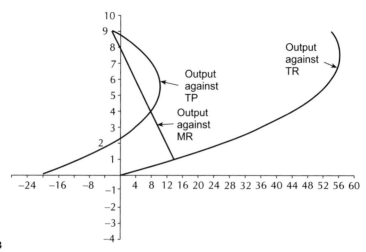

Figure 6.3

cost (MC) is the rate of change of total costs (TC) with respect to quantity sold, calculated by differentiating the total costs formula with respect to Q.

Thus, for the above example we have:

$$\text{Revenue per unit} = £(15 - Q)$$

$$\text{TR} = (\text{Revenue per unit} \times Q) = £(15Q - Q^2)$$

$$\text{MR} = \frac{dTR}{dQ} = £(15 - 2Q)$$

$$\text{TC} = \text{Total fixed cost} + \text{Total variable costs}$$

$$= £(20 + 4Q)$$

$$\text{MC} = \frac{dTC}{dQ} = £4$$

Equating MR to MC, we find the profit maximising quantity where $(15 - 2Q) = 4$, i.e. $Q = 5.5$. As we can only produce and sell whole units, profits are maximised at an output of five or six units, as found previously.

This is obviously a very simplified example, dealing with very small production volumes. In real life, both demand and cost functions are likely to be much more complex. The marginal cost is unlikely to be the same for each extra unit across the whole range of possible outputs – for instance, at a certain volume two machines may be needed instead of one, causing a jump in costs. Both demand and cost functions are likely to fluctuate over time. Nevertheless, provided that a reasonably reliable demand curve can be drawn for the product in question, marginal analysis provides a useful means of estimating optimal output volume.

Incremental Profit Analysis

Incremental profit analysis looks at the relationships between the changes in revenues and costs associated with possible courses of action, so that a company may take only those actions which will increase net profits. Only those factors affected by the decision to take a particular course of action are considered, but companies must be sure to identify all such factors, and to look at both short-term and long-term effects of the decision.

Let us look, for example, at the relevant factors in incremental analysis of a new product introduction decision. Obviously we must look at the increase in production, marketing and distribution costs, and the increase in revenues from product sales. However, the new product may directly or indirectly affect existing products – if it competes with an existing product, revenues from this product are likely to decrease, or if it complements an existing product, it may work to increase that product's sales. The extra production capacity required for the new product may affect the production of existing products, increasing their unit cost or restricting the volume that may be produced. All these factors must be considered.

Pricing Methods

Cost-plus Pricing

Cost-plus, or full-cost pricing, is the most frequently used pricing method. The typical formula for determining prices by this method would be to add together the variable costs of production, marketing and distribution, add on a sum for overheads, and then add a percentage mark-up for profits. The sum allocated for overheads, or fixed costs, is usually determined by splitting the firm's total overheads among all the products produced, in proportion to the variable costs of each product.

Although the technique is so frequently used, and is easy to apply, it does not look either at demand considerations or at marginal costs and therefore has been criticised as leading to less than optimal pricing decisions. However, it is used by many successful companies, and it is therefore worth examining in more detail.

Cost concepts in cost-plus pricing

Most firms use the 'standard' or 'normal' cost concept – that is, costs incurred at a 'normal' output level, irrespective of short-term variations. These are often based on historical accounting data. What are really needed are estimates of future costs – costs that will be incurred during the period for which prices are being set. If historical data are being used as the basis for these, it is essential that they be adjusted to reflect anticipated changes in wage levels, materials costs, etc.

Often, also, the use of fully allocated costs leads to overpricing, and the use of incremental costs would be more appropriate.

Demand analysis and cost-plus pricing
The cost-plus pricing method as previously described seems not to consider demand at all. However, surveys have shown that companies tend to adjust their percentage mark-ups depending on their perception of demand elasticity and competitive pressure. However, there is little evidence that marginal costs and revenues are considered when deciding mark-ups, so optimal prices may not be set.

The rationale for cost-plus pricing
In theory, cost-plus pricing does not appear to give optimal prices. Why is it then used by so many successful firms? The reasons lie in the differences between the basic microeconomic model of the firm and the realities of the business environment. Microeconomic theory assumes that continual maximisation of short-term profits (i.e. setting optimal prices) will lead to long-term profit maximisation. In the real world, this is seldom the case, and firms need to take a long-term view. So prices may be set lower than would be optimal in order to build market share or undercut a competitor – this would, hopefully, lead to a larger market share and, ultimately, higher long-term profits.

Another problem is that in the real world, firms rarely have precise knowledge of marginal cost and demand relationships so any calculations of optimal output based on marginal analysis can only be an approximation. Furthermore, both cost and demand functions may change frequently. Thus, the setting of optimal prices is not as simple as microeconomic theory might indicate.

Profit-based Pricing Methods

Target Profit Pricing

Here an annual monetary profit target is set, and the price established so as to make that amount of profit, given the expected demand. For instance, a soft-toy maker may wish to make a profit of £5000 per year. Assume her fixed costs (including a salary for herself) are £3500 and her variable costs £5 per toy. She believes she can make and sell 2000 toys per year and that demand is insensitive to price up to £10 per toy.

Her selling price per toy is calculated as:

$$\text{Profit} = \text{Total revenue} - \text{Total cost}$$

$$5000 = (\text{Price} \times 2000) - [3500 + (5 \times 2000)]$$

$$5000 = (\text{Price} \times 2000) - 13500$$

$$\text{Price} = \frac{18500}{2000}$$

$$= £9.25 \text{ per toy}$$

The assumption that demand is not price sensitive is critical. If less than 2000 toys are sold, the target profit will not be achieved.

Target Return-on-sales Pricing

Here the target profit is set as a specific percentage of the total sales revenue. Suppose the soft-toy maker in the last example uses target return-on-sales pricing, with a target of 20% return on sales at an annual volume of 2000 toys. Then:

$$\text{Target return-on-sales} = \frac{\text{Target profit}}{\text{Total revenue}}$$

$$20\% = \frac{\text{Total revenue} - \text{Total costs}}{\text{Total revenue}}$$

$$0.2 = \frac{(\text{Price} \times 2000) - [3500 + (5 \times 2000)]}{(\text{Price} \times 2000)}$$

$$0.2 \times \text{Price} \times 2000 = (\text{Price} \times 2000) - 13500$$

$$400 \times \text{Price} = (2000 \times \text{Price}) - 13500$$

$$\text{Price} = \frac{13500}{1600}$$

$$= £\ 8.44 \text{ per toy}$$

Target Return-on-investment Pricing

Many companies set annual targets for return on investment (ROI). Target return-on-investment pricing sets prices to a level which will achieve this target.

For example, let us suppose our soft-toy maker, having achieved an ROI of 7.5% in her first year, wishes to increase this by at least 10% on her second year. She also wishes to increase her salary from £3000 to £4000 and she has calculated that her fixed costs will rise from £500 to £600. She is considering whether to improve the quality of her toys by using better fabrics – a more expensive fur fabric, velvet for paws and ears, etc. This would increase the average unit variable cost to £5.60, but she estimates a reasonable price would then be around £8.25. If she uses the same fabrics as last year, variable cost would rise to £5.05, but she estimates price could be increased to £7.50. The toy maker feels it should be possible to achieve a small increase in sales over last year's 1800.

The easiest way to compare the various options is by means of a spreadsheet (Figure 6.4). Four possible scenarios, assuming different sales levels for each of the two materials options, are shown in the columns headed A, B, C and D. The toy maker must look at the results of the simulation projections and assess the realism of the assumptions underlying each projection. Here, she sees that the desired ROI

	Last year	A	B	C	D
Price per toy (P)	6.50	7.50	7.50	8.25	8.25
Quantity sold (Q)	1800	2000	1900	1900	1800
Unit variable cost (UVC)	4.50	5.05	5.05	5.60	5.60
Fixed costs	500.00	600.00	600.00	600.00	600.00
Salary	3000.00	4000.00	4000.00	4000.00	4000.00
Investment	1000.00	1000.00	1000.00	1000.00	1000.00
Taxes	25%	25%	25%	25%	25%
Net sales (P×Q)	11700.00	15000.00	14250.00	15675.00	14850.00
Less: cost of goods sold (Q×UVC)	8100.00	10100.00	9595.00	10640.00	10080.00
Gross margin	3600.00	4900.00	4655.00	5035.00	4770.00
Less: fixed costs	500.00	600.00	600.00	600.00	600.00
Less: salary	3000.00	4000.00	4000.00	4000.00	4000.00
Net profit before taxes	100.00	300.00	55.00	435.00	170.00
Less: taxes	25.00	75.00	13.75	108.75	42.50
Net profit after taxes	75.00	225.00	41.25	326.25	127.50
Investment	1000.00	1000.00	1000.00	1000.00	1000.00
Return on investment	7.5%	22.5%	4.1%	32.6%	12.8%

Figure 6.4   Spreadsheet for target ROI pricing

can only be achieved with the present quality of toys if well over 1900 are sold. However, with the higher quality toy the desired ROI is achieved even if she sells no more than last year. As she is reasonably confident that she will be able to do this, at the assumed price of £8.25, she selects simulation D, and has a goal of 12.8% ROI.

Product-Line Pricing

If a company has several items in one product line, it will try to set prices in order to maximise profits over the whole line. Profit margins are therefore likely to vary on the different items in the line. The higher-priced products in the line, perceived as exclusive or of very high quality, may not cost much more than the lower-priced ones to produce, but may carry a much higher mark-up. For products further down the scale, where a large part of the competition in the market may be on price, the company may have to settle for a much lower mark-up.

Products may also have interrelated costs or sales of one item in the line may be influenced by the price charged for another. If sales of Product A rise when the price of product B in the same line is increased, this would indicate that Product A was perceived as a substitute for Product B. Conversely, if sales of A rose when the price of B decreased, this would indicate that the two products were complementary (typically sold together).

   Product-line pricing would normally be done using a computer spreadsheet, inputting data on costs and demand relationships in order to achieve the most profitable combination of prices.

Variable-cost Pricing

So far we have considered pricing methods which take into account the full costs of a product – both variable and fixed. In some circumstances, it may be more realistic and profitable for a company to use variable costs only as the basis for pricing. A typical situation would be when a company is already covering fixed costs in current production, and is asked to consider producing extra volume. For example, a china manufacturer may produce 10,000 tea-sets per year which are sold at £15 each. This covers both fixed costs of £50,000 and variable costs of £7 per set, making a contribution to profits of £3 per set. A supermarket wishes to place a bulk order for 2,000 tea-sets, but is only willing to pay £10 per set. Should this order be accepted?

   If we consider full costs, currently each unit makes a contribution of £5 towards fixed costs. If production were increased to 12,000 to satisfy the supermarket order, this would be reduced to £4.50 per set. When fixed costs and variable costs are added, a price of £11.50 is required to break even. Thus, under the full costing method, £10 would be too low a price and the order would not be accepted.

   However, under variable-cost pricing, fixed costs are ignored for the additional order. The offered price of £10 covers the variable cost of £7, and therefore the order is accepted. Each tea-set contributes £3 toward profits – a total of £6000 profit that would have been lost if the firm, using the full costing method, had rejected the order.

   There are, however, other considerations that should be taken into account. Will the sales through the supermarket reduce sales at the usual outlets? Or could they increase future sales by bringing the product to the attention of new markets? Is the excess manufacturing capacity available without incurring extra costs? Could this capacity be used more profitably? If, having answered all such questions, the order still looks to be profitable, it will be accepted.

   Variable-cost pricing is often used by businesses with comparatively high fixed costs, for instance airline companies offering cheaper standby tickets, which do not cover the full cost, rather than flying with unoccupied seats.

Peak load Pricing

This is a particular type of variable-cost pricing, often used when there is a limit to the amount of products or services that can be provided, and demand is variable over time, but predictable. The price is then set to be highest at times of greatest demand and reduced during off-peak periods. Sports facilities, for instance, are often more expensive to use in the evenings and cheaper during normal working hours. Package holidays are generally most expensive during the peak holiday months of July and August. The railways offer cheaper day return tickets which are only valid outside peak commuting hours. Electricity companies have an economy tariff which charges a much reduced rate for electricity used during the night, while slightly increasing the daytime charge over the normal tariff.

Peak-load pricing makes good economic sense. The price variations tend to dampen demand fluctuations, as price-sensitive customers will not pay the higher rates unless they have no option and cheaper rates will stimulate off-peak usage – thus allowing more efficient use of facilities.

Price Discrimination

Price discrimination exists whenever different classes of customers are charged different prices for the same product where such differentials are not related to varying costs of production and distribution. For price discrimination to be practised profitably, it must be possible to segment the market into non-overlapping submarkets in order to make it possible to charge different prices to buyers in different submarkets. There must also be different price elasticities of demand for the product in the various submarkets, so that the profit-maximising prices are different – otherwise there is no point in charging different prices.

This market segmentation may be done in several ways. The market may be segmented geographically, and a lower price charged where the product faces most competition or a higher price charged where the product is the only one available in its product category. Peak-load pricing, discussed earlier, is a method of price discrimination based on time. Product use is another basis for segmentation – for instance, business users of premises pay different rates from domestic users for utilities such as electricity and water. Banks have different scales of account fees for individuals, businesses and charities. Age and income are often used as bases for price discrimination for services – half-price tickets for children, reduced entrance fees for senior citizens and the unemployed.

Maximising Profits Under Price Discrimination

We saw earlier that profits are maximised at the level of output where marginal revenue equals marginal cost. If price discrimination is being practised, then profits will be maximised where marginal revenue equals marginal cost for each submarket. This is best illustrated with an example. Let us assume that a firm sells the same product in two totally separate markets, X and Y (for instance, two different countries). The demand curves for the two markets are:

$$\text{For Market X } P_X = \pounds(40 - 0.5Q_X)$$
$$\text{For Market Y } P_Y = \pounds(90 - 2Q_Y)$$

The firm's total cost function for the product is:

$$TC = \pounds(500 + 10Q + 0.25Q^2)$$

where Q is the sum of Q_X and Q_Y.

In Market X, total revenue TR_X will be:

$$\pounds\,(40 - 0.5Q_X)\,Q_X = \pounds\,(40Q_X - 0.5Q_X^2)$$

and thus marginal revenue MR_X will be

$$\frac{d TR_X}{dQ_X} = \pounds(40 - Q_X)$$

In Market Y, total revenue TR_Y will be:

$$\pounds(90 - 2Q_Y)Q_Y = \pounds(90Q_Y - 2Q_Y^2)$$

and thus marginal revenue MR_Y will be:

$$\frac{d TR_Y}{dQ_Y} = \pounds(90 - 4Q_Y)$$

Figure 6.5 shows the demand curves, and associated marginal revenue curves, for each market. Figure 6.6 shows the aggregate demand curve representing the sum of the quantities demanded in the two markets at each price. The aggregate marginal revenue curve is interpreted in a similar fashion as the 'sum' of the marginal revenue curves for the two markets – for instance, in Market X, marginal revenue can be seen to be £10 at an output of 30 units, while in Market Y marginal revenue is £10 at an output of 20 units. Therefore, in Figure 6.6, the point where marginal revenue is £10 corresponds to an output of (30 + 20) = 50 units.

Figure 6.6 also shows the marginal cost curve, given by:

$$MC = \frac{d TC}{dQ} = \pounds(10 + 0.5Q) \text{ where } Q = Q_X + Q_Y$$

The intersection of the marginal cost curve and marginal revenue curve gives the profit maximising output, i.e. 30 units. At this point the marginal cost is £25. The optimal allocation of output between the two markets is found by taking the points on each of the separate market graphs (Figure 6.5) where the marginal cost is £25. This shows that 15 units should be sold in each market, but, from the demand curves, the selling price in Market X should be £32.50, while in Market Y it should be £60.

Calculation of the total revenue will highlight the benefits of being able to use price discrimination:

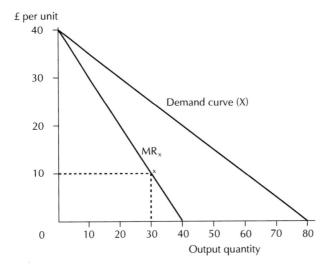

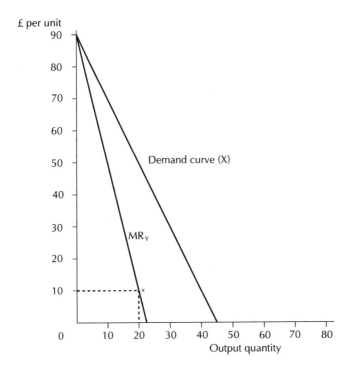

Figure 6.5 Demand curves for two separate sub-markets

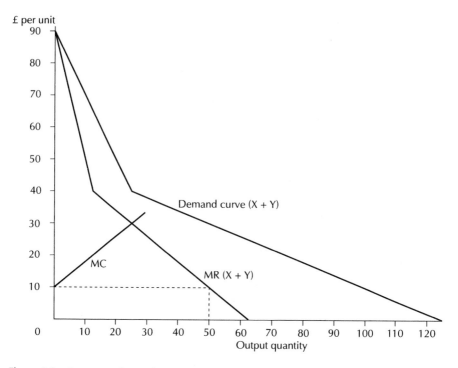

Figure 6.6   Aggregate demand curve

$$TR = £(15 \times 32.50) + (15 \times 60) = £(487.50 + 900)$$
$$= £1387.50$$

If the firm could not segment the market and had to charge a single price, the price (from Figure 6.6) would be £38, giving a total revenue of only:

$$TR_1 = £(38 \times 30) = £1140$$

Competitive-bid Pricing

This procedure is used in situations where firms are required to tender for contracts, usually by making a bid unknown to other competing firms. It is common in the construction industry and in the buying of goods and services by councils and government departments. Price is often critical for the buyer – in most cases the lowest bid will win the contract. Thus the main consideration for competing firms is 'What will our competitors bid?' Several models have been developed to help companies prepare competitive bids – here we describe one of the simpler methods.

Table 6.3 Competitive bidding example

Bid price	Profit	Probability	'Probability Profit'
700000	100000	99%	99000
750000	150000	95%	142500
800000	200000	80%	160000
850000	250000	75%	187500
900000	300000	62%	186000
950000	350000	50%	175000
1000000	400000	41%	164000
1050000	450000	33%	148500
1100000	500000	25%	125000
1150000	550000	10%	55000
1200000	600000	3%	18000

Example

A construction company are bidding for a contract to build 20 houses. They estimate that their costs will be £30,000 per house. What should they bid?

The additional information required for our calculation is the probability of winning the contract at different bid levels. This should be estimated by managers or other experts in the firm based on previous experience and any other relevant factors. Once we have an estimated probability of winning at each possible bid level, we find the optimum bid by looking for the maximum 'probability profit', i.e. maximising (profit × probability) – see Table 6.3.

Here the maximum 'probability profit' is achieved with a bid of £850,000. If the company submit this bid and win the contract, their actual profit will be £250,000.

More sophisticated methods take into account losses incurred if the firm fails to win the contract, and would refine probability predictions around the 'best' bid above – a relatively small price difference in competing bids could mean the difference between success and failure.

INVESTMENT APPRAISAL TECHNIQUES

Introduction

Investment in its simplest form is a firm making an initial cash outlay with the aim of receiving a future cash inflow. Decisions on whether to purchase a new machine, build a new factory or launch a new product are all examples of investment decisions. In order to make such decisions an investment appraisal technique is required. A good investment appraisal technique must be able to distinguish between competing investment projects and allow firms to meet their goal i.e. *the maximisation of shareholder wealth.* A good investment appraisal technique should also be able to take account of all relevant costs and cash flows, depreciation, inflation, tax, capital allowances and risk.

There are basically four different traditional investment appraisal techniques, namely: *pay back, accounting rate of return* (ARR), *net present value* (NPV) and *internal rate of return* (IRR). The use of each of these techniques varies in industry as shown by Pike (1982) who surveyed a large number of firms in the UK on which method they used. He found that 74% of UK firms use more than one investment appraisal technique and many used three techniques; that 54% of UK firms used NPV and or IRR analysis and this mirrors results found in American surveys; and that about 51% of UK firms used ARR – however this figure is likely to have fallen in recent years.

Pay Back

The pay back method looks at how quickly the incremental returns (defined as the net cash flows after tax) from a project will pay back the original capital investment. This is a fairly popular technique and is normally implemented in one of two ways. Firstly, companies may decide to only accept projects which pay back within a set period of time, e.g. 3 years or less. Secondly, if a series of different projects is being analysed, then the projects can be ranked in order of time to pay back. Then the fastest project to pay back would be chosen. The following example for an investment project lasting four years, illustrates how the pay back method works.

Example: Payback

	Cash flows	Cumulative sum of cash flows
Initial investment	−£18,000	−£18,000
Cash flow (year 1)	+£6,500	−£11,500
Cash flow (year 2)	+£8,600	−£2,900
Cash flow (year 3)	+£4,375	+£1,475
Cash flow (year 4)	+£3,999	+£5,474

Therefore for this project the cumulative cash flows will pay back the original investment of £18,000 in just under three years. Although this is a fairly popular technique it has a number of serious flaws – firstly it ignores any cash flow after the pay back point. In some industries this could easily cause false judgements to be made. A good example of this would be the mining industry which would face very heavy clean-up costs (landscaping, cleaning-up pollution, removing waste products, etc.) after the mineral has been exhausted. As these types of costs will be faced at the end of the project they will not affect the calculation of the pay back period. Secondly, pay back takes a very short-termist view, with projects with high initial returns being favoured over projects with low initial returns but higher long run returns. Thirdly, no *'time value of money'* is allowed for in the calculation.

Time Value of Money

The time value of money is based on the principle that money received in the future does not have the same value as money now. This is because money received now has a higher value than money received in the future, as money could be placed in a bank and earn interest or because inflation erodes the real value of money. To take account of the time value of money future cash flows have to be discounted by the appropriate discount factor back to the present time. The following example illustrates how an investment project is discounted back to the present day, for discounted pay back calculations.

The discount factor is calculated using the following formulae

$$1/(1+r)^n$$

where n is the year in which the cash flow takes place.
         r is the discount rate (i.e. 10% is expressed as 0.10).

Therefore the discount factor if n is equal to six and the discount rate is 12% is given by:

$$= 1/(1+0.12)^6$$
$$= \mathbf{0.5066}$$

The pay back method can be modified to allow for the time value of money by using discounted cash flows instead of undiscounted cash flows as the following example illustrates.

Example: Discounted pay back

Discount rate 10%

	Cash flows	Discount factor	Discounted cash-flows	Cumulative sum of cash flows
Initial investment	−£18,000	1.0000	−£18,000.00	−£18,000.00
Cash flow (year 1)	+£6,500	0.9090	£5,909.09	−£12,090.90
Cash flow (year 2)	+£8,600	0.8264	£7107.44	−£4,983.47
Cash flow (year 3)	+£4,375	0.7513	£3287.00	−£1,696.47
Cash flow (year 4)	+£3,999	0.6830	£2731.37	+£1,034.90

Therefore if discounted pay back is used the project will pay back in four years instead of three years if discounting was not used.

Accounting Rate of Return (ARR)

The accounting rate of return (ARR), also known as the rate of return on capital employed (ROCE), is equal to the arithmetic average of the cash flows generated by the project divided by the initial investment (however, there are a number of other formulations which can be used). Companies would choose the projects which generate the highest ARR value. The ARR technique has the advantage of being easy to calculate and generating a percentage value which could be compared to a target rate.

Example

Initial investment	=	£18,000
Average cash flow	=	(£6,500 + £8,600 + £4,375 + £3,999)/4
	=	£5,868.50
ARR	=	£5,868.50/£18,000
	=	0.3260
or	=	**32.60%**

(Note: depreciation and scrap values can be allowed for in the calculation of ARR.)

Although ARR used to be a very popular technique, recent survey evidence has tended to show a decline in its popularity and use. This decline is due to the criticisms levelled at ARR; firstly it ignores the time value of money and secondly it ignores inflation, which in high inflationary periods can be a serious problem.

Net Present Value

The net present value (NPV) technique is considered to be the best investment appraisal technique avaliable. NPV analysis will always produce the correct answer and can take account of all relevant costs and cash flows, depreciation, inflation, tax, capital allowances and risk. The NPV value is calculated by discounting the future cash flow by the cost of capital back to the present and then summing all the values up. As already shown, the discount factor is calculated using the formula

$$1/(1+r)^n$$

The NPV value will change as the cost of capital changes, and in the example shown below the project is first discounted by 10% and then 16%. Normally the higher the cost of capital the lower the NPV value will be, therefore there is normally an inverse relationship between NPV values and the cost of capital. If the locus of NPV values at different rates of the cost of capital are drawn on a graph, the NPV profile will be described. A set of discount tables are given in Appendix A on page 315.

Example: Net present value

Discount rate 10%

	Cash flows	Discount factor	Discounted cash flows
Initial investment	−£18,000	1.0000	−£18,000.00
Cash flow (year 1)	+£6,500	0.9090	£5,909.09
Cash flow (year 2)	+£8,600	0.8264	£7,107.44
Cash flow (year 3)	+£4,375	0.7513	£3,287.00
Cash flow (year 4)	+£3,999	0.6830	£2,731.37
		Net present value	**£1,034.90**

Discount rate 16%

	Cash flows	Discount factor	Discounted cash flows
Initial investment	−£18,000	1.0000	−£18,000.00
Cash flow (year 1)	+£6,500	0.8621	£5,603.65
Cash flow (year 2)	+£8,600	0.7432	£6,391.52
Cash flow (year 3)	+£4,375	0.6407	£2,803.06
Cash flow (year 4)	+£3,999	0.5523	£2208.64
		Net present value	**£−993.26**

As can clearly be seen from this example, if the cost of capital rises to 16% the project is no longer profitable as the NPV value is negative. Firms would invest in projects where the NPV value was positive but would not invest in projects where the NPV value was negative. Figure 6.7 shows the NPV profile, the locus of NPV value for different costs of capital.

Internal Rate of Return

The internal rate of return is related to the NPV technique in that it is the cost of capital which causes the NPV value to be zero. Some problems can arise from the IRR technique as it is possible to have multiple IRR values (see the articles by Longbottom and Wiper (1978) and the article by Wilkes (1980)). The technique involved in finding the IRR value precisely is very complex, involving solving a complex polynomial to degree n. The investment project used for the NPV example is written as a polynomial to degree n:

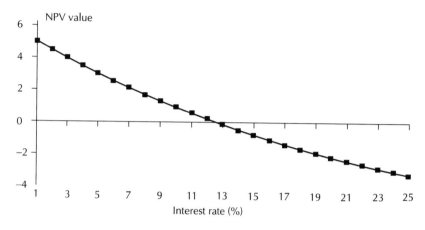

Figure 6.7 NPV profile

$$\frac{-18000}{(1+r)^0} + \frac{6500}{(1+r)^1} + \frac{8600}{(1+r)^2} + \frac{4375}{(1+r)^3} + \frac{3999}{(1+r)^4} = 0$$

If we then multiply this equation throughout by $(1+r)^4$

$$-18000^*(1+r)^4 + 6500^*(1+r)^3 + 8600^*(1+r)^2 + 4375^*(1+r)^1 + 3999 = 0$$

This equation would then be solved for values of r which cause the equation to equal zero.

One alternative is to use an approximation technique involving linear interpolation, the problem with this method is the result can be inaccurate. However the software designed by Goode and Snee (1995a) and Goode, Snee and Moutinho (1995), called Unicorn, will solve any investment appraisal problem by calculating all the NPV values over any range. Unicorn is available on the Internet on the following FTP site address:

ftp://zen.sys.ac.uk/management/CTI/NPV

New information about Unicorn is published on

http://www.sys.uea.ac.uk/cti/cti-afm.html

This software (compiled Basic and the Basic ASCII code) is also available on computer floppy disc which can be purchased separately – see the order form at the back of the book.

If the results from running Unicorn are graphed the NPV profile is shown, which will clearly illustrate all the points of interest. An example of this is shown in Figure 6.8. The IRR rate is then compared to the company's cost of capital and if the IRR rate for the particular project is greater than the cost of capital, the company would invest in the project.

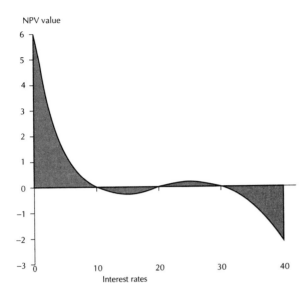

Figure 6.8   Graph of multiple internal rate of returns

Table 6.4   Investment appraisal techniques

	Advantages	Disadvantages
Payback	Quick and simple to use. Do not have to forecast cashflows over the whole life of the project. Do not need to know a cost of capital. The answer is easy to understand.	Disregards cash flows past the payback point. Disregards the time value of money.
ARR	Gives a percentage answer	No account is taken of the time value of money.
NPV	Takes account of the time value of money. Always give the correct result if the cash flows and cost of capital are correct. Analyses the whole investment project. Results can be viewed graphically on an NPV profile. Can take account of inflation, risk, tax and capital allowances. Its is the best method.	Can involve long and complex calculations. You need to know a cost of capital.
IRR	Takes account of the time value of money	Can involve long and complex calculations You can have multiple IRRs

Table 6.4 lists some of the advantages and disadvantages of the investment appraisal techniques described in this chapter.

SUMMARY

A good understanding of financial techniques is essential for any marketing manager. Managers who are able to anticipate the effects of pricing decisions on profitability, sales volume and market share, and who monitor the market situation carefully (see Chapter 7), will be able to use this factor of the marketing mix in an optimal way in pursuit of the company's objectives. Any of the four recommended books on pricing, listed at the end of the chapter, would be useful in extending the reader's understanding of the subject.

The best investment appraisal technique is NPV. IRR will normally will give similar answers to NPV analysis but not in all cases (i.e. multiple IRRs). The areas covered on investment appraisal in this chapter should only be seen as covering the major points and readers are encouraged to use other books to look in more depth into this subject. One of the best books on investment appraisal is by Lumby (1994) which provides a comprehensive coverage of all the major areas in this subject area. Another comprehensive book on the subject is by Samuels, Wilkes and Brayshaw (1995).

REFERENCES AND FURTHER READING

Devinney, T.M. (1988) *Issues in Pricing: Theory and Research*, Lexington: Lexington Books.

Goode, M.M.H. and Snee H. R. (1995) 'NPV Profiles The Easy Way: A Tale of Two Loops', *The Journal of CTI Accounting, Finance and Management*, **7**, (2), pp. 22–33.

Goode, M.M.H., Snee H. R. and Moutinho L. (1995) 'A Computer Aided Approach to Investment Decisions', *BAM Conference*, Sheffield, UK, pp. 592–3.

Longbottom D. and Wiper L. (1978) 'Necessary Conditions for the Existence of Multiple Rates in the Use of Internal Rates of Return' *Journal of Business Finance and Accounting*, **5**, (4), pp. 295–303.

Lumby, S. (1994) *Investment Appraisal and Financial Decisions*, 5th edition, London: Chapman and Hall.

Monroe, K.B. (1990) *Pricing: Making Profitable Decisions*, 2nd edition, New York: McGraw-Hill.

Morris, M.H. (1991) *Market-Orientated Pricing*, Lincolnwood: NTC Business Books.

Nagle, T.T. and Holden, R.K. (1995) *The Strategy and Tactics of Pricing*, 2nd edition, Englewood Cliffs: Prentice-Hall.

Pike, R.H. (1982) *Capital Budgeting in the 1980s*, Institute of Cost and Management Accounting, UK.

Samuels, J.M., Wilkes, F.M. and Brayshaw, R.E. (1995) *Management of Company Finance*, 6th edition, London: Chapman and Hall.

Wilkes F.M. (1980), 'On Multiple Rates of Return', *Journal of Business Finance and Accounting*, **7**, (4), pp. 569–83.

Wind, Y., Mahajan, V. and Cardozo, R. (1981) *New Product Forecasting: Models and Applications*, Lexington: Lexington Books.

PROBLEM: AVERAGE-COST PRICING

Introductory Comments

Average-cost pricing works well if the company actually sells the quantity which was used in setting the average cost-price. Ignoring demand is the major weakness of average-cost pricing. Losses may result, however, if actual sales are much lower than expected. On the other hand, if sales are much higher than expected, then profits may be very good. But this will only happen by accident – that is, because the company's demand is much larger than expected.

To use average-cost pricing, a marketing manager must make some estimate of the quantity to be sold in the coming period. But unless this quantity is related to price – that is, unless the company's demand curve is considered – the marketing manager may set a price that does not even cover the company's total cost! This can be seen in a simple example for a company with a cost structure shown in Table 6.5. The company's demand curve is shown in Figure 6.9. It is important to see that customer demands (and their demand curve) are still important – whether management takes time to analyse the demand curve or not.

Problem

Golden Taste Limited is a food manufacturer which markets an extensive product mix of fast-moving spices, herbs and sauces. The company is currently evaluating various possible price points for an improved line of food sauces, as shown by the company's demand curve in Figure 6.9.

Questions

1. Comment on your recommended price policy taking into account potential losses, units sold, total revenue, total cost and potential profit.
2. Assess the usefulness of average-cost pricing.

Table 6.5 Cost structure of Golden Taste Limited

Quantity (Q)	Total fixed costs (TFC)	Average fixed costs (AFC)	Average variable costs (AVC)	Total variable costs (TVC)	Total cost (TC)	Average cost (AC)
0	£30,000	—	—	—	£30,000	—
10,000	30,000	£3.00	£0.80	£8,000	38,000	£3.80
20,000	30,000	1.50	0.80	16,000	46,000	2.30
30,000	30,000	1.00	0.80	24,000	54,000	1.80
40,000	30,000	0.75	0.80	32,000	62,000	1.51
50,000	30,000	0.60	0.80	40,000	70,000	1.40
60,000	30,000	0.50	0.80	48,000	78,000	1.30
70,000	30,000	0.43	0.80	56,000	86,000	1.23
80,000	30,000	0.38	0.80	64,000	94,000	1.18
90,000	30,000	0.33	0.80	72,000	102,000	1.13
100,000	30,000	0.30	0.80	80,000	110,000	1.10

$$\left[\frac{110.000\ (TC)}{-80,000\ (TVC)}\right]$$
$$\frac{}{30,000\ (TFC)}$$

$$(Q)\ (100,000)\ \frac{30,000\ (TFC)}{0.30\ (AFC)}\ 0.80\ (AVC)$$

$$\frac{100,000\ (Q)}{\times 0.80\ (AVC)}$$
$$80,000\ (TVC)$$

$$\left[\frac{30,000\ (TFC)}{+80,000\ (TVC)}\right]$$
$$110,000\ (TC)$$

$$(Q)\ (100,000)\ \frac{110,000\ (TC)}{1.10\ (AC)}$$

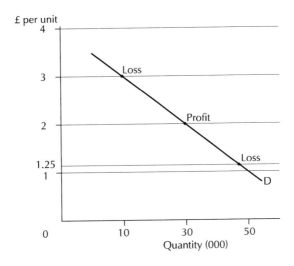

Figure 6.9 Evaluation of various prices along Golden Taste's demand curve

CASE: AVENTURA & CO.

Tom Carter is a junior accountant with Aventura & Co., a large teenagers' fashion store headquartered in Birmingham, England. Tom has three invoices on his desk that must be dealt with before his next break. In each case, he must decide whether to pay the invoice now, to take advantage of any cash discount, or to wait until the due date before paying it to allow Aventura & Co. to earn interest on the money. Aventura & Co. has a policy of taking all cash discounts yielding an annual rate in excess of 15%.

Invoice No. 1: £856 due with a stocking allowance of 3% (for ordering a full assortment of sizes and colours); terms are 2/10, net 30.

Invoice No. 2: £3,175 due with an advertising allowance of 4% and a seasonal discount of 6% (for taking merchandise earlier or later than normal); terms are 1/10, net 60.

Invoice No. 3: £4,317 due; terms are 3/5, net 45.

At this point in time, Tom decided to read the following section from one of his old university textbooks.

    'A cash discount is a discount offered on the condition that the customer will repay the credit extended within a specified period of time. A cash discount normally is expressed as a percentage discount on the net amount of the cost of goods purchased (usually excluding freight and taxes). The length of the discount period also is specified when discount terms are offered. For example, credit terms of '2/10, net 30' mean that the customer can deduct 2% of the invoice amount if payment is made within 10 days from the invoice date. If payment is not made by this time, the full invoice amount is due within 30 days from the invoice date (in some cases the discount period may begin with the date of shipment or the date of receipt by the customer). Like the length of the credit period, the cash discount varies among different lines of business.

Cash discounts are offered (or increased) in order to speed up the collection of accounts receivable and, by extension, reduce the company's level of receivable investment and associated costs. Offsetting these savings or benefits is the cost of the discounts that are taken, which is equal to the lost pound revenues from the existing unit sales volume.

The offering of a cash discount also may increase demand and sales, since some potential customers may view it as a form of price cut and be willing to purchase the product at this new, 'lower' price'.

Questions

1. Why would a manufacturer offer Aventura & Co. stocking allowances, advertising allowances, and seasonal discounts?
2. Why would a manufacturer offer Aventura & Co. cash discounts?
3. How do you think Aventura & Co. set 15% as the minimum for which a cash discount should be taken?
4. Complete the following table using the data in the case.

	Invoice No. 1	Invoice No. 2	Invoice No. 3
Original Amount			
Amount due after functional discounts			
Equivalent annual rate on discount			
Amount due after all discounts			

5. When and how much should Tom pay on each invoice? Explain your reasons for these decisions.
6. Why do most firms insist that their accounting departments pay all bills within the cash discount period?

CASE: POLYGON PUBLISHING COMPANY

Christopher Martin is an assistant editor for business publications at the Polygon Publishing Company in Devon, England. Some of his duties are to estimate the profitability of each new book proposal before a publishing contract is awarded to the author. His current assignment is to evaluate a software package, 'Computer Models for Marketing Management'. The work consists of a computer program for analysing marketing management problems and a user's manual. This assignment is particularly difficult because software publishing is such a relatively new field and Polygon Publishing Company has had very little experience with it so far. Christopher estimates the size of the market for this type of software to be between 20,000 and 30,000 copies a year. A good share of this market might be between 10% and 20%. A tentative retail price of £39 has been set, which translates into a wholesale price of £27.30. Demand is estimated to be price inelastic.

Approximately £4,000 worth of editorial support will be necessary to prepare this work for publication. An additional £3,000 should be spent on typesetting and layout. Manufacturing costs of the software disk and user's manual have been estimated at £13.75 per copy. Another £4.50 per copy is Christopher Martin's best estimate of distribution expenses. Finally, £5,000 a year will be needed after the software is published for continuing editorial and sales support.

The author has asked for a grant of £5,000 to help him complete the work. (Note: a grant is different from an advance against royalties in that a grant is given to the author, whereas an advance could be viewed as a loan to be paid back out of future royalties as sales occur). In addition, the author will receive a 10% royalty on the wholesale price of all sales made.

Polygon Publishing Company has a minimum profit goal of £20,000 that must be earned before it will consider publishing any work. The numbers in Table 6.6 have been derived from Christopher Martin's calculations:

Table 6.6   Christopher Martin's Data Calculations

	(£)
New investment needed	12,000
Fixed costs	25,000
Variable costs	20.98/unit
Selling price	27.30/unit
Industry sales	25,000 units (range 20,000 – 30,000)
Market share	15% (range 10 – 20%)

Questions

1. Why do you think Polygon Publishing Company might want to have a minimum profit goal before considering a new product?
2. Looking at Table 6.6, how accurate do you think the various estimates used in this case are? Explain why?
3. You have the choice of several different trial break even calculations that can be performed in this situation. The results of one of these calculations can be compared to the values in Table 6.6 to determine if Polygon Publishing Company is likely to break even in this situation. Frequently we calculate a break even value for the quantity about which we have the greatest uncertainty. Sensitivity analysis can then be used to determine whether or not our estimate lies within an acceptable range. Which quantity in this situation do you see as hardest to estimate? Why will this value be so hard to estimate?
4. Using the data available, calculate the break even values for each of the following quantities:

    Break even volume in units
    Break even market share
    Break even selling price
    Break even manufacturing cost/unit
    Break even new investment
    Break even fixed costs

    Based on this result, would you recommend publishing the software? Why or why not?
5. Try different values for the quantities in this situation. By how much must each quantity change before you would make a different decision about publishing or not publishing the software? What should Christopher Martin recommend? Why?

CASE: GEOFFREY HANSEN LIMITED

Geoffrey Hansen Limited makes 1,000 units per annum of each of five products. The overall profit level for the company is deemed to be unsatisfactory. The cost structure and sales per unit are given in Table 6.7.

The fixed overheads for the year are: £25,000 (factory) £20,000 (selling).

   You should note that local skill-base constraints mean that you can not expand the labour force. You can, however, obtain as much raw material as you wish to purchase.

Table 6.7

Product	Selling Price	Material	Labour	Variable factory overhead	Variable selling overhead
	£	£	£	£	£
A	25	10	5	2	—
B	35	20	8	2	—
C	40	15	5	2	5
D	50	23	10	5	6
E	60	25	15	5	7

Questions

1. Draft a table to enable management to decide which products justify most concentrated effort and production activity.
2. The Fixed Selling Overhead comprises salaries of salespeople and related expenses. The directors propose to replace the salespeople with agents who are only paid commission. Draft a report to the directors to show what product mix and commission agreement you would propose to give a satisfactory return.

7
Budgeting and control

Contents

Objectives

After reading this chapter you should know:

- The considerations to be taken into account when allocating a marketing budget.
- The characteristics of three types of control system (after-the-fact, steering, and adaptive).
- How to use various measurement tools for marketing control.
- How marketing effectiveness may be evaluated.

MARKETING BUDGET PLANNING

Budget allocation is a fundamental part of marketing planning. A marketing plan cannot be carried out unless adequate financial resources are allocated to it. This section considers, firstly, the process of determining the total marketing budget, and, secondly, methods of allocating this among the different components of the marketing mix.

In most companies, budgeting begins at the lowest managerial level, with managers submitting budgets to increasingly higher management levels for approval or modification, until the top level decision makers approve the final budgets. It is common to base a current year's budget on that of the previous year, with adaptations to allow for inflation, market changes, etc. Once the overall budget is known, managers can adjust the amounts allocated to specific products, markets and marketing activities. Generally, a product or market in the growth stage would have budgets increased, whereas declining products or markets would have their budgets reduced.

A method often used for allocating resources among different products and markets is to allocate in proportion to the current sales of each product in each market – thus a product accounting for 30% of the company's sales in a particular market would be allocated 30% of the planned expenditure in that market. This method, however, does not take into account products' market potentials – their relative capacity to increase their market share – as it only looks at the individual company's sales data. Some companies, in an attempt to consider market potentials, base budgets on industry figures rather than their own sales figures. However, this still may not fully take into account the relative potential of each of the company's products. Also, of course, budget allocation based on past data is impossible for new products or new markets, since no past data exist.

Budget Allocation

We are therefore going to consider alternative methods of budget allocation, which, after an overall budget is set, is a three-step process:

1. Allocate resources among the four major marketing mix components – product, pricing, promotion, distribution.
2. Allocate the resources for each of these four areas among their sub-components. e.g. the promotion budget may need to be allocated among advertising, personal selling, sponsorship, etc.
3. Allocate resources to specific markets, e.g. sales territories, target market segments, etc.

Allocating to Major Marketing Mix Components

Here, a manager needs to consider alternative combinations of expenditure on the four marketing mix components in order to achieve the optimal combination. There will, of course, be a minimum that needs to be spent on each component, but above that level the manager needs to consider the likely relative gains from different spending plans. A useful method often used to do this is based on isoquant curves. Suppose we wish to divide part of our budget in the most efficient way between promotion and distribution. Our company's annual sales range from £1.5 million to £2.25 million. Based on experience and analysis of previous figures, the company has been able to determine the levels of expenditure on promotions and distribution which are necessary to achieve sales of £1.5 million, £2 million and £2.5 million. Figure 7.1 shows these graphically – for instance, spending of £40,000 on promotions and £18,000 on distribution leads to sales of £2 million (point X). So does spending of £32,000 on promotions and £22,000 on distribution (point Y). The isoquant curve for each sales level is the curve specifying all combinations of promotion and distribution spending that will achieve this sales level.

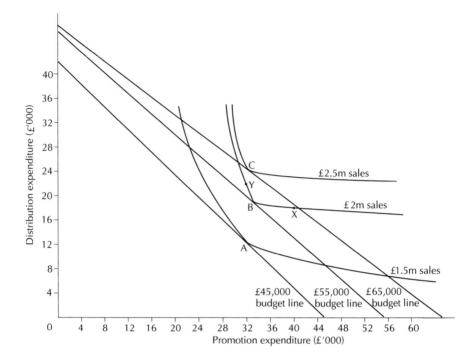

Figure 7.1   Isoquant curves

Having drawn the isoquant curves, a straight line representing all the possible combinations of expenditure between the two variables, given the available budget, can be superimposed. Figure 7.1 shows such budget lines for budgets of £45,000, £55,000 and £65,000. The optimal combination of expenditure then lies at the point where the budget line is tangential to the isoquant curve, i.e. at points A, B and C for the three budget levels shown.

The success of this approach will of course depend on the isoquant curves being reasonably accurate. Later in this chapter we will discuss ways of estimating response functions in order to predict sales.

Allocating Within Marketing Mix Components

The next step is to allocate the budget for each main component of the mix among its sub-components. The promotional spending, for instance, may need to be allocated among media advertising of different types, direct mail and personal selling. Isoquant curves may again be employed here using analysis of sales generated by different spending combinations. Another method which can be used is called the incremental matrix. Here, again based on experience and analysis, a table is drawn up showing the extra sales revenue which can be generated by

Table 7.1 Media allocation using an incremental matrix

Increments in media budget (£)	Additional revenue generated (£)		
	Television	Radio	Magazines
5,000	100,000	30,000	60,000
5,000	70,000	18,000	30,000
5,000	40,000	12,000	15,000
5,000	25,000	8,000	10,000
5,000	15,000	4,000	7,000
5,000	10,000	2,000	5,000
30,000	260,000	74,000	127,000

successive budget increments when spent on the different sub-components of the mix. Table 7.1 is the type of incremental matrix which might be used to allocate media expenditure, given a total media budget of £30,000.

Obviously, if the whole budget were to be spent on one medium, the best choice would be television. However, better results are achieved by using a combination of media, selected by considering each £5,000 increment separately. The first £10,000 is spent on television, but then we can get a better return for our third £5,000 by spending it on magazine advertising (£60,000 as opposed to £40,000 if we bought more television advertising). Our next £5,000 goes on television, and our final two increments are spent on radio and magazine advertising (£30,000 each), giving a total revenue of £100,000 + 70,000 + 60,000 + 40,000 + 30,000 + 30,000 = £330,000 − £70,000 more than by using television alone.

Again, this method of resource allocation depends on managers estimating figures which may be difficult or even impossible to determine accurately. Managers need to find out as much data as they can on the reach and effectiveness of the advertising media under consideration, and then use this, along with their experience, to estimate incremental revenues.

Allocation Among Target Markets

Finally, decisions have to be made about the precise allocation of resources among different target markets. With regard to advertising and promotion, in which geographical areas should local media be used and how much should be spent? Should all stores have the same point of sale advertising or should it be varied according to the locality? Should product distribution be national, or limited to major cities or certain areas initially? Should the product be priced and packaged similarly for all target markets, or not? These sorts of questions must be considered, in the light of the company's experience and market knowledge, in order to achieve an optimal allocation of resources.

Further Considerations in Resource Allocation

The main problems with the methods we have discussed relate to the changing nature of markets, and the non-availability of precise and accurate data from which to predict. There are also other aspects which managers must take into account, and these considerations fall into six categories.

Measurement

It is impossible to tell precisely how much of an increase in sales revenue is due to increased expenditure on specific aspects of the marketing mix. Many factors affecting sales, such as competitor activity or changing consumer tastes, are uncontrollable by the firm.

Number of alternatives

Each of the four main elements of the marketing mix have so many sub-components that managers have to consider a vast array of different combinations of expenditure. A computer spreadsheet is essential to compare these.

Time lag

Budgets may be determined annually or as often as quarterly, but there is still a time lag between the determining of the budget and the actual spending, and between the expenditure and its effects. Changes to different aspects of the marketing mix may take a long time to be reflected in sales revenue, and the longer the time lag, the harder it is to determine the strength of the link between budget changes and sales revenue increase or decrease.

Market evolution

Managers must always be alert to changes in the market, such as introduction of new products which render existing ones obsolete, changes in consumer tastes or product perceptions and competitor activity. Budgets may need to allow for items not previously necessary, such as product modification or new types of advertising.

Market saturation

The typical S-shaped product life cycle curve means that, when sales have reached a certain saturation level, it may not be possible to boost them any higher, however high the marketing expenditure. Managers need to spot when this is the case, in order not to waste marketing resources which would be better spent elsewhere.

Economies of scale

Economies of scale can be achieved in many ways in mass marketing, e.g. through efficient methods of distribution, or cooperation between manufacturers and sellers of a product with regard to advertising and promotion. Such possibilities need to be considered during budget allocation.

We now return to the question raised earlier - how can we predict the level of sales that will result from different marketing mixes? Such prediction is made easier if managers can estimate the sales-response functions for different marketing mix variables.

Sales-response Functions

Sales of a product are affected by many factors. Some of these are under the control of the company (e.g. price, advertising, product quality) and others are out of the company's control (e.g. competitors' prices, the size and demographic profile of the target market). The effect of the latter on sales must be estimated for forecasting purposes. Effective allocation of the marketing budget then means setting the variables in the first category so as to maximise sales. In order to allocate resources in this way among the various elements of the marketing mix, a manager must have some idea as to how sales are affected by changes in each variable. The term sales-response function is used to describe the relationship between sales volume and a particular element of the marketing mix, when all other elements of the mix are held constant. Figure 7.2 shows some possible sales-response functions.

Figure 7.2(a) shows a demand curve – a relationship between price and sales volume as discussed in Chapter 4. The slope of the curve indicates that a lower price will increase sales, which is the usual situation. Demand curves may be either linear or curvilinear.

Figure 7.2(b) shows a possible relationship between product quality and sales volume. The elongated S-shape indicates that when a certain quality level (Q1) is reached, sales begin to increase quickly, until at a high level of quality (Q2), further improvements become progressively less effective in increasing sales.

Figure 7.2(c) is again an S-shape and is a possible relationship between advertising expenditure and sales volume. Below point A1, advertising spending is too low to create more than a minimal awareness. As advertising spending increases, it creates a higher level of awareness and interest, which should lead to increased purchase and therefore increased sales. However, once the market has become very familiar with the product, or becomes saturated, further increases in advertising spending (beyond point A2) may not produce many extra sales and thus the curve levels out.

Finally, Figure 7.2(d) shows a possible relationship between sales force size and sales volume. Sales increase, but at a progressively decreasing rate, with increases in sales force size. This could be explained by reasoning that a company with only one sales representative would send that person to call on the best prospects, so there would be large increases in sales over the situation with no representatives. If the company hired a second sales representative, this would allow them to cover the second best tier of prospects as well. The expectation of sales from these would be high, but not so high as from the best prospects, so the rate of sales volume increase

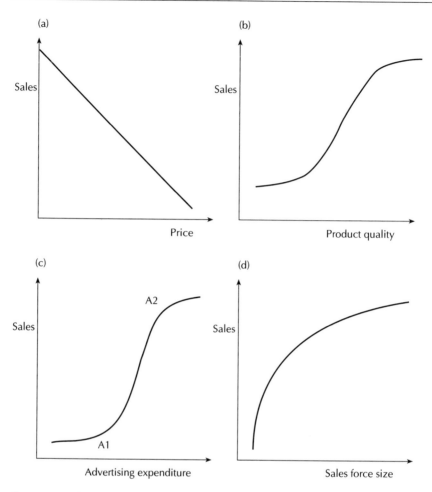

Figure 7.2   Sales-response functions

would be lower. As successive representatives are added to the sales force, they begin to cover less and less attractive prospects, so the expected increase in sales from each additional representative would be lower than from the previous one, leading to the concave curve shown.

One way in which the relationship between sales volume and a particular element of the marketing mix is often expressed is by using a response coefficient. For instance, if we said that we expected advertising to have a response coefficient of 0.25, this would mean that we would expect a percentage increase in advertising spending to have the effect of increasing sales by a quarter (25%) of that percentage. For instance, a 40% increase in advertising spending would result in a 10% increase in sales, or, conversely, a 20% decrease in advertising spending would result in a 5% decrease in sales. However, we must be careful not to extend this type of relationship outside the bounds of its validity. We saw previously that a typical sales-response function for advertising spending was an S-shaped curve, indicating that the relationship between advertising spending and sales volume varies depending on the absolute values of advertising expenditure and sales. We might therefore be justified in claiming that, for a product with normal annual sales of around £800,000 for advertising expenditure of £10,000, that a 20% increase in advertising spending to £12,000 would increase sales by 5% to £840,000, or even that a 40% increase to £14,000 would increase sales by 10% to £880,000 – but it is rather unlikely that an 800% increase in advertising spending to £90,000 would result in a 200% increase (i.e. a trebling) of sales volume.

Another important concept is that of synergy between the effects of changes in two or more variables in the marketing mix. Often, marketing variables interact, producing greater effects on sales volume when changes are made to two (or more) of them than the sum of the effects of changes in each variable alone. For instance, a washing powder manufacturer may estimate that advertising spending, as above, has a response coefficient of 0.25, and that price changes from the current price level have a response coefficient of -2 (as sales generally increase with decrease in price, response coefficients for price are normally negative).

Suppose the price is decreased by 5% and advertising spending increased by 20%. This should lead to an increase in sales of 10% plus 5% = 15%. But if the company decides to use the extra advertising spending to advertise the price reduction, increased awareness of this may further increase sales volume. If the actual sales volume increases by more than 15%, then we can conclude that the two variables, advertising spending and price, show synergy.

The classic equation for estimating the joint effects of several marketing mix variables was first proposed by Kotler in the early 1960s (see Kotler, 1997), and is of the form:

$$Q = kP^a A^b S^c$$

where Q = sales volume
      k = a scale factor, representing the size of the market prior to changes in marketing mix variables
      P = price
      A = advertising
      S = personal selling
      a = price response coefficient
      b = advertising response coefficient
      c = personal selling response coefficient.

Other variables and their coefficients may of course be included in the equation or may replace any or all of those given.

Estimating Sales-response Functions

There are three methods of estimating sales-response functions. The first is the statistical method, using data on past sales and levels of marketing mix variables to estimate relationships using statistical techniques. The method's effectiveness very much depends on the availability and quality of past data, and on whether the market is stable enough for the past to adequately predict the present. The second method, the experimental method, uses sample test markets in which the marketing mix is varied in a controlled fashion and the effect on sales volume noted. This method produces the most reliable results, but is complex and costly to administer properly.

Finally, the judgemental method relies on market experts' estimation of sales volume under given variations of the marketing mix. Questions such as 'What do you think sales would be in area A if we increased television advertising on the regional television station by 20%?' and 'What do you think sales would be if we decreased such advertising by 20%?' can be used to obtain estimates of sales for different levels of marketing mix elements. A procedure such as the Delphi method (see Chapter 5 – Forecasting) would be used for combining the expert opinions, and finally different types of functional relationships would be tested for goodness of fit to the estimates, in order to derive an equation for the sales-response function. It is preferable to obtain estimates of sales for several levels of the marketing mix variable, sufficiently far from the current level to fit a meaningful curve through the estimates.

The estimation procedure may be enhanced by asking the experts how confident they are of their predictions, with questions such as 'What is the probability that, given this level of advertising, sales will be greater than £500,000/greater than £600,000, etc.?'. This additional information is useful in calculating the expected values of alternative strategies and the levels of risk associated with them.

Customer Profitability Analysis

A successful company must attract and retain profitable customers. Therefore, another important aspect of marketing resource allocation is that the budget should be targeted toward those markets which will provide the highest profitability. It is impossible for a company to satisfy the needs of every potential customer and so the company needs to be clear about where it is positioning itself in the market. It needs to know the level of product or service quality expected by customers in possible target markets and the price they are prepared to pay for this. For instance, airlines target very different types of customer with business class and economy fares. Although economy passengers would no doubt like to have the increased comfort and service of business class, they would not be prepared to pay a premium price for it and therefore it would be unprofitable for airlines to provide it.

Customer profitability is a long-term concept. A profitable customer is one who, over time, yields a profit which substantially exceeds the company's costs of marketing to and servicing that customer. Thus companies should seek to engender brand loyalty to their products among profitable customers, and to maintain a high profitable customer retention rate. They should also be continually monitoring customer satisfaction – if dissatisfied customers go elsewhere and develop loyalty to a competitor, not only are the customers' lifetime revenues lost, it is also extremely likely that they will tell others of their dissatisfaction, turning other existing or potential customers away.

In order to discover who are the most profitable customers, a company needs to know, firstly, what each customer buys, and, secondly, how profitable is each purchase. This information is much easier to obtain for a business serving corporate customers, who will have accounts showing their purchases, or for marketers of products which are major purchases, such as cars. Marketers of mass market products, such as groceries, will generally not be able to identify individual customers and will have to look at the profitability of specific market segments, considering such aspects as retailer mark-up and distribution costs.

There are, however, many companies whose customers have multiple transactions with them, and who have the data available to analyse individual customer profitability. The task is made much easier with the use of customer databases, and companies who do this analysis may be surprised at the results. The recent introduction by most credit card companies of an annual fee may well have been prompted by a realisation of how many unprofitable customers they had – those who paid their accounts on time and incurred no interest charges.

Figure 7.3 shows a simple but useful type of profitability analysis. The columns

Customers

	C_1	C_2	C_3	C_4	C_5	
P_1	++			++		Highly profitable product
P_2	+	+	+		+	Profitable product
P_3			–	–	–	Losing product
P_4	+			–	–	Mixed-bag product (may or may not be profitable)
	High profit customer	Profitable customer	Mixed bag customer	Losing customer		

Figure 7.3 Customer and product profitability analysis

represent individual customers and the rows individual products. Each cell contains a symbol for the profitability of selling that product to that customer. The columns can then be analysed to rank customers by profitability. If too many customers are shown by such analysis to be unprofitable, the company may decide to raise the price of its unprofitable products or to increase efforts to cross-sell its more profitable products to currently unprofitable customers. Another option, of course, is to eliminate unprofitable products entirely, but for many companies this is not realistic as the product fits into a portfolio – banks, for instance, would not be popular if they decided to stop offering cheque accounts which are generally unprofitable.

MARKETING CONTROL

We have already referred several times in this chapter to market variables outside the control of the firm which may affect sales and the changing nature of markets which may make it necessary to continually revise or refine marketing strategy and budget allocations. It is therefore essential that constant control is kept over the firm's marketing strategy and its implementation. In this section we discuss the concept of control and how it can be established, and consider control variables and standards.

What is Marketing Control?

The purpose of control is to match the firm's performance as closely as possible to its objectives. Thus, all marketing activities must be closely monitored and if planned performance levels are not being achieved, action must be taken either to improve performance or to set more realistic objectives. Tactical control involves actions to keep the current marketing plan on course, while strategic control refers to the monitoring and adjustment of future plans.

Control systems may be categorised into three types: after-the-fact control systems, steering control systems and adaptive control systems. After-the-fact control systems are used at the end of a planning period in order to evaluate actual performance against planned performance. Steering control systems attempt to identify problems during the period, rather than at the end, by monitoring performance and regularly predicting end-of-period figures from current performance. If this shows that end-of-period performance is likely to deviate substantially from the plan, corrective action can be taken at once to steer the plan back on course. Finally, adaptive control systems also try to identify problems at an early stage, but, rather than reacting to performance figures, they attempt to identify changes in the marketing environment which are likely to cause deviations from planned performance. Thus the marketing plan can be adapted to cope with such changes before they affect performance.

Controlling Implementation of the Marketing Plan

An efficient system for controlling the marketing plan must be able to:

- Detect deviations from planned results.

- Measure the extent of such deviations to determine their seriousness.

- Determine the cause of such deviations.

- Take action – this may be by taking corrective action to bring results into line with the plan, or, if this is not possible, by changing plans to adapt to the new situation. For minor deviations, firms may choose not to take action, but to learn from their experience when it comes to preparing future plans.

In order that these activities can be carried out, the system must provide yardsticks by which performance can be measured against the plan, and a feedback system by which planners are informed of performance against such yardsticks. For instance, annual planned sales may be broken down into a monthly profile so that planners may check monthly whether the firm is on target. It is important that such yardsticks are at frequent intervals so that any problem may be detected early and corrective action taken. Enough information must also be held for planners to be able to identify the causes of problems – the main source of such information would normally be the firm's MkIS (marketing information system).

Measurement Tools for Marketing Control

Ratio Analysis

There are several ratios which measure profitability, activity and sales performance of a company. These can be used to compare the company's performance over time or to compare its performance to that of similar firms. Some of those most commonly used are listed below.

Profitability ratios

$$\text{Return on investment (ROI)} = \frac{\text{Profit after taxes}}{\text{Total assets}}$$

$$\text{Return on sales (ROS)} = \frac{\text{Profit after taxes}}{\text{Sales}}$$

$$\text{Return on equity} = \frac{\text{Profit after taxes}}{\text{Net worth}}$$

Activity ratios

$$\text{Inventory turnover} = \frac{\text{Sales}}{\text{Inventory}}$$

$$\text{Fixed assets turnover} = \frac{\text{Sales}}{\text{Fixed assets}}$$

$$\text{Total assets turnover} = \frac{\text{Sales}}{\text{Total assets}}$$

$$\text{Average collection period} = \frac{\text{Average outstanding debt}}{\text{Average sales per day}}$$

Sales ratios

$$\frac{\text{Production cost of sales}}{\text{Sales}}$$

$$\frac{\text{Marketing cost of sales}}{\text{Sales}}$$

$$\frac{\text{Distribution cost of sales}}{\text{Sales}}$$

It is important to remember, however, that ratios can be affected by environmental factors outside the control of the company and therefore the causes of increase or decrease in ratios should be closely examined.

Variance Analysis

If performance is evaluated against standards or yardsticks laid down in the marketing plan, analysis of the variance of final figures from their planned values can identify problem areas. Hulbert and Toy (1977) developed such a framework for performance analysis which we shall illustrate with a hypothetical example. Table 7.2 shows sales, costs and contributions from Product X over one planning period.

Sources of variance from Product X's planned performance may derive from three sources:

1. Actual market size differs from planned market size.
2. Actual market share differs from planned market share.
3. Contribution per unit differs from planned contribution due to difference in price, cost, or both (price/cost variance).

Table 7.2 Variance between planned and actual performance for Product X

Item	Objective	Actual	Variance
Sales			
Units sold	50,000	48,000	(2,000)
Price per unit (£)	1.99	2.09	0.10
Sales (£)	99,500	100,320	820
Total market			
Units	500,000	520,000	20,000
Market share (%)	10	9.23	(0.77)
Costs			
Variable cost per unit	1.50	1.62	0.12
Contribution			
Per unit	0.49	0.47	(0.02)
Total	24,500	22,560	(1,940)

The total variance, i.e. a shortfall of £1,940 on total contribution, may be decomposed into these three parts using the following formulae:

$$\text{Total variance} = Q_a C_a - Q_p C_p$$

where Q = quantity sold in units
M = total market in units
S = share of total market
C = contribution per unit
a = actual
p = planned

This is first split into price/cost variance and quantity variance:

Price/cost variance = $Q_a(C_a - C_p)$

Quantity variance = $C_p(Q_a - Q_p)$

The quantity variance may further be split into market size variance and market share variance:

Market size variance = $C_p S_p(M_a - M_p)$

Market share variance = $C_p M_a(S_a - S_p)$

Figure 7.4 shows these calculations for Product X.

These figures can now give a clearer idea of why Product X failed to make its planned contribution to profits, falling 8% short of its objective. The first decomposition of variance into price/cost variance and quantity variance shows that these were almost equally responsible for the deviation. However, when we divide

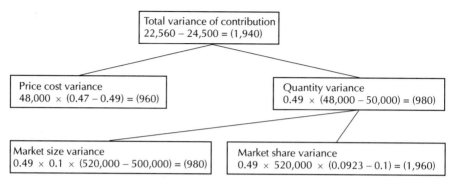

Figure 7.4   Calculation of variance decomposition for Product X

the quantity variance again, we see that the increased market size tended to increase profit contribution (positive variance), while the negative effect of not gaining the planned market share was twice as great. Thus the major cause of deviation was failing to meet the market share target, while the secondary cause was the lower contribution per unit due to increased variable costs not being fully covered by the price rise from the planned price.

The company should now attempt to analyse the situation as fully as possible. Why did variable costs rise? Will they continue to rise? Can prices be increased to cover rises in costs or will this cause further loss of market share? Why has industry demand risen? Could this have been forecasted? Will it continue to rise? Was the shortfall in market share due to inaccurate forecasting, or to other factors such as increased competitor marketing activity or new firms entering the market? Having performed such an analysis, corrective action may be taken.

Marketing Audit

This is a regular and comprehensive review of all the company's marketing operations appraising what is being done and recommending what should be done in future. It should consider allocation of marketing resources, strategy and tactics, the marketing environment and how it is changing, and marketing systems and procedures. We now go on to consider specific areas of the marketing mix and how they should be evaluated.

Evaluating Marketing Effectiveness

Product

Any firm which markets several products is likely to group them into one or more lines of related products, usually packaged in a recognisably similar way. This makes for efficiency in advertising by:

- Creating economies of scale – one product line advertisement can advertise several products and one product can advertise another.

- Providing corporate advertising along with product advertising if the line uses the company name.

Product lines of similar products also reduce manufacturing costs as standardised components can be used, and facilitate sales and distribution as a whole range of product alternatives is offered to customers or retailers.

There are three factors on which a product line should be evaluated: depth, length and consistency.

Depth

The depth of a product line refers to the extent to which it covers the product category. Some companies aim to carry a full product line in order that customers have a range of alternatives and there are no gaps in the line which could cause lost sales. A detergent product line, for instance, may include products suitable for hand and machine washing, for white and coloured items, and powder and liquid formulations. Other companies may decide to specialise in one or two items – the Lux brand, for instance, is recommended for the handwashing of delicate items.

It is important to review the product line regularly, analysing profits on each separate product and considering whether it is worth carrying any unprofitable products for the sake of having a complete product line. If, on the other hand, there are found to be gaps in the line, new product introduction should be considered carefully. Will the new product steal sales from others in the line (cannibalisation)? How will costs increase with its introduction? How many new customers will we gain and how many will we lose if it is not introduced? The product should only be introduced if such analysis of costs warrants it.

Length

The length of a product line refers to its diversity – the range of products that it covers. Brand leveraging – using a strong brand name to introduce related items to the market – is an important way of lengthening a product line. Kelloggs, for example, used their strong brand name in cereals to introduce Pop-Tarts, positioned initially as a breakfast product. Product managers must bear in mind that in lengthening a product line they may be going into a market of which they have less experience, and therefore that market must be well researched and reliable sales projections done before a decision is made. Experience shows that the most successful cases of product line lengthening are those where the new product is most closely related to the known branded product.

Consistency

Consistency considers how similar the product line items are in terms of end use. Greater length tends to lead to a lower level of consistency. Consistent lines lead to economies in advertising as they can be advertised under one umbrella. To some extent, therefore, the product-line manager makes a trade-off between length and consistency.

Price

If sales goals are not being met, the company must find out whether price plays a part in this and adjust their pricing strategy accordingly. They may have wrongly estimated the demand curve showing the effect on sales of a price increase or decrease, or their price may position the product unfavourably against competitors. Consumer surveys will indicate opinions on price and reasons for non-purchase or switching to a competitive product.

Continuous monitoring of the market may alert managers to other circumstances requiring adjustment of pricing strategy. Competitors may be offering discounts to retailers or money-off coupons to customers. Additions to the product line may require adjustment of prices so that they reflect the relative value of the products. Price may not accurately reflect the value of the product, or may not be sufficient to cover increased variable costs.

Finally, pricing strategy must be coordinated with other aspects of the marketing mix to ensure that the image of the product's value, as conveyed by price and advertising, is consistent.

Distribution

Evaluation of the distribution system should cover three areas: the distribution channel system, the performance of channel members, and the physical distribution system.

Evaluation of the channel system

The marketing plan should show projected sales through different types of distribution channels, e.g. for a confectionery product these might be supermarkets, independent grocers, newsagents, vending machines, etc. If actual revenues do not reach those projected, or distribution costs for the channel are higher than estimated, distribution policy may require to be changed. A channel audit should be carried out, comprehensively evaluating each class of intermediary. The findings may point to a need to change distribution policy radically, but they may show that smaller changes, such as changes in the margins offered to channel members, could achieve the desired results.

Evaluation of performance of channel members

This should be done regularly and may be part of a periodic channel audit. There are three sales criteria which may be used for evaluation:

1. Actual sales compared to projected sales.
2. Current sales compared to past sales.
3. Sales compared to other intermediaries of the same type.

In addition, the evaluator may look at service factors (such as delivery times to customers and fulfilment of service contracts), efficiency of re-ordering procedures and cooperation with company strategy with regard to advertising, pricing, etc.

If performance is unsatisfactory, the company should investigate and help the intermediary to improve performance. If performance continues to be sub-standard then the company may have to consider replacing the intermediary.

Evaluation of the physical distribution system

This covers areas such as order handling, inventory management, storage and transportation, both in the manufacturing company and throughout the distribution channels. Managers should be alert for findings which may signal problems with control of the distribution system, such as:

1. Large numbers of incomplete orders being sent out, which may indicate problems with inventory management.
2. Frequent use of express transport services at the company's expense showing either a disregard for costs or inefficient order handling.
3. Slow inventory turnover – in most companies distribution inventory turns over between six and twelve times a year. Less frequent turnover may indicate that too much stock is held or that it is not adequately controlled.

Again, such problems should be investigated and the causes corrected.

Advertising

Although the ultimate goal of advertising is to increase sales, it is extremely difficult to measure directly the effect of a particular advertising campaign on sales figures. There are so many factors impacting on sales that the effect of advertising cannot be isolated, and it is also impossible to tell if buyers have been influenced solely by the current advertising campaign or whether a cumulative effect has built up from past advertising.

Marketers therefore measure advertising effects indirectly – have consumers seen or heard the advertisement, did they pay attention to it and absorb the intended message, for how long will they remember it? Figure 7.5 shows the series of steps through which consumers are assumed to proceed between first exposure to an advertisement and purchase of the advertised brand – this is known as the hierarchy of effects. At each step the probability of purchase is assumed to increase.

Marketers evaluate the effectiveness of an advertisement at each stage in this hierarchy. Exposure is measured by the circulation of print media or the reach of a television or radio programme. Attention and comprehension are measured by asking

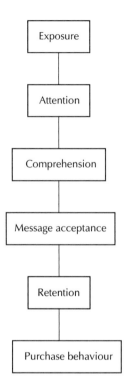

Figure 7.5   Hierarchy of effects

consumers if they have noticed the advertisement and what they remember of it. To evaluate message acceptance, questions are asked on consumers' opinions of the brand and their intentions to purchase it. Retention is measured by asking consumers, some time after exposure to the advertisement, what they remember of it.

Advertisements are evaluated both to test them before an advertising campaign (pre-testing) and to evaluate the effectiveness of a current or past campaign (post-testing). For advertisements in print, the most commonly used pre-tests are portfolio tests where respondents look through a portfolio of advertisements, or a magazine containing several advertisements, and are asked what they remember of them. Physiological techniques may also be used, such as measurement of pupil dilation on looking at the advertisement – dilation is believed to indicate interest. Comprehension is tested by asking respondents to describe the advertisment and its message or asking specifically if they noticed certain key words or images (aided recall). For broadcast advertisements, pre-testing is generally done by inviting respondents to watch television shows with test advertisements and asking them both before and after viewing about brand preferences and buying intentions. In this way the advertisements which seem to have most influence in changing respondent attitudes can be selected. The most common post-test for all media is a recognition or recall test where respondents are asked if they remember seeing or hearing the advertisement and what they recall of it.

Advertising effect on sales
There are a few situations where direct measurement of advertising effect on sales is possible. For instance, sales of products sold only by direct mail or through a television advertisement can only be due to advertising. Marketers have tried various other ways of direct measurement, the most useful of which has been field experiments. Here the target market is divided into different geographical areas, receiving different levels of advertising or different campaigns. Differences in sales levels in the various areas are then analysed. The use of historical data linking advertising and sales, using econometric methods, has also been tried as have various quantitative models similar to the sales-response curves discussed earlier. The main difficulty with any direct approach, however, is the existence of other influencing factors which can never be totally controlled.

Personal Selling

Salespeople have many roles. They need to find out what the customer wants or needs, select the right products or services to meet those needs, ensure that the customer is satisfied and continues to be satisfied with the purchase, and report customer information back to the company. Sales managers need to evaluate the sales effort by comparing performance with objectives – comparing sales for each customer, product line and territory with those projected. If sales are below projections, the sales manager must investigate the reasons for this – e.g. inefficient salespeople, too large territories which cannot be adequately covered, ineffective advertising, badly designed products, or market factors, such as competitor activity, which are outside the company's control. Attempts have also been made to relate sales efforts directly to sales in similar ways to those described above for advertising, but have run into the same problems of inability to isolate the effects of sales efforts.

Evaluation of Retail Performance

A retailer will not only be concerned with overall sales levels, but, in order to control operations efficiently, will set performance objectives such as stock turnover and return on investment, assets or sales. A retail information system, usually computerised, will allow performance against these objectives to be continuously monitored. The system will record sales data by product, store and price, and also data on inventory, accounts and assets. It should also enable comparison with competitors. If performance is shown to be significantly below objectives, management must determine the reasons for this and take corrective action.

Retailers should also evaluate the effectiveness of overall marketing strategy, both at corporate and store level. This will include evaluation of product line, advertising and distribution effectiveness, as previously discussed.

Evaluation and Control in International Marketing

A multinational firm will monitor and evaluate its marketing efforts in the ways already described. However, there are several factors which make evaluation and control more difficult in international marketing. The firm has less control over its operations, due to its physical distance from foreign subsidiaries and distributors, and the various environments in which it operates, with different business customs, laws and trade regulations. The company may be affected by factors outside its control such as economic or political instability in its overseas markets. And reliable market data is unlikely to be available in a format which enables direct comparison of all the firm's overseas markets.

It is therefore essential that multinational firms have a multinational marketing information system. This will include market information for all the countries in which the firm operates, in a form which enables comparability between estimates of market potential and projected sales. The system should also monitor economic and political trends.

CONCLUSION

Almost every company nowadays operates in a fast-changing environment. Customers' needs and preferences change, competitors adapt their products and services or offer completely new ones, companies diversify into different areas, and external factors such as technological advances, new advertising regulations or economic recession can radically change the market for a product or service. The company which continuously monitors its markets and its position in them will be the company best placed to be proactive, to anticipate future problems or opportunities and work out in advance how to deal with them. This type of company, rather than one which merely reacts after changes have happened, is the most likely to succeed in today's business environment.

The case study 'Arctic Power', at the end of this chapter, shows a company using the data which it has gathered through monitoring the performance of its brand and competing brands, in formulating future brand strategy – a good example of how continuous monitoring of performance can inform future decision making.

REFERENCES AND FURTHER READING

Clarke, D.G. (1987) *Marketing Analysis and Decision Making: Text and Cases*, Redwood City: Scientific Press.
Cooper, L.G. and Nakanishi, M. (1988) *Market-Share Analysis*, Norwell: Kluwer Academic Publishers.

Dalrymple, D.J. and Parsons, L.J. (1989) *Marketing Management*, Chichester: John Wiley and Sons.

Dyer, R.F. and Forman, E.H. (1991) *An Analytical Approach to Marketing Decisions*, Englewood Cliffs: Prentice-Hall.

Hanssens, D.M., Parsons, L.J. and Schultz, R.L. (1990) *Market Response Models: Econometric and Time Series Analysis*, Boston: Kluwer Academic Publishers.

Hulbert, J.M. and Toy, N.E. (1977) 'A Strategic Framework for Marketing Control', *Journal of Marketing*, April, pp. 12–20.

Kotler, P. (1997) *Marketing Management: Analysis, Planning, Implementation and Control*, (9th edition), Upper Saddle River: Prentice-Hall International

Lilien, G.L., Kotler, P. and Moorthy, K.S. (1992) *Marketing Models*, Englewood Cliffs: Prentice-Hall.

Vidale, M.L. and Wolfe, H.C. (1957) 'An Operations-Research Study of Sales Response to Advertising', *Operations Research*, June, pp. 370–81.

PROBLEM: ADVERTISING IMPACT MEASUREMENT

Introduction

Marketing managers need to have a dynamic advertising budgeting model since in most cases, advertising expenditures present the largest outlay within the overall marketing budget. Some of these best models incorporate the analysis of the sales response to advertising. Vidale and Wolfe (1957) proposed an interesting model in which they sought to explain not the level of sales directly but the rate of change in sales. Their studies of the sales–advertising relationship in several major companies led them to formulate the following differential equation:

$$\frac{dS}{dT} = \left(\frac{rA(M-S)}{M}\right) - \lambda S$$

where: S = rate of sales at time T
dS/dT = change in the rate of sales at time T
A = rate of advertising expenditure at time T
r = sales response constant (sales generated per advertising pound when $S = 0$)
M = saturation level of sales (the maximum sales that can be profitably achieved via a given campaign)
λ = sales decay constant (proportion of sales lost per time interval when $A = 0$)

The right-hand side of the equation shows that the increase in the rate of sales depends on several factors: it will be greater for higher levels of sales response, advertising expenditure and the percentage of the non-saturated portion of the market; and it will be smaller for higher levels of the sales decay and the rate of sales. In words, the equation says that the increase in the rate of sales is equal to the response of sales per pound of advertising times the number of advertising pounds being spent, reduced by the percentage of non-saturated sales, less the sales being lost through decay.

The parameters r, M, and λ, are taken as constant for a given product and advertising campaign. The response coefficient, r, can be measured by observing the rate of change in sales that takes place under controlled conditions with a given campaign. The saturation level M is estimated from data on the absolute size of the market. The sales decay constant, λ, is measured by observing sales declines in areas where A has been set at zero for measurement purposes.

Thus more advertising expenditure would be necessary the higher the desired sales growth rate, the higher the sales decay constant, the higher the present sales level, the lower the sales response constant or the lower the remaining sales potential. All of these relations accord with intuition.

The sales decay constant is presumably low for well-established brands and these brands need not spend as much to maintain their sales level. Brands with a high sales decay constant must be continuously supported by advertising money to offset competitive inroads. Furthermore, the sales decay constant is likely to vary over the product's life cycle, probably decreasing as the product passes from the introductory stage to the maturity stage, and then increasing as the product passes to the saturation and decline stages.

The closer the sales are to the saturation level M and the higher the ratio λ/R, the greater the advertising investment A in order to maintain the desired sales level S. These effects can be analysed by using the following formula:

$$A = \frac{\lambda S}{r} \cdot \frac{M}{M - S} = \lambda \cdot \frac{SM}{M - S}$$

In another modelling approach – Koyck's Model – the author proposed a weighting pattern for the coefficients of previous advertising expenditures that could be described with two parameters. He proposed that the initial sales effect of a previous expenditure is b and that this effect declined each period by a constant percentage, c, that is:

$$b_{T-1} = cb_T$$

where c is the carryover effect and $0 < c < 1$. The impact of advertising expenditures on company sales can then be seen in the following equation (using a least squares regression):

$$Q_T = a + bX_t + cbX_{T-1} + c^2bX_{T-2} + \ldots + c^nbX_{T-n} + \ldots$$

where: Q = sales
X = advertising expenditures
b = current effect of today's advertising expenditure
c = carryover effect, $0 < c < 1$
c^nb = current effect of an advertising expenditure made n periods ago
(assumes that every advertising expenditure has a constant effect b)

Rearranging the equation shown above, we get:

$$Q_T = (1 - c)a + bX_T + cQ_{T-1}$$

This yields the important result that if the current influence of past advertising expenditures decreases at a constant rate, the current sales level (Q_T) is related to a constant $(1-c)\, a$, the current advertising expenditure level (X_T), and a fraction c is last period's sales level, where c represents the carryover effect. To discover the sizes of the current and carryover effects, current sales are fitted to current advertising expenditures plus last period's sales. Last period's sales, Q_{T-1}, acts in the equation as a weighted moving average of all past advertising expenditures. The parameter c may measure the carryover effect only if we assume that managers decide on the level of advertising expenditure without reference to current sales. If they set advertising expenditures as a strict function of current sales, then the equation may be reflecting the dependence of expenditure levels on sales levels as much as the reverse effect.

Checklist of Key Points

- The change in the rate of sales at time T is a function of four factors:
  1. advertising budget
  2. sales-response
  3. saturation level of sales
  4. sales-decay constant.

- Measuring the impact of advertising expenditures.

- Advertising budgeting.

- Response of sales per pound of advertising.

- Advertising investment needed in order to maintain the desired sales level.

- Advertising carryover effects.

- Current effect of today's advertising expenditure.

- Current effect of a past advertising expenditure.

Case Examples and Questions

1.   A company's advertising expenditures average £50,000 a month. Current sales are £290,000 and the saturation sales level is estimated at £420,000. The sales-response constant is £2 and the sales-decay constant is 6% per month.

Use the Vidale–Wolfe formula and the spreadsheet model to estimate the probable sales increase next month.

2.   Another company, Gilmar Limited, estimate the saturation sales level of £400,000 per month. Current sales are £100,000 per month. The sales-response constant is £2 and the sales-decay constant is 6% per month.

Calculate the amount that the company has to invest per month in advertising in order to maintain present sales stabilised around £100,000 per month.

3.   The Argent C.S. Company wants to apply the Koyck's Model taking into consideration the following input data:

- Last period sales: £100,000

- Current advertising: £60,000
- Immediate advertising impact: 0.5
- Proportionate effect of previous sales: 0.75.

Calculate the future sales trend (for the next six periods) and the respective rates of change in sales.

CASE: CHOCOHOLIC CAKE MIX

Peter Williams, a young and relatively inexperienced product manager for Chocoholic Cake Mix, is in the office of Mary Jones, advertising manager of the company.

'Mary', he says, 'I want to talk to you about the allocation of our advertising and sales promotion funds for our cake mix. As you know, our advertising and promotion allowance for next year is £1.30 a case against anticipated sales of 1,671 thousand cases. Company practice has been to allocate 70% of this amount for consumer advertising and 30% of it for sales promotion. For the past three years the brand manager on the cake mix has followed this practice in all regions. I've just taken over as product manager and I'm not sure that's the best way to do it.' 'I've had the research department break-down next year's estimated sales in terms of our six regions, and also provide me with information on the total number of retail outlets in each region as well as the number of stores stocking our product. Here is the data (see Table 7.3). Now that I have it, I'm not sure what it means.'

Mary looked over the data. 'Well, Peter, the first thing you have to do is to analyse it. After you have done that, allocate the funds the way you think it should be done. Then come back and we'll talk about it. Why don't you come back at 3.00 tomorrow afternoon, and we'll spend some time together to see if we can figure out what you have here.'

As he walks out of Mary's office, Peter is thinking, 'Well, there goes another evening shot. If I'd paid more attention to these issues of marketing resource allocation and promotion budgeting, I'd have a better idea about how to make sense of this data.'

Questions

1. Analyse the data and define the problems.
2. Allocate advertising and promotion funds by region, and justify your allocations.

Table 7.3 Sales and distribution for cake mix by sales region

Regions	1	2	3	4	5	6
Total market ('000 cases)	897.8	1,605.6	676.0	3,242.6	2,640.6	1,499.9
Company sales ('000 cases)	269.3	240.8	135.2	389.1	369.6	267.0
Retail outlets ('000)	18.7	33.7	14.0	67.6	55.0	31.3
Stores stocking company's cake mix ('000)	15.0	28.4	13.3	60.8	33.0	28.3

CASE: ARCTIC POWER*

'We've got some important decisions to make on Arctic Power for 1988,' said Linda Barton, Senior Product Manager for the brand. 'As I see it, we can continue to develop our strong markets in Québec, the Maritimes, and British Columbia or we can try to build market share in the rest of Canada.' Barton was discussing the future of Arctic Power, one of Colgate–Palmolive Canada's leading laundry detergents, with Gary Parsons, the Assistant Product Manager on the brand.

'Not only do we have to consider our strategic direction,' replied Parsons, 'but we also have to think about our positioning strategy for Arctic Power. I'm for running the Québec approach in all our markets.' Parsons was referring to the Québec advertising campaign, which positioned Arctic Power as the superior detergent for cold water cleaning.

'I'm not sure, given the mixed results achieved with our 1986 Western campaign,' said Linda. 'However, we are making great progress with our current advertising in British Columbia. It might be more effective outside of Québec. Remember, cold water washing is a newer concept for the western provinces. We have to overcome that obstacle before we can get people to buy Arctic Power. Let's go over the data again, then make our decisions.'

The Company

Colgate–Palmolive Canada (CPC) is a wholly owned subsidiary of Colgate–Palmolive, a large multinational with divisions in 58 countries. Worldwide company sales in 1986 were $4.9 billion, with profits of $178 million. The Canadian subsidiary's sales exceeded $250 million annually. CPC manufactures a range of household, health, and personal care products. Among CPC's major brands are ABC, Arctic Power, and Fab (laundry detergents), Palmolive (dishwashing liquid), Ajax (cleanser), Irish Spring (bar soap), Ultra Brite and Colgate (toothpastes), Halo (shampoo) and Baggies (food wrap).

Under the product management system at CPC, product managers are assigned responsibility for specific brands, like Arctic Power. Their overall goals are to increase the sales and profitability of their brand. To meet these goals, the product manager supervises all marketing functions including planning, advertising, selling, promotion and market research. In planning and executing programs for a brand, the product manager usually is assigned as assistant product manager and they work closely together to accomplish the brand goals.

* This case was prepared by Gordon H.G. McDougall of Wilfrid Laurier University in Waterloo, Ontario, and Douglas Snetsinger of the University of Toronto. Copyright © 1989 by the North American Case Research Association. Reproduced by permission.

Prior to the late 1970s, CPC essentially followed the strategy of nationally supporting most of its brands. The result was that CPC was spread too thin with too many brands. There were insufficient resources to properly promote and develop all of the CPC line, and profits and market share were less than satisfactory. Beginning in the late 1970s and continuing into the early 1980s, the Canadian division altered its strategy. An extensive review of the entire product line was conducted and CPC moved to what was referred to as a *regional brand strategy*. Where a brand had regional strength, resources were focused on that area, with the objective of building a strong and profitable brand in that region. For example, Arctic Power had a relatively strong market share in Québec and the Maritimes, where the proportion of consumers using cold water to wash clothes was considerably higher than the national average. Promotional support was withdrawn from the rest of Canada and those resources were focused on Québec and the Maritimes.[1] Arctic Power was still distributed nationally but by the end of 1981, national market share was 4%, consisting of an 11% share in Québec, a 5% share in the Maritimes and a 2% share in the rest of Canada. Over the next four years, marketing efforts were concentrated primarily on Québec and to a lesser extent in the Maritimes. This approach worked well for Arctic Power. By the end of 1985, Arctic Power's national share had increased to 6.4%, share in Québec had risen to 18%, share in the Maritimes was 6% and less than 2% in the rest of Canada. With the increase in sales and profitability, the decision was made to target Alberta and British Columbia for 1986. The results of these efforts exceeded expectations in British Columbia but were less than satisfactory in Alberta.

The Laundry Detergent Market

The laundry detergent market was mature, with unit sales increasing by approximately 1% annually and dollar sales increasing by about 5% each year between 1983 and 1986 (Table 7.4). Three large consumer packaged goods companies – Procter and Gamble (P&G), Lever Detergents, and CPC – dominated the market. All three were subsidiaries of multinational firms and sold a wide range of household and personal care products in Canada. Procter and Gamble Canada had annual sales exceeding $1 billion, and some of its major brands included Crest (toothpaste), Ivory and Zest (bar soaps), Secret (deodorant), Pampers and Luvs (disposable diapers) and Head & Shoulders (shampoo). P&G held a 44% share of the laundry detergent market in 1986, due primarily to the large share (34%) held by Tide, the leading brand in Canada.

---

[1] The Maritimes contained the four Eastern provinces: Newfoundland, Nova Scotia, Prince Edward Island, and New Brunswick. In 1988, the population of Canada was estimated at 25.8 million people: Maritimes (2.3 million), Québec (6.6 million). Ontario (9.4 million), Manitoba and Saskatchewan (2.1 million), Alberta (2.4 million), and British Columbia (3.0 million).

Table 7.4 Laundry detergent market

	1983	1984	1985	1986
Colgate				
ABC	6.0	9.8	11.8	13.9
Arctic Power	4.7	5.6	6.4	6.5
Fab	2.1	1.3	1.6	1.4
Punch	2.0	0.7	0.4	0.3
Dynamo	1.0	0.8	0.6	0.5
Total Colgate	15.8	18.2	20.8	22.6
Procter and Gamble				
Tide	34.1	35.1	32.6	34.1
Oxydol	4.9	4.2	4.0	3.3
Bold	4.8	4.2	3.2	2.3
Other P&G brands	4.7	4.8	4.4	4.3
Total P&G	48.5	48.3	44.2	44.0
Lever				
Sunlight	13.9	12.2	14.2	13.4
All	4.1	3.7	3.8	3.2
Surf	2.6	2.6	2.7	2.2
Wisk	3.8	4.1	4.1	4.4
Other Lever brands	0.9	0.8	0.6	0.4
Total Lever	25.3	23.4	25.4	23.6
All other brands	10.4	10.1	9.6	9.8
Grand total	100.0	100.0	100.0	100.0
Total Market				
Metric tonnes ('000)	171.9	171.9	173.6	175.3
(% change)	2.0	0.0	1.0	1.0
Factory sales ('000,000)	$265.8	$279.1	$288.5	$304.7
(% change)	6.2	5.0	3.0	6.0

Source: Company records.

Lever Detergents, with annual Canadian sales in excess of $400 million, operated primarily in the detergent, soap and toiletry categories. Major brands included Close-up (toothpaste) and Dove and Lux (bar soaps). Lever held a 24% share of the laundry detergent market and its leading brand was Sunlight, with a 13% share.

CPC was the only one of the three companies to gain market share in the laundry detergent market between 1983 and 1986. In 1986, CPC's total share was 23%, up from 16% in 1983. ABC, a value brand, positioned to attract consumers interested in 'value for less money,' more than doubled its share between 1983 and 1986 and was the second leading brand, with a 14% share.

Competitive Rivalry

Intense competitive activity was a way of life in the laundry detergent business. Not only did the three major firms have talented and experienced marketers, but they competed in a low-growth market where increased sales could be achieved only by taking share from competitive brands. A difficult task facing any product manager in this business was to identify the marketing mix that would maximise share while maintaining or increasing brand profitability, a task that had both long- and short-term implications. In the long term, competitors strove for permanent share gains by building a solid franchise of loyal users based on a quality product and a strong brand image or position. The positioning strategies were primarily executed through product formulation and advertising campaigns. However, companies also competed through consumer and trade promotions (e.g., coupons, feature specials in newspaper ads), tactics that were more short term in nature. Trade and consumer promotions were critical to maintain prominent shelf display and to attract competitors' customers. Virtually every week of the year, at least one brand of detergent would be 'on special' in any given supermarket. The product manager's task was to find the best balance between these elements in making brand decisions.

Reformulating brands, changing the branch ingredients, was a frequent activity in the laundry detergent business. Reformulating a brand involved altering the amount and kind of active chemical ingredients in the detergents. These active ingredients cleaned the clothes. Each of these cleaning ingredients was efficacious for particular cleaning tasks. Some of these ingredients were good for cleaning clay and mud from cotton and other natural fibres, while others would clean oily soils from polyesters, and still others were good for other cleaning problems. Most detergents were formulated with a variety of active ingredients to clean in a wide range of conditions. As well, bleaches, fabric softeners, and fragrances could be included.

Thus, laundry detergents contained different *levels* and *mixes* of active ingredients. The major decision was the *amount* of active ingredients that would be used in a particular brand. In simple terms, the greater the proportion of active ingredients, the better the detergent was at cleaning clothes. However, all detergents would get clothes clean. For example, in a recent test of 42 laundry detergents, *Consumer Reports* concluded: 'Yes, some detergents get clothes whiter and brighter than others, but the scale is clean to cleanest, not dirty to clean.'

The Canadian brands of laundry detergent contained various amounts of active ingredients. As shown in Table 7.5, Tide and Arctic Power had more active ingredients than any other brand.

In fact, Tide and Arctic Power were equivalent brands in terms of the level of active ingredients. These two brands, referred to as the 'Cadillacs' of detergents, had considerably higher levels of active ingredients than all other detergents. While the actual mix of active ingredients differed between the two brands (with Arctic

Table 7.5 Level of active ingredients of laundry detergents

1	2	3	4	5
Some private labels	Bold III Oxydol Surf All	ABC Fab Cheer 2 Sunlight	—	Arctic Power Tide

Power having a greater mix of ingredients that were more suited to cold water washing), the cleaning power of Tide and Arctic Power was equal.

As the amount of active ingredients in a brand increased, so did the cost. Manufacturers were constantly facing the trade-off between cost and level of active ingredients. At times they had the opportunity to reduce unit costs by switching one type of active ingredient (a basic chemical) for another, depending on the relative costs of the ingredients. In this way, the level of ingredients remained the same; only the mixture changed. Manufacturers changed the physical ingredients of a brand to achieve an efficient per unit cost, to provide a basis for repositioning or restaging the brand; and to continue to deliver better consumer value.

Maintaining or increasing share through repositioning or other means was critical because of the profits involved. One share point was worth approximately $3 million in factory sales, and the cost and profit structures of the leading brands were believed to be similar. While some economies of scale accrued to the largest brands, the average cost of goods sold was estimated at 54% of sales, leaving a gross profit of 46%. Marketing expenditures included trade promotions (16%), consumer promotions (5%), and advertising expenditures (7%), leaving a contribution margin of 18%. Not included in these estimates were management overheads and expenses (e.g., product management salaries, market research expenses, sales salaries and factory overheads), which were primarily fixed. In some instances, lower share brands were likely to spend higher amounts on trade promotions to achieve their marketing objectives.

One indication of competitive activity was reflected in advertising expenditures between 1982 and 1986. Total category media advertising increased by 12% to $14.4 million (Table 7.6). As well, substantial increases in trade promotions had occurred during that period. While actual expenditure data were not available, some managers felt that twice as much was being spent on trade promotions versus advertising. As one example in Montréal, in a nine-month period in 1986, Tide was featured in weekly supermarket advertisements 80 times and Arctic Power was featured 60 times. Typically, the advertisement cost for a feature was shared by the manufacturer and the retailer. At times during 1986, consumers could have purchased six litres of Arctic Power or Tide for $3.49 (regular price of $5.79). There was also a strong indication that the frequency and size of price specials on detergents were increasing. The average retail price of laundry detergents (based on

Table 7.6   Share of national media expenditures (1982–6)

	Percentages				
	1982	1983	1984	1985	1986
ABC	6.4	8.9	12.3	14.0	13.6
Arctic Power	6.1	6.1	6.7	7.2	9.3
Tide	21.0	17.8	19.1	16.4	29.7
Oxydol	5.1	4.5	5.9	6.6	6.4
Sunlight	14.1	10.8	10.5	9.1	11.3
All	10.3	5.5	6.9	7.7	4.0
Wisk	9.9	12.8	10.3	10.4	14.6
All other brands	27.1	33.6	28.3	28.6	12.1
Total	100.0	100.0	100.0	100.0	100.0
Total spending ('000)	$12,909	$13,338	$14,420	$13,718	$14,429
% Change	N/A	3.3	8.1	−4.9	5.2

Source: Company records.

the volume sold of all detergents at regular and special prices) had increased by only 4% in the last three years, whereas the cost of goods sold had increased by 15% during the same period.

One final observation was warranted. Between 1983 and 1986, the four leading brands – Tide, ABC, Sunlight, and Arctic Power – had increased their share from 58.7% to 67.9% of the total market. The three manufacturers appeared to be focusing their efforts primarily on their leading brands and letting the lesser brands decline in share.

Positioning Strategies

While positioning strategies were executed through all aspects of the marketing mix, the strategy was most clearly seen in the advertising execution.

Tide was the dominant brand in terms of share of market and share of media expenditures. Tide's strategy was to sustain this dominance through positioning the brand as superior to any other brand on generic cleaning benefits. In 1986, four national and four regional commercials were aired to support this strategy. These commercials conveyed that Tide provided the benefits of being the most effective detergent for 'tough' situations such as for ground-in dirt, stains and bad odours. Tide also aired copy in Québec claiming effectiveness in all temperatures. Most of Tide's copy was usually developed around a 'slice of life' or testimonial format.

Other brands in the market faced the situation of going head-to-head with Tide's position or competing on a benefit Tide did not claim. Most had chosen the latter route. CPC's ABC brand had made strong gains in the past four years, moving from sixth to second place in market share based on its value position. ABC was positioned as the low-priced, good-quality cleaning detergent. Recent copy for ABC utilised a demonstration format whereby the shirts for twins were as clean when washed in ABC versus a leading higher-priced detergent with the statement 'Why pay more? I can't see the difference.' Sunlight, a Lever's brand, had for several years attempted to compete directly with Tide and build its consumer franchise based on efficacy and lemon-scent freshness. Advertising execution had been of the upbeat, up-scale lifestyle approach and less of the straightforward problem solution or straight-talking approaches seen in other detergent advertising. More recently, Sunlight had been moving toward ABC's value position while retaining the lemon freshness heritage. Sunlight was positioned in 1986 as the detergent which gave a very clean, fresh wash at a sensible price. The final brand which attempted to compete for the value position was All. The advertising for All also claimed that the brand particularly whitened white clothes and had a pleasant fragrance.

Arctic Power had been positioned as the superior cleaning laundry detergent especially formulated for cold water washing. For the Eastern market, Arctic Power advertising had utilised a humorous background to communicate brand superiority and its efficacy in cold water. For the Western market, a non-traditional, upbeat execution was used to develop the cold water market.

Wisk, which had received much attention for its 'ring around the collar' advertising, competed directly with Tide on generic cleaning qualities and provided the additional benefit of a liquid formulation. Tide Liquid was introduced in 1985 but received little advertising support in 1986.

Fab and Bold 3 competed for the 'softergents' market. Both products, which had fabric softeners in the formulation, were positioned to clean effectively while softening clothes and reducing static cling. Another detergent with laundry product additives was Oxydol, which was formulated with a mild bleach. Oxydol was positioned as the detergent which kept colours bright while whitening whites.

The other two nationally advertised brands were Cheer 2 and Ivory Snow. Cheer 2 was positioned as the detergent which got clothes clean and fresh. Ivory Snow, which was a soap and not a detergent, was positioned as the laundry cleaning product for infants' clothes which provided superior softness and comfort.

The positioning strategies of these brands reflected the benefit segmentation approach used to market laundry detergents. Most brands attempted to appeal to a wide target (primarily women in the 18 to 49 age group) based on benefits rather than specific demographic segments.

The Cold Water Market

Every February, CPC commissioned an extensive market research study to identify trends in the laundry detergent market. Referred to as the *tracking study*,

Table 7.7   Proportion of households washing in cold water (1981–6)

	Percentages					
	1981	1982	1983	1984	1985	1986
National	20[a]	22	26	26	26	29
Maritimes	23	25	32	40	32	33
Québec	35	41	49	48	53	55
Ontario	35	41	49	48	53	55
Prairies	12	12	13	11	10	17
British Columbia	13	19	20	17	22	21

Source: Tracking study.
[a] 20% of respondents did 5 or more out of 10 washloads in cool or cold water.
N = 1800.

approximately 1800 personal interviews were conducted with female heads of households across Canada each year. Among the wealth of data provided by the tracking study was information on cold water usage in Canada. Regular cold water usage was growing in Canada and, by 1986, 29% of households were classified as regular (five or more times out of ten) cold water users (Table 7.7). Due to cultural and marketing differences, Québec (55%) and the Maritimes (33%) had more cold water users than the national average.[2] A further 25% of all Canadian households occasionally (one to four times out of ten) used cold water for washing.

Four households that washed regularly or occasionally with cold water, the most important benefits of using cold water fell into two broad categories (Table 7.8). First, it was easier on or better for clothes in that cold water stopped shrinkage, prevented colours from running, and colours stayed bright. Second, it was more economical in that it saved energy, was cheaper, saved hot water and saved on electricity. Households in Québec, the Maritimes and British Columbia mentioned the 'economy' benefit more frequently, whereas households in the rest of Canada mentioned the 'easier/better' benefit more often.

Arctic Power

Having achieved reasonable success in Eastern Canada and returned the brand to profitability, Linda Barton decided to increase the brand's share in Alberta and British Columbia for 1986. That brand plan is reported below.

---

[2] Canada has two major cultural groups, the English (who emigrated primarily from the British Isles) and the French (who emigrated from France). Of the 6.2 million French-speaking Canadians, most reside in Québec (5.3 million) and the Maritimes (264,000). Historically, many French-speaking Canadians had washed clothes in cold water.

Table 7.8 Most important benefit of cold water washing (1986)

Reason	National	Maritimes	Québec	Ontario	Manitoba/ Saskatchewan	Alberta	British Columbia
Stops shrinkage	22.7[a]	19.4	5.2	32.7	35.4	35.4	30.2
Saves energy	16.5	12.5	32.1	8.2	2.1	9.9	12.9
Prevents colours from running	11.6	17.4	0.0	21.8	21.3	9.9	2.9
Cheaper	11.1	19.4	10.4	10.2	2.8	9.3	16.5
Saves hot water	9.7	9.7	15.5	6.8	11.3	3.1	3.6
Colours stay bright	8.8	4.2	7.8	11.6	9.2	6.8	7.9
Saves on electricity	8.7	19.4	0.5	8.2	5.7	16.1	25.9
Easier on clothes	8.5	11.1	6.7	8.8	10.6	13.7	5.0

Source: Tracking study.
[a] When asked what they felt was the most important benefit of cold water washing, 22.7% of all respondents said 'stops shrinking.'
Sample includes all households that washed one or more times out of last 10 washes in cold water.
N = 956.
Only the eight most frequent responses are reported.

The 1986 brand plan for Arctic Power

Objectives
Arctic Power's overall objective is to continue profit development by maintaining modest unit volume growth in Québec and the Maritimes while developing the Alberta and British Columbia regions.

Long term (by 1996) The long-term objective is to become the number three brand in the category, with market share of 12%. Arctic Power will continue to deliver a minimum 18% contribution margin. This will require (1) maintenance of effective creative/media support; (2) superior display prominence, particularly in the key Québec market; (3) continued investigation of development opportunities; and (4) cost of goods savings programs where possible.

Short term The short-term objective is to sustain unit growth while building cold water washing dominance. This will require current user reinforcement and continued conversion of warm water washing users. Specifically, in fiscal year 1986, Arctic Power will achieve a market share of 6.5% on factory sales of $22.0 million and a contribution margin of 18%. Regional share objectives are: Maritimes – 6.3%; Québec – 17.2%; Alberta – 5%; and British Columbia – 5%.

Marketing strategy
Arctic Power will be positioned as the most effective laundry detergent especially formulated for cold water washing. The primary target for Arctic Power is women 18 to 49 and skewed towards the 25 to 34 segment. The secondary market is all adults.

Arctic Power will defend its franchise by allocating regional effort commensurate with brand development in order to maintain current users. In line with the Western expansion strategy, support will be directed to Alberta and British Columbia to enhance the acceptance of cold water washing and thereby broaden the appeal among occasional users and nonusers of Arctic Power.

Media strategy

The media strategy objective is to achieve high levels of message registration against the target group through high message continuity and frequency/reach. Media spending behind regional television will be allocated 75% to brand maintenance and 25% to investment spending for brand and cold water market development. Arctic Power will have the number five share of media expenditure position nationally while being the number three detergent advertiser in Québec.

Arctic Power's 1986 media spending of $1.35 million is a 36% increase over 1985 (Table 7.9). This returns Arctic Power to its reach objective of 90% in Québec, five points ahead of a year ago. In addition, two new television markets have been added, with enhanced support in British Columbia and Alberta. Reach objectives will be achieved by skewing more of Arctic Power's spending into efficient daytime spots, which cost less than night network and are more flexible in light of regional reach objectives.

Scheduling will maintain continuous flighting established in 1985, with concentrations at peak dealing time representing 40 weeks on air in the East and 32 weeks in the West.

Copy strategy: Québec/Maritimes

The creative objective is to convince consumers that Arctic Power is the superior detergent for cold water washing. The consumers' benefit is that when they are washing in cold water, Arctic Power will clean clothes and remove stains more effectively than other detergents. The support for this claim is based on the special formulation of Arctic Power. The executional tone will be humorous but with a clear, rational explanation.

Table 7.9

	TV spending	GRP's week
1985 plan	$1,010,000	92
Actual	$990,000	88
1986 plan	$1,350,000	95

GRP (Gross Rating Points) is a measurement of advertising impact derived by multiplying the percentage of the target population exposed to an advertisement by the average number of exposures per person.

Copy strategy: British Columbia/Alberta
The creative objective is to convince consumers that cold water washing is better than hot and, when washing in cold water, to use Arctic Power. The consumer benefit is that cold water washing reduces shrinkage, colour run and energy costs. The executional tone needs to be distinct from other detergent advertising to break through traditional washing attitudes and will be young-adult oriented, light, 'cool' and upbeat.

Consumer promotions
The objective of consumer promotions in Québec/Maritimes is to increase the rate of usage by building frequency of purchase among existing users. The objective in British Columbia/Alberta is to increase the rate of trial of Arctic Power. In total $856,000 will be spent on consumer promotions.

1. January: $.50 in-pack Coupon – to support trade inventory increases and retain current customers in the face of strong competitive activity; 400,000 coupons will be placed in all sizes in the Québec/Maritimes distribution region. The coupon is for 6-litre (6l) or 12l sizes, and expected redemption is 18% at a cost of $50,000.
2. April: To generate a 17% recent trial of regular-sized boxes of Arctic Power in British Columbia and Alberta, a 500 ml saleable sample prepriced at $.49 will be distributed through food and drug stores. In addition, a $.50 coupon for the 6l or 12l size will be placed on the pack of all samples. The offer will penetrate 44% of households in the region at a total cost of $382,000.
3. June: $.40 coupon through free-standing insert – to sustain interest and foster trial, a $.40 coupon will be delivered to 30% of homes in Alberta/British Columbia. The coupon is redeemable on the 3l size, and expected redemption is 4.5%, at a cost of $28,000.
4. April/July: Game (cool-by-the-pool) – Five in-ground pools and patio accessories will be given away through spelling 'POWER' by letters dropped in boxes of Arctic Power. Two letters will be placed in each box through national distribution, and will coincide with high trade activity and the period in which the desirability of the prizes is highest, at a cost of $184,000.
5. September: $.75 direct mail national coupon pack (excluding Ontario) – to maximise swing buyer volume (from competition) in Québec and encourage trial in the West, a $.75 coupon for the 6l or 12l size will be mailed to 70% of households in the primary market areas, generating a 3% redemption rate at a cost of $212,000.

Trade promotions
The objective of the trade promotions is to maintain regular and feature pricing equal to Tide and encourage prominent shelf facing. An advertising feature is expected from each key account during every promotion event run in Québec and

Table 7.10   Arctic Power 1986 promotional schedule

Trade promotions	J	F	M	A	M	J	J	A	S	O	N	D
Maritimes	X			X	X				X		X	
Québec	X	X		X		X			X		X	X
Alberta/British Columbia	X			X	X			X	X			
Consumer promotions												
East $.50 coupon	X	X										
West sample/coupon				X								
West $.40 coupon						X						
National game				X	X	X	X					
National $.75 coupon										X		

the Maritimes. Distribution for any size is expected to increase to 95%. In the West, maximum effort will be directed at establishing display for the 6l size, and four feature events will be expected from each key account. Distribution should be developed to 71% in British Columbia and 56% in Alberta. Average deal size will be 14% off the regular price or $5.00 per 6l case. In addition, most trade events will include a $1.00 per case allowance for coop advertising and merchandising support. The total trade budget is $3.46 million, which includes $1 million investment spending in the West. The promotion schedule is presented in Table 7.10.

Results of the Western campaign
In August 1986, during the middle of the Western campaign, a 'minitracking' study was conducted in the two provinces to monitor the programme. The results of the August study were compared with the February study and reported in Table 7.11. Market share for Arctic Power was also measured on a bimonthly basis, and the figures are shown in Table 7.12.

The campaign clearly had an impact, as brand and advertising awareness had increased, particularly in Alberta Table 7.11. Brand trial within the last six months had more than doubled in Alberta and was up over 25% in British Columbia. However, market share had peaked at 2.8% in Alberta and by the end of the year had declined to 1.9%. Market share in British Columbia had reached a high of 7.3% and averaged 5.5% for the year.

In attempting to explain the different results in the two provinces, Linda Barton and Gary Parsons isolated two factors. First, British Columbia had always been a 'good' market for Arctic Power with share figures around 4%, whereas Alberta was less than half that amount. Second, there had been a considerable amount of competitive activity in Alberta during the year. Each of the three major firms had increased trade and consumer promotions to maintain existing brand shares.

Table 7.11 Results of Western campaign

	Pre-launch (February 1986)		Post-launch (August 1986)	
	Alberta	British Columbia	Alberta	British Columbia
Unaided brand awareness[a]				
Brand mentioned total (%)	13.3	20.3	18.1	24.2
Advertising awareness				
1. Advertising mentioned (unaided)[b] (%)	1.9	7.9	20.3	11.5
2. Advertising mentioned (aided)[c] (%)	18.5	27.9	31.4	34.6
Brand trial				
1. Ever tried[d] (%)	25.0	43.0	36.3	48.0
2. Used (last six months)[e] (%)	6.8	15.1	17.1	19.4
Image measure[f]				
• Cleaning and removing dirt	1.0	1.2	1.2	1.5
• Removing tough stains	0.7	0.9	0.9	1.4
• Being good value for the price	0.5	0.9	1.0	1.4
• Cleaning well in cold water	1.2	1.3	1.7	1.8
Conversion to cold water				
• Average number of loads out of 10 washed in cold water	1.8	2.2	2.0	2.3

Source: Tracking study.
[a] Question: When you think of laundry detergents, what three brands first come to mind? Can you name three more for me? *Brand mentioned total* is if the brand was mentioned at all. On average respondents mentioned 4.5 brands.
[b] Question: What brand or brands of laundry detergent have you seen or heard advertised? *Advertising mentioned (unaided)* is of brand advertising mentioned.
[c] Question: Have you recently seen or heard any advertising for *brand*? *Advertising mentioned (aided)* is if respondent said yes when asked.
[d] Question: Have you ever tried *brand*?
[e] Question: Have you used *brand* in the past six months?
[f] Respondents rated the brand on the four image measures. The rating scale ranged from −5 (doesn't perform well) to +5 (performs well).

Table 7.12 Arctic Power market share

				1986						Total
	1983	1984	1985	D/J	F/M	A/M	J/J	A/S	O/N	1986
Alberta	0.7	2.3	1.7	1.4	1.1	2.8	2.8	2.4	1.9	2.1
British Columbia	3.2	4.0	3.9	4.0	4.0	6.1	6.1	7.3	5.4	5.5

Arctic Power – 1987

The 1987 brand plan for Arctic Power was similar in thrust and expenditure levels to the 1986 plan. Expenditure levels in Alberta were reduced until the full implications of the 1986 campaign could be examined. Market share in 1987 was expected to be 6.7%, up marginally from the 6.5% share achieved in 1986 (Table 7.13).

Each year, every product manager at CPC conducted an extensive brand review. The review for Arctic Power included a detailed competitive analysis of the four leading brands on a regional basis and was based primarily on the tracking study. In July 1987, Linda Barton and Gary Parsons were examining the tracking information which summarised regional information on four critical aspects of the market – brand image (Table 7.14), brand and advertising awareness (Table 7.15), brand trial and usage in the last six months (Table 7.16) and market share and share of media expenditures (Table 7.17). Future decisions for Arctic Power would be based, in large part, on this information.

The Decision

Prior to deciding on the strategic direction for Arctic Power, Barton and Parsons met to discuss the situation. It was a hot Toronto day in early July 1987. Barton began the discussion. 'I've got some estimates on what our shares are likely to be for 1987. It looks like we'll have a national share of 6.7%, broken down as follows: Maritimes (6.3%), Québec (18%), Ontario (1%), Manitoba/Saskatchewan (0.1%), Alberta (2%), British Columbia (6%).'

Table 7.13 Arctic Power: market share and total volume by region (1983–7)

Region	Market share					1986 total volume[a] ('000 litres)
	1983	1984	1985	1986	1987E	
National	4.7	5.6	6.4	6.5	6.7	406,512
Maritimes	5.3	5.7	6.3	6.3	6.3	32,616
Québec	12.3	13.8	17.7	17.5	18.0	113,796
Ontario	0.9	1.1	1.1	0.8	1.0	158,508
Manitoba/Saskatchewan	0.2	0.2	0.1	0.1	0.1	28,440
Alberta	0.7	2.3	1.7	2.1	2.0	40,644
British Columbia	3.2	4.0	3.9	5.5	6.0	32,508

Source: Company records.
[a] All laundry detergent.
1987E = estimated.

Table 7.14 Brand images by region (1986)

Image measure[a]	National	Maritime	Québec	Ontario	Manitoba/ Saskatchewan	Alberta	British Columbia
Arctic Power							
• Cleaning and removing dirt	1.4	2.0	2.5	0.8	0.4	1.0	1.3
• Removing tough stains	1.1	1.6	1.9	0.7	3.0	0.7	0.9
• Being good value for the price	1.1	1.4	2.6	0.3	0.2	0.5	0.9
• Cleaning well in cold water	1.6	2.1	2.8	1.0	0.4	1.2	1.3
ABC							
• Cleaning and removing dirt	1.0	1.9	0.5	0.9	1.1	1.2	1.6
• Removing tough stains	0.5	1.1	0.0	0.6	0.8	0.7	0.9
• Being good value for the price	1.5	2.4	0.8	1.5	1.3	1.7	2.1
• Cleaning well in cold water	0.6	1.0	0.1	0.7	0.7	0.7	0.7
Sunlight							
• Cleaning and removing dirt	2.0	1.9	1.8	2.4	1.9	1.6	1.6
• Removing tough stains	1.6	1.6	1.5	1.9	1.4	1.2	1.2
• Being good value for the price	2.0	1.7	1.9	2.4	1.8	1.7	1.5
• Cleaning well in cold water	1.4	1.1	1.5	1.7	1.2	1.1	0.7
Tide							
• Cleaning and removing dirt	3.4	3.7	3.2	3.6	3.5	3.3	3.2
• Removing tough stains	3.0	3.1	2.8	3.3	3.0	2.7	2.7
• Being good value for the price	3.1	3.1	3.3	3.1	2.8	3.0	2.4
• Cleaning well in cold water	2.4	2.3	2.6	2.5	2.4	2.3	1.9

Source: Tracking study.
[a] Respondents rated each brand on the four image measures. The rating scale ranged from −5 (does not perform well) to +5 (performs well).
$N = 1816$.
A difference of 0.2 is likely to be significant in statistical terms.

Table 7.15 Brand and advertising awareness by region (1986)

		Percentages					
	National	Maritime	Québec	Ontario	Manitoba/ Saskatchewan	Alberta	British Columbia
Unaided brand awareness[a]							
1. Brand mentioned first							
Arctic Power	4.4	7.0	12.5	0.0	0.0	1.0	2.6
ABC	8.1	18.4	4.6	7.3	4.7	8.4	12.8
Sunlight	9.3	8.4	9.6	9.3	12.0	9.1	7.9
Tide	57.9	55.5	41.9	69.7	63.1	59.7	54.4
2. Brand mentioned total							
Arctic Power	23.0	43.5	49.8	5.0	3.0	13.3	20.3
ABC	61.3	82.6	47.9	64.0	56.1	67.5	64.9
Sunlight	58.1	60.2	50.8	65.0	58.5	62.0	46.6
Tide	94.8	95.7	88.8	98.0	97.3	97.4	94.4
Advertising awareness							
1. Advertising mentioned (unaided)[b]							
Arctic Power	7.0	10.7	17.5	0.7	0.0	1.9	7.9
ABC	25.2	32.8	20.8	27.0	17.3	30.5	24.9
Sunlight	8.6	4.7	5.9	13.0	5.0	6.8	8.2
Tide	44.0	40.1	32.7	55.0	46.2	48.4	35.4
2. Advertising mentioned (aided)[c]							
Arctic Power	29.2	38.8	55.1	15.3	5.6	18.5	27.9
ABC	56.1	61.5	55.1	56.0	51.5	60.4	53.4
Sunlight	29.9	20.1	26.4	40.3	21.3	21.1	24.9
Tide	65.3	60.9	54.8	78.0	68.1	65.3	48.4

Source: Tracking study.
[a] Question: When you think of laundry detergents, what three brands first come to mind? Can you name three or more for me? *Brand mentioned first* is the first brand mentioned. Brand mentioned total is if the brand was mentioned at all. On average, respondents mentioned 4.5 brands.
[b] Question: What brand or brands of laundry detergent have you seen or heard advertised? *Advertising mentioned (unaided)* is of brand advertising mentioned.
[c] Question: Have you recently seen or heard any advertising for *brand? Advertising mentioned (aided)* is if respondent said yes when asked.
N = 1816.

Table 7.16 Brand trial in last six months by region (1986)

Brand trial	National	Maritime	Québec	Ontario	Manitoba/Saskatchewan	Alberta	British Columbia
1. *Ever tried*[a]							
Arctic Power	42.4	67.9	75.6	19.7	20.3	25.0	43.0
ABC	60.4	83.9	50.8	60.0	53.5	62.7	67.9
Sunlight	66.3	65.6	59.4	75.0	67.1	58.1	58.7
Tide	93.6	91.0	90.1	97.3	95.0	91.9	92.1
2. *Used (last six months)*[b]							
Arctic Power	19.4	29.8	46.5	4.3	2.3	6.8	15.1
ABC	37.2	56.2	34.7	32.3	29.2	39.3	47.5
Sunlight	38.3	29.8	38.0	44.3	36.2	36.7	28.5
Tide	68.1	66.6	66.0	73.3	67.8	69.5	54.8

Source: Tracking study.
[a] Question: Have you ever tried *brand*?
[b] Question: Have you used *brand* in the past six months?
Note: On average, respondents had 1.3 brands of laundry detergents in the home.
N = 1816.

Table 7.17 Market share of media expenditures by region (1986)

				Percentages			
	National	Maritime	Québec	Ontario	Manitoba/ Saskatchewan	Alberta	British Columbia
Market share							
Arctic Power	6.5	6.3	17.5	0.8	0.1	2.1	5.5
ABC	13.9	27.8	8.6	13.8	11.6	16.1	21.5
Sunlight	13.4	7.7	12.1	16.4	14.2	10.4	11.3
Tide	34.1	24.5	28.3	39.3	40.0	36.9	28.5
All other brands	32.1	33.7	33.5	29.7	34.1	34.5	33.2
Total	100.0	100.0	100.0	100.0	100.0	100.0	100.0
Share of media expenditures[a]							
Arctic Power	9.3	13.1	16.1	0.5	1.4	16.0	13.1
ABC	13.6	14.7	9.1	18.4	17.3	12.1	12.1
Sunlight	11.3	11.1	11.1	12.6	10.2	10.1	9.8
Tide	29.7	27.8	25.1	33.1	38.1	30.2	28.7
All other brands	36.1	33.3	38.6	35.4	33.0	31.6	36.3
Total	100.0	100.0	100.0	100.0	100.0	100.0	100.0
Total $('000)	14,429	695	4,915	4,758	928	1,646	1,487

Source: Company records.
[a] The total amount of advertising spent by all brands was determined. The amount spent by each brand as a percentage of total spending was calculated.

Parsons responded, 'I think our problem in Alberta was all the competitive activity. Under normal conditions we'd have achieved 5% of that market. But the Alberta objective is small when you think about what we could do in our other undeveloped markets. I've been giving it a lot of thought, and we should go national with Arctic Power. We've got a brand that is equal to Tide, and we've got to stop keeping it a secret from the rest of Canada. If we can duplicate the success we had in British Columbia, we'll turn this market on its ear.'

'Wait a minute Gary,' said Linda, 'in 1986 we spent almost $2,000,000 on advertising, consumer and trade promotions in the West. Even though spending returned to normal levels this year, that was a big investment to get the business going, and it will be at least four years before we get that money back. If we go after the national market, you can well expect Tide to fight back with trade spending which will make your share or margin objectives even harder to achieve. On a per capita basis, we'd have to spend at least as much in our underdeveloped markets as we spent in the West. We've got a real problem here. Our brand may be as good as Tide, but I don't think we can change a lot of consumers' minds, particularly the loyal Tide users. I hate to say it, but for many Canadians, when they think about washing clothes, Tide is the brand they think will clean their clothes better than any other brand. I agree that the size of the undeveloped market warrants another look. But remember, any decision will have to be backed up with a solid analysis and a plan that senior management will buy.'

Gary replied, 'I know that even if I am right, it will be a tough sell. I haven't got it completed yet, but I'm working out the share level we would need to break even if we expanded nationally.'

Linda responded, 'Well, when you get that done, we will talk about national expansion again. For the moment, we have to resolve this positioning dilemma. I don't like a two-country approach but it does seem to make sense in this case. I think we might still want to focus on the brand in the East and continue to develop the cold water washing market in the West.'

Gary would have preferred to continue the discussion of national expansion but realised he would have to do some work and at least produce the share estimate before he raised the subject again, so replied, 'I agree that Canada is not one homogeneous market but that perspective can be taken to extremes. I worry that all of this data we get on the regional markets is getting in the way of good marketing judgement. I prefer a unified strategy, and the Québec campaign has a proven track record.'

Linda concluded, 'Let's go over the data again, then start marking our decisions. Remember, our goal is to develop a solid brand name for 1988 for Arctic Power.'

8
Decision techniques

This chapter is divided into four main sections which look at critical path analysis, queuing theory, linear programming and games theory.

Contents

Critical path
Queuing theory
Linear programming
Game theory

Objectives

After reading this chapter you should:

• Know what critical path analysis is and how to apply it.

• Know what PERT is and how to apply it.

• Understand the basic concepts in queuing theory.

• Know what the assumptions are of linear programming, queuing theory and CPM/PERT.

• Know how to construct and apply linear programming models.

• Understand the importance of game theory.

• Understand some of the simple games and dilemmas in game theory.

INTRODUCTION

This chapter reviews four key decision-making techniques which have numerous applications in industry, namely critical path analysis, queuing theory, linear programming and game theory. Each section includes the key assumptions implicit in that technique and an explanation of its use as well as one or more worked examples of its use in practice.

CRITICAL PATH

PERT/CPM

Several marketing activities – for instance, new product development – involve a series of interrelated tasks which need to be performed. Some may need to be performed sequentially, while it may be possible to carry others out concurrently. For example, the screening of new product ideas obviously follows sequentially from the idea generation stage, but it would be possible to manufacture products to be used in test marketing at the same time as organising participating retailers. PERT (Project Evaluation and Review Technique – designed by the US military to control the Polaris missile project) and CPM (Critical Path Method – designed by Dupont to control their chemical plants) are project management tools which can provide a systematic approach to scheduling complex products. Both these techniques were developed independently in the 1950s and originally differed in their treatment of times and costings – however, nowadays the best features of both techniques tend to be blended, particularly in computerised solutions, to produce a 'PERT/CPM' technique.

Planning with PERT/CPM requires three steps: firstly, all project activities are identified and put into sequence; secondly, a network is drawn showing the activities in sequence; and finally, activity times and costs are estimated. The planning procedure will be illustrated with an example of the organisation of a presentation to launch a new software product.

Example

A software company are going to hold a presentation at a London hotel, inviting representatives from the computer press and major companies who would be interested in using the software. Computers and copies of the new software are to be available for all participants.

The first task, then, is to sequence all activities, listing, for each activity, its immediate predecessor. Table 8.1 shows this for our example. This table then helps us to carry out the second step, that of constructing a network of activities. A PERT/CPM network is made up of activities represented by arrows, and events represented by circles, often called nodes. The activities are the tasks which have to be carried out, while the events are project milestones, representing starts and/or finishes of activities. The basic rules which should be followed in drawing the network are:

- Every activity is represented by one and only one arrow, and each arrow begins and ends at a node.

- The network begins with a single node, on the left of the page, and grows toward the right, ending with a single node.

Table 8.1 Sequencing of activities

Activity code	Activity	Immediate predecessor
A	Arrange location	–
B	Make list of whom to invite	–
C	Hire computers	–
D	Design and print invitations	A
E	Mail invitations	B,D
F	Take reservations until capacity filled	E
G	Prepare presentation outline	–
H	Prepare slides and handouts	G
I	Copy handouts	F,H,C
J	Copy software onto computers	C,F,H

- Lengths of arrows have no relation to the duration of the activity represented.
- Each activity arrow starts at the node where its immediate predecessor(s) ended.
- Two nodes may not be directly connected by more than one arrow, as this would cause confusion when it came to considering the duration of activities. Dummy activities are used to avoid this situation.

A very simple example will serve to illustrate a dummy activity. Table 8.2 shows the sequence of activities involved in serving a microwave meal. The resulting network is shown at Figure 8.1. Activities B and C are concurrent. In order not to have two arrows connecting the same two nodes, we put a dummy activity into the network. Dummy activities are represented with a broken line, use up no time and no resources, and incur no costs.

We can now return to our software presentation example and draw up the network for it. We start by drawing a node at the left of the page and labelling it Node 1. All activities with no immediate predecessors – i.e. A, B, C and G – will start at this node, so four lines are required to emerge from it (Figure 8.2).

We then see that activity A is the immediate predecessor to D, so at the end of

Table 8.2 Activity list for serving microwave meal

Activity code	Activity	Immediate predecessor
A	Select meal from freezer	–
B	Cook meal in microwave	A
C	Lay table	A
D	Serve meal	B,C

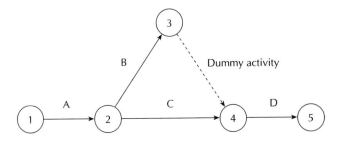

Figure 8.1 PERT/CPM network for serving microwave meal

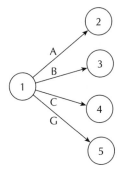

Figure 8.2 Starting the network

arrow A we draw a node from which D can start. Activity E is immediately preceded by both B and D, thus B and D must terminate at the same node, from which E must start. Considering each activity in turn, we build up the complete network (Figure 8.3). Note that the two final activities, I and J, are concurrent. Therefore we have to put in an extra node, 7, and a dummy activity.

The final stage of PERT/CPM planning is to estimate activity times and costs,

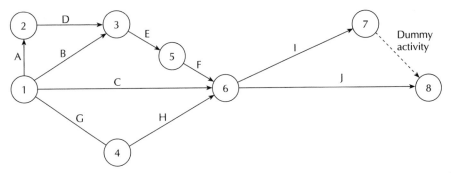

Figure 8.3 Network for software presentation

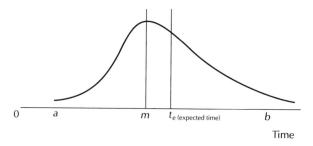

0   a   m $t_{e \text{ (expected time)}}$ b

Time

Figure 8.4   The beta probability distribution

and incorporate these into the network. For some activities, it may be possible to estimate the activity duration accurately – in our example, the mailing of invitations is a task that should easily be completed in one day, provided an up-to-date address list is available. However, for many activities, especially those involving design, development or testing, it is likely that times will be uncertain. The PERT technique allows for time uncertainty by assuming activity time to be random, with a beta probability distribution (Figure 8.4).

The lower and upper bounds of the beta distribution are represented by estimates of an optimistic time (minimum possible), a pessimistic time (maximum possible) and a most likely time – a realistic estimate. These are denoted on Figure 8.4 by a, b and m respectively. The expected time is then calculated using the formula

$$\text{Expected time} = \frac{a + 4m + b}{6}$$

Table 8.3 shows activity time estimates and expected times for the activities in our example and Figure 8.5 then shows the network redrawn, including times.

Table 8.3   Calculation of expected activity times

Activity code	Optimistic time (a)	Most likely time (m)	Pessimistic time (b)	Expected time (e)
A	1	3	5	3
B	3	7	9	7
C	1	3	9	4
D	8	12	24	13
E	1	2	3	2
F	2	8	21	9
G	1	3	5	3
H	3	5	7	5
I	2	3	5	3
J	1	1	2	1

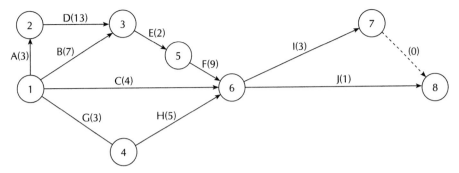

Figure 8.5   Network for software presentation including times

Scheduling Activities

The first calculation which can be made from the network at Figure 8.5 is the expected project completion time. To determine this, we need to consider all paths (activity sequences) through the network. The path which takes the longest time will determine the completion time – this path is known as the critical path. Table 8.4 shows the paths through our network, with their times computed by adding up the expected times for their component activities.

The critical path is therefore ADEFI. Its duration is long enough to ensure that all other sequences of activities will be completed. A delay on any of the activities on this path will delay the whole project, while delays on activities not on the critical path can be accommodated without affecting project completion time, provided that the delay is not so much as to make another path longer than ADEFI (i.e. to change the critical path).

When analysing a network, we may wish to determine an expected finishing date, or work out when a project needs to start in order to meet a deadline, or purely to estimate the duration of the project – if, for instance, casual staff are required. Within the project, we will also need to establish times at which specific activities

Table 8.4   Alternative paths through network

Path	Component times	Total time
ADEFI	$3+13+2+9+3$	30
ADEFJ	$3+13+2+9+1$	28
BEFI	$7+2+9+3$	21
BEFJ	$7+2+9+1$	19
CI	$4+3$	7
CJ	$4+1$	5
GHI	$3+5+3$	11
GHJ	$3+5+1$	9

should start and finish. The two algorithms for network analysis are known as activity analysis and event analysis. Both are based on the principle of establishing time boundaries, i.e. the earliest and latest times by which an activity can or must be completed or at which an event (completion of all activities leading to an event node) can occur. From these can be determined how much time leeway, or slack, there is for each activity. Network analysis, for all but the smallest networks, is a fairly complicated task, and is thus normally carried out by computer. There are hundreds of project management software packages available, many designed for use on a personal computer.

Cost Considerations – PERT/Cost

So far, we have only looked at the times taken by the various project activities. However, each activity also has a cost associated with it. In order to budget properly for the project, the manager needs to know the cost of each activity and when this cost will occur. The PERT/cost system is an accounting system which is designed to predict budget demands and cash flow, and to monitor project spending. It is included in most project management software packages.

The PERT/cost system assumes that the cost of an activity is expended at a constant rate, thus, a task taking three weeks and costing £600 is costed at £200 per week. Two tables are drawn up, showing the cash flow required if all activities start at their earliest possible start times and the cash flow required if all activities start at their latest possible start times. This gives upper and lower bounds for weekly expenditures, so budget demands can be anticipated. As the project proceeds expenditure can be closely monitored by checking that it is within the predicted bounds.

Time-cost Trade-offs – Crashing a Project

The cost of performing each activity in the expected time is known as the normal-time cost. If the project manager decides that the project completion time given by PERT/CPM analysis is too long, it may be possible to shorten this by giving more resources to activities on the critical path, thus lessening their completion time (usually to the most optimistic estimate) and shortening the critical path. This is known as 'crashing' the project. Obviously, putting more resources into the activity will increase its cost – the new cost estimate is known as the crash-time cost.

Difficulties in Applying PERT/CPM

The difficulties most often found in the application of PERT/CPM techniques are as follows:

* It may be hard to divide the project into independent activities or to decide where one activity ends and the next starts.

- It may be difficult to draw up a precedence table if relationships between activities are not firmly established, for instance new product development may only proceed to test marketing if concept testing has been successful, otherwise product modifications will be required.

- It may be hard to make accurate estimates of activity times.

However, it is generally believed that the benefits of the PERT/CPM technique outweigh such difficulties.

QUEUING THEORY

We are all familiar with the idea of a queue or waiting line. We queue to be served at the bank or supermarket, we wait for a suitable table in a restaurant, we queue up in our cars to enter a car park. A queue, of course, does not have to have a human element – cars could be waiting on a garage forecourt for servicing or components waiting for machine assembly. However, most queuing situations encountered by marketers will concern human queues for customer service of some sort.

The analysis of queues attempts to describe the waiting process by producing statistics such as the average time a person can expect to have to wait for service, the average length of the queue and the amount of time the server is idle. Analysis can help marketers to achieve an acceptable balance between customer satisfaction and costs. If customers have to wait too long for service, they may leave the queue. Prospective customers seeing a large queue may not even join it at all. If the service is obtainable elsewhere, the custom of these dissatisfied people may be lost entirely. However, providing so many servers that nobody has to queue may be prohibitive in terms of costs.

Terms Used in Queuing Theory

Before explaining how to derive useful measures to describe queues, we must specify standard terms used in queuing theory. The calling population is the source of arrivals at the queue. In most customer service situations it is assumed to be infinite, but finite calling populations are possible – for instance, the number of arrivals for dinner service at a factory workers' canteen should be no more than the number of workers.

The way in which people arrive in the queue can be described by either the mean arrival rate (average number arriving in a specified time period) or the mean interarrival time (average time between arrivals). The arrival rate is often assumed to follow a Poisson distribution, that is, the probability of n arrivals in a particular time period is:

$$P_n = \frac{\lambda n e^{-\lambda}}{n!}$$

where λ is the expected number of arrivals in the time period and $e = 2.71828$.

Queue discipline refers to the way in which the next customer is selected for service. Most queues we encounter will be first-come, first-served – customers are served in the order in which they join the queue. However, marketers may also come across situations where a priority queue discipline applies – in an accident and emergency department of a hospital, for instance, the most seriously injured people are likely to be treated first. The other two possibilities are last-come, first-served – often used with inanimate objects such as parts for machining, but unlikely to be tolerated by people – and random service.

The actual service facility can be described in terms of the number of servers and the number of steps that a customer must pass through within the system. Thus we can distinguish between single-server and multiple-server systems, and between single-phase and multi-phase systems. Most systems we come across will be single-phase – one interaction only between customer and server – but an example of a multi-phase system would be a well-person clinic, where a patient first waits to see the nurse to check weight and blood pressure, then waits again to see the doctor about a specific problem and finally may have to wait a third time to book a further appointment.

The time taken for a customer to be served may be described simply as an average service time (e.g. 5 minutes) or in terms of an average service rate (e.g. 12 customers per hour).

Use of Queuing Analysis

We will now show how queuing analysis could be used in marketing decision making by looking at two examples, one from banking and one from a fast-food takeaway restaurant. We shall consider use of the bank's single automated teller machine (ATM) in a busy shopping centre – a single-server, single-phase model – and the queuing situation at the fast-food takeaway, where there are three serving-staff – a multi-server, single-phase model. For each situation we are assuming:

- Arrivals, having a Poisson distribution (mean = λ), from an infinite calling population.
- A single queue with infinite capacity.
- Patient customers who stay in the queue until served.
- Queue discipline is first-come, first-served.
- An exponential distribution of service time with a mean service rate of μ, i.e. mean service time is $1/\mu$.
- Overall, service rate is greater than arrival rate.

Single-server Model

Here are the formulae for the operating characteristics of the single-server model. (Derivation of these formulae is beyond the scope of this book.)

Arrival rate	$=$	λ
Service rate	$=$	μ
Probability of system being busy	$=$	λ/μ
Probability of system being idle	$P_o =$	$1 - (\lambda/\mu)$
Probability of n customers in the system	$P_n =$	$P_o(\lambda/\mu)^n$
(being served or in queue)		
Average waiting time	$W_q =$	$\lambda/[\mu(\mu - \lambda)]$
Average time customer spends in system	$W =$	$1/(\mu - \lambda)$
or		$W_q + 1/\mu$
Average number of customers in queue	$L_q =$	$\lambda^2/[\mu(\mu - \lambda)]$
or		λW_q
Average number of customers in system	$L =$	$\lambda/(\mu - \lambda)$
or		λW

Example

During the day, an average of 45 customers per hour arrive to use the ATM. The average length of transaction is one minute. The bank manager wonders if a second ATM should be installed to reduce waiting times.

Arrival rate = 0.75 customers per minute
Service rate = 1 customer per minute
Probability of ATM being in use = λ/μ = 0.75/1 = 0.75
(ATM is in use for 75% of the time, and thus it is idle for 25% of the time)
Average waiting time $W_q = \lambda/[\mu(\mu - \lambda)]$ = 0.75/(1(1 − 0.75)) = 0.75/0.25 = 3 minutes
Average time in system = $W = W_q + 1/\mu$ = 3 + 1 = 4 minutes
Average number in queue = $L_q = \lambda W_q$ = 0.75 × 3 = 2.25 customers
Average number in system = $L = \lambda W$ = 0.75 × 4 = 3 customers

On average, a customer will have to wait for three minutes to use the ATM. This does not appear excessive, so there does not seem to be a need for another ATM.

Multiple-server Model

Here are the formulae for the operating characteristics of the multiple-server model. They are considerably more complicated than those for the single-server model.

Arrival rate $= \lambda$
Service rate $= \mu$
Number of servers $= s$

Probability of system being idle $P_o = \dfrac{1}{\displaystyle\sum_{n=0}^{s-1} \dfrac{(\lambda/\mu)^n}{n!} + \dfrac{(\lambda/\mu)^s}{(s-1)!}(s\mu/(s\mu - \lambda))}$

Probability of n customers in the system $P_n = (\lambda/\mu)^n/(s!\, s^{n-s}) * P_o$ for $n > s$
(being served or in queue)

$P_n = (\lambda/\mu)^n/(n!) * P_o$ for $0 \leq n \leq s$

Average number of customers in queue $L_q = \dfrac{(\lambda/\mu)^s \lambda\mu}{(s-1)!(s\mu - \lambda)^2} P_o$

Average number of customers in system $L = L_q + \lambda/\mu$
Average waiting time $W_q = L_q/\lambda$
Average time customer spends in system $W = W_q + 1/\mu$

Example

The fast-food takeaway has three serving staff. Customers queue in a single line and go to the first available server. The average number of customers per hour is 30 and they take an average of five minutes to be served. Serving staff make up the orders themselves and there is assumed to be no problem, in terms of the food being ready, with fulfilling these orders even if an extra server was hired. The manager has noticed that there are queues and wants to analyse the benefits of hiring an extra member of staff.

Arrival rate = 0.5/minute
Service rate = 0.2/minute

Here we must work out the probability of the system being idle before we can find out the average number in the queue, because we need the value of P.

Probabililty P of system being idle

$$= \frac{1}{\displaystyle\sum_{n=0}^{2} \frac{(0.5/0.2)^n}{n!} + ((0.5/0.2)^3/2!)(0.2/(3*0.2) - 0.5)}$$

$$= \frac{1}{1 + 2.5 + 3.125 + (7.8125 \times 2)}$$

$$= 0.045$$

$$\text{Average number waiting} = L_q \quad = \quad \frac{(0.5/0.2)^3 (0.5)(0.2)}{2! \left[(3 * 0.12) - 0.5\right]^2} \times 0.045$$

$$= \quad \frac{1.5625}{0.02} \times 0.045$$

$$= \quad 3.5$$

$$\text{Average number in system} \quad = \quad 3.5 + 2.5 = 6$$

$$\text{Average waiting time} \quad = \quad \frac{3.5}{0.5} = 7 \text{ minutes}$$

$$\text{Average time in system} \quad = \quad 7 + 5 = 12 \text{ minutes}$$

The system is only idle 4.5% of the time. A new customer coming into the premises is most likely to find a queue of three or four people, and waits an average of seven minutes. The manager may wish to ask further questions before making a final decision on this – for instance, do customers think a seven-minute wait is reasonable, how does it compare with the waiting time in competing fast food outlets, are staff able to take adequate breaks? Queuing theory can give managers descriptive statistics about queues, but it is up to managers to interpret their significance.

Summary

The examples have shown how queuing analysis can provide operational statistics which can help a manager by providing figures as a basis for decision making. We have looked at only two fairly simple queuing situations, but hope that they will assist in showing how queuing analysis can be useful. Sometimes, however, we may come across types of queue so complex that they defy mathematical analysis – these are often analysed by means of a simulation (usually computerised) which is set up to imitate the behaviour of the queue.

LINEAR PROGRAMMING

Concepts and Definition

Linear programming is a member of a group of optimisation techniques which include integer programming, transportation programming, non-linear programming and assignment programming (also called Hungarian programming), all of which seek to maximise or minimise a single goal. This goal could be profits, costs, revenue or advertising effectiveness. Linear programming will solve problems which maximise or minimise this single goal subject to all the constraints the firm faces. Linear programming has a number of uses which include:

- Deciding on the product mix a company should make.
- Determining the maximum level of capacity of a firm.
- Deciding on the profit maximising position for a firm.
- Deciding on the optimum use and mix of an advertising budget.

Linear programming has two basic approaches, namely, the graphical approach and the simplex method. The graphical approach is fully explained in the next example. The simplex method involves an iterative technique to search for the optimal solution, which can be used to solve complex problems. Simplex problems can be solved by hand, however the best way to solve these problems is by a computer program.

Although linear programming is a powerful technique and has many uses there are a number of critical assumptions, as listed below, which need to be fully understood if it is to be used effectively.

1. The firm can follow the maximisation or minimisation of a single goal.
2. The constraints the firm faces can be measured and expressed.
3. The constraints the firm faces are linear or approximated by linear relationships.
4. The prices and constraints faced by the firm do not change and there is no differential pricing.
5. All resources are fully available and there is no waste of scrap in the process.
6. Everything the firm manufactures can be sold to the market at once. (Similar to the concept of perfect competition in economics.)
7. Parts of products can be manufactured (e.g. 2004.52 cars).
8. The right-hand side coefficients for the constraint equations are measured with 100% accuracy and there is no set-up time between processes or in processes. This assumption becomes more important the greater the quantities manufactured.

The more important assumptions are 1, 2 and in particular 6. Most of the other assumptions can be relaxed if other techniques are used or they are coded into the constraints. Assumption 7 can be relaxed if integer programming is used and Assumption 1 can be relaxed if goal programming is used.

The Two-product Firm and the Graphical Approach

Example

A company manufactures two products X1 and X2 which yield a profit contribution of £10 and £9 respectively. To manufacture these two products a total of four

Table 8.5

	X1	X2	Total available processing time (in minutes)
Department 1	42	60	18900
Department 2	30	50	18000
Department 3	60	40	21240
Department 4	6	15	4050

departments is used and each product needs a number of minutes of processing time before moving on to the next department. The time in minutes is given in Table 8.5.

The decision variables are X1 and X2 which stand for the levels of products manufactured. The first step is to form the objective function, which will be a single goal the firms seeks to maximise.

Profit = 10X1 + 9X2

This equation states that for every X1 sold £10 profit will be earned and for every X2 sold £9 profit is earned. The second step is to form the constraints on the system, in this case there will be four constraints. The first constraint is for department one.

42X1 + 60X2 <= 18900 C1

The total available time in department one is 18900 and each X1 takes 42 minutes and each X2 takes 60 minutes, therefore any combination of X1 and X2 can be manufactured as long as we do not use more than 18900 minutes.

The other three constraints can be formed in a similar manner taking the information from Table 8.5.

30X1 + 50X2 <= 18000 C2
60X1 + 40X2 <= 21240 C3
 6X1 + 15X2 <= 4050 C4

These four constraints can be shown graphically by calculating the end points of each constraint line. This is achieved by first setting X1 to zero in each constraint equation and calculating the value of X2. Secondly the values of X2 are set to zero and the values of X1 are calculated.

In constraint line one

42X1 + 60X2 <= 18900 C1

if X1 is set to zero the equation will simplify to:

60X2 <= 18900

Table 8.6 End points of the constraint lines

	X1 = 0		X2 = 0	
Department 1	X2 =	315	X1 =	450
Department 2	X2 =	360	X1 =	600
Department 3	X2 =	531	X1 =	354
Department 4	X2 =	270	X1 =	675

and at the end point of the line

$$60X2 = 18900$$

Therefore

$$X2 = 18900/60$$
$$= \textbf{315}$$

If the same process is now done for X2 being set to zero, in equation C1, the equation will simplify to:

$$42X1 = 18900$$

Therefore

$$X1 = 18900/42$$
$$= \textbf{450}$$

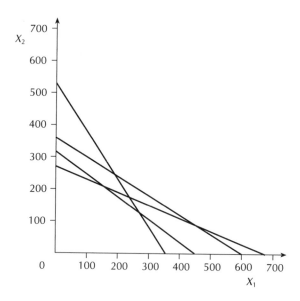

Figure 8.6

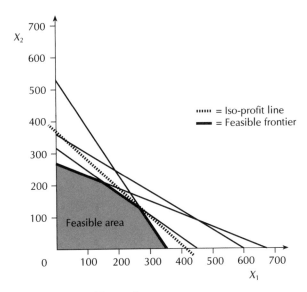

Figure 8.7 Feasible frontier and iso-profit

If this process is carried out for all the constraints the results will be as shown in Table 8.6. The results are shown graphically as Figure 8.6.

The area enclosed by all the constraint lines is called the feasible area and the outermost part of the feasible area is called the feasible frontier (see Figure 8.7). It is on this feasible frontier that the optimal solution to the problem will lie.

The next step is to use the objective function (Profit = $10X1 + 9X2$) to find the optimal solution; this is achieved by calculating the slope of the objective function, also called an iso-profit line. The optimal point will be the point where the iso-profit line cuts the outmost point of the feasible area on the feasible frontier. Therefore the optimal solution is given by the intersection of constraint lines 1, 3 and the objective function.

$$42X1 + 60X2 <= 18900 \ C1$$
$$60X1 + 40X2 <= 21240 \ C3$$

These two equations can be solved by using simultaneous equations, if the equations are set to equals:

Multiply equation C1 by 2

$$84X1 + 120X2 = 37800$$

Multiply equation C3 by 3

$$180X1 + 120X2 = 63720$$

Subtract C3 from C1

$$96X1 = 25920$$
$$= \mathbf{270}$$

Substitute into C1

$$180*270 + 60X2 = 18900$$
$$60X2 = 18900 - 270*42$$
$$X2 = \mathbf{126}$$

Therefore the optimal solution for this problem is X1=270 and X2=126. The level of profit earned can be found by substituting these values into the objective function

$$Profit = 10X1 \quad + 9X2$$
$$= 10*270 + 9*126$$
$$= \mathbf{3834}$$

Shadow Costs and Shadow Prices

The shadow cost or shadow price is the imputed opportunity cost for each constraint in the system. Each shadow cost measures the marginal effect of a small change in the available resource. These shadow costs can be used as a guide to where extra resources should be channelled. If a constraint is non-binding it will have a shadow cost of zero as there is already unused capacity and more capacity will not yield any further profits. In the above example only constraints 1 and 3 are binding so constraints 2 and 4 will have a zero shadow cost. The shadow costs for binding constraints are calculated by increasing the available resource by one unit and resolving the problem, i.e.

$$42X1 + 60X2 <= 18900 + 1 \quad C1$$
$$60X1 + 40X2 <= 212400 \quad C3$$

These two equations can be solved by using simultaneous equations, by setting each equation to equals rather than less than or equals:

Multiply equation C1 by 2

$$84X1 + 120X2 = 37802$$

Multiply equation C3 by 3

$$180X1 + 120X2 = 63720$$

Subtract C3 from C1

$$96X1 = 25920$$
$$= \mathbf{269.98}$$

Substitute into C1

$$180*270 + 60X2 = 18901$$
$$60X2 = 18901 - 269.98*42$$
$$X2 = \textbf{126.03}$$

Therefore the optimal solution for this problem is X1=269.98 and X2=126.03

$$\text{Profit} = 10X1 \quad\quad + 9X2$$
$$= 10*269.98 + 9*126.03$$
$$= \textbf{3834.07}$$

If this new profit is subtracted from the original profit level (i.e. £3834.07 − £3834.00) the shadow cost of constraint 1 is 0.07 or 7p. If the same process is repeated for constraint 3, the new solution is X1 = 270.03 and X2 = 125.98 giving a new profit level of £3834.12, leading to a shadow cost of 0.12 or 12p.

GAME THEORY

Game theory was first put forward by John von Neumann and Oskar Morganstern (1947) in their classic book *Theory of Games and Economic Behaviour*. John von Neumann was a mathematical genius and was one of the three inventors of the Hydrogen Bomb in the mid 1940s. The theory of games is concerned with what is the best strategy for a firm/player to adopt in an attempt to gain a competitive advantage over other firms (such as increased market share or increased profit levels). However the choice of which strategy to adopt becomes complex as other firms can adopt counter strategies which could affect the first strategy's effectiveness. Furthermore, there will normally be uncertainty as to what other firms are considering or planning as well as whether the chosen strategy will have the desired effect. Therefore the strategy a firm chooses will depend on what strategy they think the opposition will adopt as well as the effectiveness and cost of the chosen strategy. There are many different types of games and a summary of some of the simpler games is detailed below. The first type of game is called the zero-sum or constant-sum game as the winner's gains are offset by the loser's losses. There are also positive and negative sum games as well as cooperative and non-cooperative games.

The Zero or Constant-sum Game

In a duopoly situation (two firms dominate the market) every percentage point gained by one firm will be lost by the other firm. This situation is called a two-person zero-sum game (another example of this type of game is poker as the winner's gains are offset by the loser's losses).

Positive-sum Game

A voluntary exchange is a good example of a non-zero sum game. When you purchase a bottle of wine from a supermarket you are better off because you would rather have the bottle of wine than the £3.79 it cost (otherwise you would not have purchased it). However the supermarket that sold the wine would rather have the money so when they sell the wine they are better off.

Negative-sum Game

War is an example of a negative sum game, as one country wins and the other country loses, but people in both countries die.

Cooperative Games

In a cooperative game the players or firms make binding agreements forming a cartel. This could happen with oligopolists (a few large firms and many small firms in the market) where the large companies make an agreement to divide a market into segments and then practise joint profit maximisation by controlling supply or by controlling price. This type of behaviour happened in the 1970s when OPEC (Oil Producing and Exporting Countries) set quotas on the level of oil each member of OPEC could produce, so maximising the price and therefore the profit from selling oil. However, there is always a tendency for players/members of a cooperative game to cheat, particularly in the long run, so maximising their own profit levels. Within OPEC, many of its members did cheat by not sticking to the agreed limits. In some countries, such as America, collusive cartels are illegal and deemed to be not in the consumer's interest.

Non-cooperative Games

Non-cooperative games do not allow agreement of binding contracts. Normal competition between firms is an example of a non-cooperative game.

Nash Equilibrium

Nash equilibrium exists when there is no tendency for change once an equilibrium has been established, however, there may be no dominant strategy within a situation.

Aggressive Price-Cutting Games

One of the more simple games is aggressive price cutting and in some extreme cases prices can fall below costs. There have been many real-life cases of this type of game, which normally ends in one company either facing financial ruin or in being taken over in a merger. Real-life examples of this type of strategy are as follows:

- Vanderbilt & Drew in the USA used to cut and re-cut shipping rates on their parallel rail networks.

- John D. Rockefeller used to undercut competitors prices to drive them into mergers.

- Petrol companies and supermarkets have reduced prices to force competitors out business.

However, this is a very dangerous strategy to use as its short-term effect is to drive prices and profit levels down. This is good for the customers in the short run, however, in the long term, if one firm merges with another prices will rise back to their previous levels or higher.

Pay-off Matrices

A pay-off matrix (or joint-strategy diagram) shows all the possible results from two player, two strategy games. Once both players have chosen their strategies from the rows and columns within the matrix the overall result will be found. This process can be illustrated with the following example.

Example

Two companies, STAR Plc and SUN Plc, both manufacture electronic semi-conductors. These two companies have two pricing strategies for the ED-145 product, which they could use for this product. The effect of each strategy on profitability is shown in the matrix in Table 8.7.

Each cell in the matrix shows the combination of profit levels for each company, if Star Plc chooses strategy P_1 and Sun Plc also chooses strategy P_1, they would each gain, earning a joint profit level of $10+10 = 20$ (thousand pounds). At this point profits are maximised at the monopoly price of £2.40. However, this is not a stable result because if Sun Plc knew that Star Plc was going to choose strategy P_1, Sun Plc would be better off by choosing P_2. Star Plc would now have to follow suit choosing P_2 where excess profit is minimal. One important point to note is that if both parties collude and both charge P_1 they will maximise profit levels. However this is not in the best interest of the customer, due to higher prices, and in some countries such as the United States of America anti-trust laws stop companies from

Table 8.7

		STAR Plc	
		$P_1 = £2.40$	$P_2 = £1.60$
S U N Plc	$P_1 = £2.40$	A Star (10)/Sun(10)	B Star(15)/Sun(0)
	$P_2 = £1.60$	C Star(0)/Sun(15)	D Star(5)/Sun(5)

Numbers in brackets are the effect on profits.

colluding (Sherman Act (1890), Clayton Act (1914) and the Federal Trade Commission Act (1914)). The only way to guarantee customer interests is through competition and having numerous suppliers in the industry. It should be clear that all these types of games assume perfect information and knowledge which in the real world is not normally the case.

Example: The Prisoners' Dilemma

Another classic example of game theory is the 'Prisoners' Dilemma'. Two people have been caught in a joint crime. The police interview each person separately and say that they have enough evidence on both of them to send them to jail for a year. However, if one of the criminals confesses to the crime, a deal where he only serves a three-month sentence will be given, while the partner will get the full 10-year sentence. If both criminals confess they will both get a five-year jail sentence. This problem can be shown in the pay-off matrix as shown in Table 8.8.

Table 8.8

		Prisoner 1	
		Not confess	Confess
Prisoner 2	Not confess	A Prisoner 1 (1 year)/2 (1 year)	B Prisoner 1 (3 months)/2 (10 years)
	Confess	C Prisoner 1 (10 years)/2 (3 months)	D Prisoner 1 (5 years)/2 (5 years)

Numbers in brackets are the length of jail sentence.

What should Prisoner 2 do, confess hoping to get a shorter sentence? That must be better than not confessing. However, if Prisoner 1 also confesses they will both get a five-year sentence, which would be much worse than a short three-month sentence. If Prisoner 2 does not confess then he could end up with a 10-year jail sentence. The only answer is to collude, i.e. both prisoners know what the other is going to decide. The optimal strategy for both prisoners is not to confess and get a year each in jail. However, there is a great temptation for either prisoner to be selfish and confess, and if both confess then they will both serve a five-year jail sentence.

Game theory can be applied to many situations and the examples given here are only a very brief introduction to a very wide field. Von Neumann has developed many other classic game situations and those of particular interest include the theory of collusion. For a complete review of the foundations of game theory the three-volume set by Dimand and Dimand (1997) includes over 120 articles on game theory from its beginnings in the 1940s to the present day.

CONCLUSION

Four basic decision techniques have been discussed in this chapter, namely, CPM/PERT, queuing theory, linear programming and game theory. All these techniques have been and are used to solve real-world problems. However, it is important for you to understand the key assumptions implicit in all these techniques to make sure they yield the correct results, as things like changes in prices, timings or constraints can have important knock-on effects on the results these techniques give. Most of these techniques are available within computer software programs or can be modelled using standard spreadsheet packages. One very useful computer programme is 'SOLVER' available in Microsoft Excel spreadsheet. This very flexible routine can be used to solve complex linear programming problems by utilising all the constraints and objectives given by the user. Finally, readers should remember that all these techniques will yield sensible results only if the data used is accurate; if it is not the results will be meaningless (GIGO – garbage in garbage out). The following references will provide interested readers with further work which will expand on the subjects covered in this chapter.

REFERENCES AND FURTHER READING

Baumol, W.J. (1972) *Economic Theory and Operations Analysis*, 3rd edition, London: Prentice Hall International.

Charnes, A., Cooper, W.W. and Henderson A. (1953) *An Introduction to Linear Programming*, New York: John Wiley and Sons.

Cooper R.B. (1972) *Introduction to Queuing Theory*, New York: Macmillian.

Dennis, T.L. and Dennis L.B. (1991) *Management Science*, St Paul: West Publishing Company.

Dimand M.A. and Dimand, R.W. (1997) *The Foundations of Game Theory*, Cheltenham: Edward Elgar.

Koutsoyiannis, A. (1982) *Modern Microeconomics*, Hong Kong: Macmillan Press.

Luce R.D. and Raiffa, H. (1957) *Games and Decisions*, New York: John Wiley and Sons.

Meredith, J.R. and Mantel, S.J. (1985) *Project Management*, New York: John Wiley and Sons.

Payne, J.A. (1982) *Introduction to Simulation: Programming Techniques and Methods of Analysis*, New York: McGraw-Hill.

Silver, M. (1997) *Business Statistics*, 2nd edition, New York: McGraw Hill,

Von Neumann, J. and Morgenstern, O. (1947) *Theory of Games and Economic Behaviour*, 2nd edition, Princeton: Princeton University Press.

Waters, C.D.J. (1989) *A Practical Introduction to Management Science*, Wokingham: Addison-Wesley Publishing Company.

Weist, J.D. and Levy, F.K. (1977) *A Management Guide to PERT/CPM*, 2nd edition, Englewood Cliffs: Prentice Hall.

PROBLEM: GAME THEORY

Introductory Comments

This is an approach used to evaluate decision alternatives. Like statistical decision theory, it calls for an identification of the decision alternatives, uncertain variables and the value of different outcomes. It differs from statistical decision theory in that the major uncertain variable is assumed to be a competitor, nature, or some other force. The probability is 1.00 that each actor will do what is in its best interest.

Problem

A car manufacturer is trying to decide whether to restyle a particular car model. The company knows that its main competitor is also trying to make the same decision. The company estimates that if neither restyles, neither will gain anything over the normal rate of profit. If the company restyles, and the competitor does not, the company will gain £20 million over its competitor. It is assumed that the competitor loses £20 million – the gain to one company is a loss to the other. If the company decides not to restyle and the competitor does, the company loses £10 million. Finally, if both restyle, the company gains £5 million and its competitor loses £5 million, because the company is assumed to be better at restyling. A solution is possible if we assume that both opponents will want to take the course of action that will leave them least worst off. This is called the minimax criterion – in minimising that maximum loss. It also assumes that both opponents are conservative.

Competitor

	Do not restyle	Restyle
Do not restyle	£0	−£10
Restyle	£20	£5

Company

Figure 8.8

Question

Given the game matrix in Figure 8.8 (values in millions), find the decision associated with the least worst outcome.

PROBLEM: MARKETING DECISION MODEL – STATISTICAL OR BAYESIAN DECISION THEORY

Introductory Comments

This model would call for the following:

- Identifying major decision alternatives facing the company.
- Distinguishing the events (states of nature) that might, with each possible decision, bring about a distinct outcome.
- Estimate the probability of each state of nature.
- Estimate the value (payoff) of each outcome to the company.
- Determine the expected value of each decision.
- Choosing the decision with the highest expected value.

Problem

Given the payoff matrix in Figure 8.9, find the decision that maximises the expected value of the payoffs to the company. Suppose a product manager is trying to decide

	Recession (0.7)	Prosperity (0.3)
Do not raise price	£500,000	£700,000
Raise price	−£1,000,000	£1,000,000

Figure 8.9

between raising a price or leaving it alone. The outcome will be affected by whether the economy slides into a recession, of which the product manager believes there is a 0.7 chance. If a recession occurs and price is not raised, the profits will be £500,000. But if price is raised, there will be a loss of £100,000. If the economy is prosperous, and the price is unchanged, then the profits will be £700,000; if the price is raised here, profits will go up to £1,000,000. The expected value is the weighted mean of the payoffs with the probabilities serving as the weights.

PROBLEM: MARKETING DECISION MODEL

Introductory Comments

An important type of marketing decision model is mathematical programming. Here, the objective of the decision maker is expressed as some variable to be optimised subject to a set of explicitly expressed constraints.

Problem

This problem shows a profit function relating to profits to the amount of funds spent on advertising and distribution.

Given the objective function $Z = 10A + 20D$ and the constraints

(1) $A + D \leq 100$
(2) $A \geq 40$
(3) $A \leq 80$
(4) $D \geq 10$
(5) $D \leq 70$

A pound spent on advertising contributes £10 to profits and a pound spent on distribution contributes £20. A set of policy constraints is also introduced: (1) the marketing budget, divided between advertising and distribution, should not exceed £100,000; (2) of this, advertising should receive at least £40,000; (3) and no more than £80,000; (4) distribution should receive at least £10,000; (5) and no more than £70,000. This is a simple problem, so the best marketing programmes can be found without any higher mathematics. Since the distribution investment is twice as effective as the advertising investment, it would make sense to spend all that is permitted within the constraints on distribution.

Question

Find the allocation of the £100,000 budget between advertising (A) and distribution (D) that will maximise profits (Z).

CASE: KANTER PRODUCTS LIMITED

The management of Kanter Products Limited, based in Fort William, Scotland, were facing a problem to be solved which called for the use of decision theory. The problem focuses on the evaluation of sales prospects who were considering the purchase of a high-value durable goods item with a good deal of necessary presale effort. The problem of selecting the prospects that hold greatest profit potential was of prime importance in order to focus a limited sales force on an expanding marketplace. Considerable selectivity had to be exercised, and the importance of the judgement underlying this selectivity was extremely important.

In analysing the situation, the following questions had to be tackled one at a time and an economic evaluation made of each.

- What is the payoff or profit potential of each prospect?
- What are the costs involved in bidding for the account?
- What are the odds on getting the account?

The profit potential is based on the revenue that can be expected over a five-year period. A five-year period is selected because a customer can be expected to contribute add-on business after the initial sale. If installation is not anticipated before 12 months, the profit potential must reflect this factor. For example, this multidivision company which is expecting to sign a contract for one machine (£110,000 revenue) to be installed in 12 months with two similar machines to be installed two years after the first would have a five-year revenue potential of £880,000 (£110,000 × 4 + £220,000 × 2). The revenue potential must then be viewed in light of its profit contribution (based on the company's accounting methods) and must be discounted in light of the fact that revenue does not accrue the first year.

The next question to answer is the presale effort that must be expended in an attempt to sign the account. This figure covers the cost of special engineering, system analysis, special training courses, demonstration programmes, proposal preparation and other support needed to bid for the business. Kanter's marketing department has prepared an elaborate proposal taking into account that considerable special engineering is also required. The costs involved were as follows:

Two engineers for four months (8 man-months × £2,000)	= £16,000
Two illustrators/designers for four months (£1,500 per man month)	= £12,000
Supplies and proposal material	= £ 1,000
	£29,000

The next step is the determination of the betting odds or the probability that the business can be closed. This is a rather subjective valuation, but an analysis of competitive factors, plus past experience, can be used to establish the odds. The result is stated in terms of a percentage probability. To see how decision theory works, assume that there were two prospects for Kanter and that it is desired to rank them according to priority as it is not possible to expand a major sales effort on each.

	Account A (the account described above)	Account B
Revenue potential	£880,000	£560,000
Profit potential	170,000	90,000
Sales cost	−29,000	−6,000
Net Profit Potential	£141,000	£ 84,000

Decision table statement of problems

Alternatives	Bid on Prospect A	Probability (%)	Bid on Prospect B	Probability (%)
Get the sale	+£170,000	20	+£90,000	40
Lose the sale	−29,000	80	−6,000	60

Decision theory is a systematic method of facilitating decision making under conditions of uncertainty. The example used here has but a few variables and there are only two alternative courses of action. As the variables and alternatives are multiplied severalfold, as is the case in most business decisions, the need for techniques like decision theory becomes more apparent. Decision theory analyses the factors underlying a decision and allows the decision maker to quantify the major parts of the problem so that he or she is free to concentrate on those factors that cannot be readily quantified. The human mind has a difficult time handling multidimensional problems. Decision theory divides a problem into its logical parts, analyses each part separately and then puts the parts back together in their proper perspective in order to reach a decision. Decision theory follows the philosophy of 'divide and conquer'; that is, divide a problem into its logical components, analyse and quantify each component, and thereby conquer the overall problem. Thus, the example of choosing between two sales prospects by use of decision theory illustrates in a simplified manner the way information systems are impacting top management decision making. Although it is only the leading edge of companies who are effectively utilising such approaches today, the success that the relatively few are experiencing augurs well for greatly extended use in the future.

Questions

1. Comment on the technique of risk analysis/decision theory.
2. What is the resultant discounted contribution margin derived from the sale of three (one plus two) initial machines?
3. Calculate the expected monetary values for both prospects A and B, and comment on the decision table statement of problems.

9
Operations management

This chapter is divided into four main sections which look at capacity, inventory control, quality and production systems.

Contents

The task of operations
Capacity control
Inventory control
Quality
Production management systems

Objectives

After reading this chapter you should:

- Know what capacity is and how to measure it.
- Know some of the strategies to control capacity problems.
- Understand the basic concepts in inventory control.
- Know some of the strategies to reduce inventories.
- Understand the importance of quality.
- Know what SPC and TQM are.
- Know the key concepts behind MRP, JIT and OPT.
- Know the advantages and disadvantages of the different production systems (MRP, JIT and OPT).

INTRODUCTION

New concepts in business and management are drawing together previously separate areas like finance, marketing, operations management and human resource management into a much more co-ordinated approach. One way this has been achieved is by the use of Manufacturing Resource Planning (MRP II) which takes a much more global view of the firm. This change in thinking has meant a sharing of key ideas, concepts and most importantly information across many different areas of the firm. It is therefore becoming much more important in setting *marketing strategy* to be aware of the causal effects on other areas of the firm of new strategies.

This chapter outlines four of the key areas in operations management that all areas of the business should be aware of: firstly capacity control and measurement, secondly inventory control, thirdly quality and fourthly production systems. Three production systems are discussed, namely: materials requirement planning, optimum production technology and just-in-time. However we start by looking at the task of any operation whether it be in the manufacturing or service sector.

THE TASK OF OPERATIONS

The task of most operations is to produce goods and services which are needed by customers in terms of quantity, quality and delivery at the minimum overall cost. Production systems are usually complex and, until computerised, most production systems worked at only a very simple level and normally carried high levels of inventories. The key problems any system has to address are the sheer complexity of the production system, poor information flow, constantly changing demand patterns and supply difficulties. Before computers were available to solve production problems the best approach was to:

- Carry large inventory levels to allow for any unforeseen changes.

- Run large batches to reduce unit manufacturing costs by spreading set-up costs.

- Attempt to minimise planning difficulties which often led to high work-in-progress and bottlenecks.

There are basically two approaches to production systems, namely push systems and pull systems. Push systems 'push' products through the production system normally in large batches. These batches are pushed whether the next work station is ready for them or not. The result is normally delays in the production system and an increase in stocks of work-in-progress. MRP is an example of a push system. Pull systems 'pull' products through the production system – when a preceding work station finishes its process the product moves directly on to the next work station. Therefore work in progress is minimised. Pull systems work with small batches of products.

CAPACITY CONTROL

Capacity and the control of it is of prime importance to any company. If a company operates at only 20% of their capacity they will have a lot of unproductive resources which will all have to be paid for. If they operate at or close to 100% they will face many problems particularly in the event of machine breakdown, as they will not be able to meet promised demand.

Capacity can be generally defined as the maximum level of production that can be achieved with the present level of resources. It has been formally defined by the American Production and Inventory Control Society (APICS), as 'the highest reasonable output rate which can be achieved with the current specifications, product mix, workforce, plant and equipment'. Therefore capacity utilisation can be defined as the ratio of actual production to this maximum level, as shown in the following equation:

$$\text{Capacity utilisation} = \frac{\text{actual output}}{\text{maximum output}} * 100$$

Within a manufacturing environment actual production poses no problem as you can simply count the number of products you have made. However, the problem of defining actual output in a service sector is much more complex and it normally revolves around some form of input measure.

The measurement of maximum output is a very difficult concept to measure, as it changes over time due to technological advances. For example the introduction of an MRP system can cause as much as a 15% increase in production for firms which successfully implement it.

There are two basic approaches to measuring maximum output, firstly survey-based methods and secondly data-based methods.

Survey-based Methods

Survey-based approaches work by asking managers in firms 'at what level of capacity are you presently working?'. This information is then used to calculate average utilisation rate for industries. This approach is used by the US Bureau of the Census and MITI index of operating ratio of Japan. However, the implicit assumption is that managers will actually know what their maximum level of capacity is – this is very questionable. This major problem could be further added to if there were a biased sample of firms in the survey.

Data-based Methods

There are numerous data-based methods available for estimating capacity utilisation. Three of the more commonly used approaches are given below.

Production Function Frontier Method

This method estimates a production function which links actual output to all the factor inputs used in the manufacture of the product(s).

$$Y = f(K, L, La, E, \text{ etc.})$$

where Y = production
K = capital
L = labour
La = land
E = energy

The functional form of this equation can take numerous forms (Cobb–Douglas, CES or Translog). After the equation has been estimated the maximum available factors of production (K, L, La, E) can be substituted into the equation and the maximum or potential capacity estimated. However, there are three important assumptions, firstly that the maximum or potential capacity will be parallel to the estimated one (as the estimated slope coefficients will remain the same). Secondly that the data has been measured without error. Thirdly that the estimated equation fits the data well.

Electricity Approach

This is based on the work of Foss (1963) and Jorgenson and Grilliches (1967) and works on the principle that services from the stock of capital are only released by the application of energy or power. Therefore, each piece of capital will have an installed rated wattage, which defines a maximum amount of electricity that can be consumed (E_t^o). The index of capacity utilisation can therefore be calculated by the ratio of actual electricity (E_t) used to the maximum aggregated rated wattage.

$$CU_e = E_t/E_t^o$$

OPT Bottle-neck Approach

This is by far the best method with the most realistic assumptions. Within the production system there will be one or a small number of machines which are the bottle-neck. The maximum level of production is simply the maximum work rate of the bottle-neck process. Therefore any firm can easily find out what is determining their capacity constraint by finding the bottle-neck process.

As we have seen, all the above methods have some seriously restrictive assumptions built into them. The most practical and by far best is the OPT bottle-neck approach.

One other important factor is that a firm may be working at a rate fairly close to full capacity, but, due to high waste or defective items being manufactured, actual output may be much lower. Therefore these types of firms must attempt to improve the quality of the items produced, as only good items will be sold. The three production systems (MRP, OPT, and JIT) discussed later in this chapter will help firms to work smarter rather than simply harder.

Ways of Controlling Capacity

There are many ways of controlling capacity and these can be divided into temporary and permanent changes. Permanent changes will normally involve building or changing existing facilities. There are four temporary methods which are commonly used and are detailed below.

Production Rate Changes

One of the most common ways of increasing capacity without changing existing resources is to use overtime, however this normally requires a wage premium to be paid. Another way is to use subcontracting during periods of high or peak demand. However the subcontractor must be able to produce the products at the correct quality and at the correct time.

Work-force Changes

This involves changing the size of the work-force through either hiring or layoffs. In many industries this is used due to high peak demand, i.e. harvesting agricultural products, tourism industry and extra postal workers required around Christmas. However one problem in work-force changes is that the workers will not have specialised skills so this method can not be used for highly skilled jobs.

Inventory Smoothing

Inventories can be allowed to build up in slack periods and then held for peak periods. However, to do this the manufacturer must have the warehouse space to store all the products, the cash to fund the inventory and also be fairly certain they can sell the products. This type of strategy can be very dangerous if there is a technological change and new products supersede the old products. If this happens the value of the inventory will fall to a fraction of its value.

Another strategy is to manufacture complementary products which use the same technology but have opposite seasonal patterns. Examples of such products are snow skis and water skis or heating systems and air conditioners. If complementary products can be manufactured then the seasonal peaks can be smoothed out. One other strategy which may be available to firms who have strong seasonal demand, is to export more of their products in the low-demand period.

Demand Shifting

This uses various marketing strategies to influence or change demand patterns. One example of this is to charge a higher price at the peak of demand and a lower price at other times. This practice is often used by the transportation industry (a train ticket will normally cost more before 9.00am than after). Other strategies involve the use of advertising promotions like coupons to stimulate demand in low demand periods.

With all of these techniques temporary changes can be made to cope with or change demand patterns. However forward planning is of the utmost importance and forecasting is often used to predict future demand peaks.

INVENTORY CONTROL

An inventory is defined as a store of raw materials, work-in-progress and/or finished products. To illustrate the importance of controlling inventory levels and the ever increasing competitive pressure we need only look at Table 9.1. This shows how inventory turnover (i.e. yearly turnover level/yearly inventory level), quality and product cycles have dramatically changed over the last few years.

As Table 9.1 clearly shows, the best companies in the world, such as Toyota, have accelerated the competitive race to such a level, that any other company which does not improve in line to this new standard will be swept away in the tidal wave of competitive pressures. One very important side effect of this ever increasing competitive flywheel is the increase in managerial stress.

Therefore inventory control is a very important area for any business, particularly for those businesses which are manufacturing high numbers of products. Techniques such as MRP, OPT and JIT (see sections in this chapter) will all reduce inventory levels by better planning and control; in fact, JIT views inventories as evil. All these techniques attempt to control production and inventories and in the case of JIT, companies produce products only when they are needed.

One of the major problems in running any inventory is knowing when a product/raw material will be required. If the future demand levels for the company are fairly uniform or highly predictable this problem disappears. However, few companies have this luxury and small companies can face huge swings in demand levels. If

Table 9.1

Year	Product life cycles	Inventory turnover	Quality
1970	Decades	3	Defects 10%
1975	Many years	6	Defects < 10%
1980	A few years	15	Defects < 1%
1985	A year	32	Parts per million
1990	< 12 months	101	Zero defects

orders are placed by customers in a random pattern this leads to peaks and troughs in the demand pattern and therefore the production process. Some firms use inventories to smooth out this problem; however, this is not a cost-effective strategy and can be very dangerous if new technology makes your inventory out of date.

Once companies realise that inventories cost money to purchase, control and store, the cost-saving of not holding large levels of raw materials, work in progress or finished goods is clearly apparent. For some companies reducing inventory levels can save millions of pounds. When the problems of shortening product life cycles (i.e. how long a product is sold before being withdrawn or replaced – many electronic products have a life cycle of less than a year) are added to the equation, high levels of finished products soon become out-dated by new, better and cheaper products. The only thing left to do for a company holding high stocks of last year's product(s) is to heavily discount them (sometimes even at or below cost) and sell them as soon as possible. Sometimes the only option is to scrap all these out-dated products and try to salvage any raw materials that may be useful. For an excellent discussion of the issues of inventory control see Goldratt & Fox (1986) and Lee & Schniederjans (1994).

The following ten strategies will all reduce inventories; however, some will be more effective than others depending on the type of company which adopts them. All these strategies if properly implemented will have positive effects on many aspects of the company; however, they are not often painless to implement in the short run. The primary and secondary effects of each strategy are also discussed.

1. *Man the bottle-neck at all times the production process is working*   The bottle-neck is an OPT term and refers to any production process whose capacity is lower than the other parts of the production system. It is fairly obvious that it is the bottle-neck that determines the overall level of capacity of any production system. Therefore any time wasted at the bottle-neck is time wasted for the whole production system. Things like lunch breaks for staff at the bottle-neck and bottle-neck set-up times should be staggered so as to minimise any down time.

2. *Place quality control before the bottle-neck*   The major effect of this strategy is *not* to continue to process a bad or defective item as it will be rejected later. This will lead to lower finished goods scrap levels, higher utilisation of available capacity, increased throughput and higher profit levels.

3. *Know the lead and process times of all the operations in the production system*   This strategy will allow better planning of the product system, reduce the build up of work-in-progress, give better and more accurate delivery times and increase competitive ability.

4. *Use statistical process control (SPC)*   This strategy applies some of the basic principles of probability and has been successfully used for over 50 years. SPC allows the production system to be constantly monitored. If any problems start to arise, like making a product too large or too small, SPC control charts will

alert management to the problem straight away. This type of strategy is particularly useful in situations of mass production.

5. *Reduce set-up times for production processes*   This strategy will allow faster change over between different products. Any time taken in changing a machine over from the manufacture of one product to another which stops the production process means the company is not making any products which can be sold. If set-up times can be reduced it will lead to better utilisation of available capacity, increased throughput and higher profit levels.

6. *Improve training and education of the work-force*   This strategy will improve quality, increase job satisfaction and make the work-force more flexible, particularly if workers can work on more than one process. This strategy is particularly useful for small companies like jobbing shops.

7. *Reduce the distances between the operations in the system*   This strategy will increase throughput by reducing travel and waiting times, which will in turn reduce lead times, improve productivity and increase profitability.

8. *Develop a close trust and cooperation between you and your suppliers*   This strategy can lead to improved quality for raw materials and more flexibility in terms of ordering and delivery.

9. *Improve the distribution system*   This strategy will lead to the faster delivery of products to customers, lower holding costs for finished goods and faster payment for goods and services.

10 *Use statistical forecasting techniques to predict future demand levels*   This strategy will lead to better prediction of future demand peaks, which can be accordingly planned for.

One of the most important books on management thinking and inventory control has been written by Goldratt and Cox (1993) and is called *The Goal*. Anyone studying a business subject should read it (once you start reading you will not want to stop – it is that good). There is also a video of the same title available published by Melrose which summarises the key points contained within the book and lasts about an hour.

Not only can manufacturing companies benefit from reduced inventory holding, services companies can also reap the rewards.

QUALITY

Every product or service which is provided has to be designed to satisfy customers' demands and expectations. Customers judge products and services not only in terms of price but in terms of quality, availability and flexibility. Products and services which are not of the required standard will not be demanded by people. Therefore in its widest sense quality can be defined as the ability of a product or service to meet, and preferably exceed, customers expectations. Products and services which do not meet customers' expectations will not be purchased again and can cause negative word-of-mouth effects on other potential customers.

Quality management is the management function concerned with all aspects of product or service quality. Two approaches to improving quality are discussed below, namely statistical process control (SPC) and Deming's 14 principles for total quality management.

Statistical Process Control

SPC has been used for around 50 years and is based on the laws and principles of probability. SPC can be used to control the quality of everything from cream cakes to plastic bowls, in fact anything which is mass produced. SPC uses samples drawn from current production to calculate statistical characteristics (mean, range and variance). These characteristics can be plotted on statistical quality control (SQC) charts on a regular basis over time. An upper control limit and a lower control limit are drawn on the SQC chart to specify the acceptable levels of variation which the product must not go outside. The results of each sample can then be placed on the chart. The mean of a sample is plotted on an Xbar-chart (see Figure 9.1) and the range is plotted on an R-chart; P-charts are also used to chart the proportion of defective units in a sample. The beauty of these charts is that they give an instant visual picture of what is going on within the production system.

If any of the calculated characteristics start to develop into patterns like those shown in Figure 9.1(b), (c) or (d) then this is considered to be abnormal behaviour and a problem is developing. It is very important to regularly monitor the control charts so action can be taken as soon as a problem starts to occur.

Total Quality Management

The basic principle behind total quality management (TQM) is that the whole organisation works together to systematically improve product quality. TQM was developed by Deming, an American who visited Japan in the late 1940s to improve productivity and quality. Within TQM quality is a strategic issue with everyone in the organisation responsibile for it. TQM emphasis is on preventing defects rather than detecting them with the goal of TQM being zero defects. Deming compiled a list of 14 points which need to be followed to implement TQM – no time frame is attached to this.

Deming's 14 Principles of TQM

1. Create constancy of purpose towards product quality.
2. Refuse to accept customary levels of mistakes, delays, defects and errors.

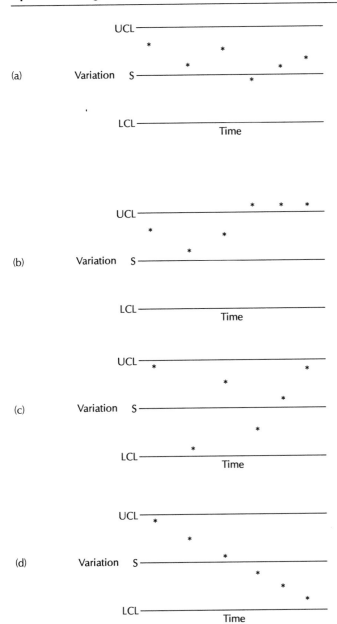

Figure 9.1   SQC X bar chart showing (a) normal behaviour; (b) abnormal behaviour – samples close to UCL; (c) abnormal behaviour – samples very erratic; (d) abnormal behaviour – samples trending

3. Stop depending on mass inspection, but build quality into the product in the first place.
4. Stop awarding business on the basis of price only – reduce the number of suppliers and insist on meaningful measures of quality.
5. Develop programmes for continuous improvement of costs, quality, productivity and service.
6. Institute training for all employees.
7. Focus supervision on helping employees to do a better job.
8. Drive out fear by encouraging two-way communication.
9. Break down barriers between departments and encourage problem solving through team-work.
10. Eliminate numerical goals, posters and slogans that demand improvement without saying how these should be achieved.
11. Eliminate arbitrary quotas that interfere with quality.
12. Remove barriers that stop people having pride in their work.
13. Institute vigorous programmes of life-long education, training and self improvement.
14. Put everyone to work on implementing these 14 points.

Source : Deming (1986)

These 14 principles give the organisation a new way of thinking, they emphasise that managers are responsible for improving overall performance and quality.

There are numerous examples of the successful introduction of TQM. One occurred in 1984 when Ford America had been running its 'Quality is Job 1' programme for about five years. During that period the number of warranty repairs dropped by 45%, faults reported by owners fell by 50% and the company's share of the US market rose by 19.2%.

In the UK a quality standard was developed called BS5700; this has now been brought under the international quality standard called ISO 9000 certification. This has five separate levels:

ISO 9000   defines quality and quality characteristics which an organisation should aim for.

ISO 9001   deals with the whole range of TQM, from product design all the way through to the testing of the finished product/service.

ISO 9002   deals with quality management during the production process and how this quality can be documented for ISO certification.

ISO 9003   deals with final inspection and testing.

ISO 9004   states what needs to be done within the operations to develop and maintain quality, including management responsibilities.

An excellent review of the key issues in TQM is provide by Powell (1995).

PRODUCTION MANAGEMENT SYSTEMS

Materials Requirement Planning

With the advent of computers in the 1960s and 1970s came the development of materials requirement planning (MRP). This was a great step forward and led to lower inventories, better planning, improved quality and better due date delivery. MRP is a push system where resources are pushed through the production system and it acts like a large jigsaw of information. This system allows the correct scheduling of resources, and its basic principle is to make sure the resources or sub-assemblies are available for other processes in the production system. The jigsaw puzzle is built up from information as shown in Figure 9.2.

Demand and Stocks

This details what orders are on the order book, what levels of work-in-progress there are and what levels of raw materials and finished products are in the inventory. This information can be used to develop forecasts and plans for the future.

Aggregate Production Plan

This is developed on a monthly or quarterly basis for product groups or product families that will mean the estimated levels of demand. For example, a company that manufactures sport shoes would look at tennis shoes but not sizes of tennis

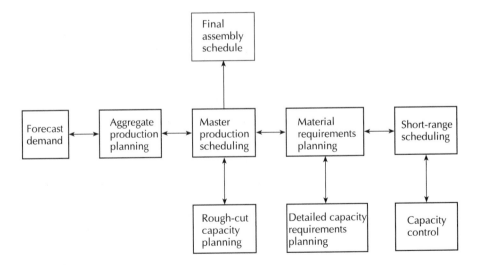

Figure 9.2   The production planning and scheduling process

shoes within the aggregate production plan. Manufacturing, marketing and financial managers will all be involved in the development of this plan. Gross capacity constraints must be taken into account in this plan. If demand outstrips current capacity the firm may want to outsource some of the work to other companies or use overtime to meet demand levels.

The Master Production Schedule

The master production schedule (MPS) provides a weekly product requirement over a 6- to 12-month time horizon. It is not a forecast but a schedule of production that should be completed to meet demand. The MPS is used by the operating staff to make detailed plans for procurements of materials, the production of sub-components and the final assembly of finished goods.

Rough Cut Capacity Planning

This provides general capacity information that can be used to plan and correct resource shortages as well as provide general guidelines which are used in the MPS.

Final Assembly Schedule

The final assembly schedule (FAS) is a statement of the final products that must be assembled from the MPS schedule. The FAS is not prepared very far into the future (a few weeks to a month).

Example: MRP in practice – the example of Western-Star plc

Western-Star plc manufacture televisions and have just had an order for 2,800 Model 15 televisions from a large rental company. The Model 15 is divided into four separate stages of production with the time to complete each task shown in Table 9.2.

The televisions must be manufactured in the order of dependence (a), (b), (c) and finally (d). This is because sub-components are assembled either in or on top of earlier components. At present Western-Star plc has some inventories as shown in

Table 9.2

	Stage	Time to compete	Inventory level
(a)	Manufacture the screen	4 days	991
(b)	Assemble screen components	5 days	234
(c)	Assemble all components	2 days	141
(d)	Package finished product	3 days	140

Table 9.3 Time-phased requirement processing chart

Day number	1	2	3	4	5	6	7	8	9	10	11	12	13	14	15
Finished product															
Demand															2800
Inventory															2800
Package finished product															
Inventory	140	140	140	140	140	140	140	140	140	140	140	140	140	140	
Net requirement												2660	2660	2660	
Assemble all components															
Inventory	141	141	141	141	141	141	141	141	141	141	141				
Net requirement										2519	2519				
Assemble screen components															
Inventory	234	234	234	234	234	234	234	234	234						
Net requirement					2285	2285	2285	2285	2285						
Manufacture screen															
Inventory	991	991	991	991											
Net requirement	1294	1294	1294	1294											

Table 9.4 Net requirements

	Total order	2800	
Package finished product	Inventory	140	Subtract
	Net requirement	2660	
Assemble all components	Inventory	141	Subtract
	Net requirement	2519	
Assemble screen	Inventory	234	Subtract
	Net requirement	2285	
Manufacture screen	Inventory	991	Subtract
	Net requirement	1294	

Table 9.2. If the order for 2,800 Model 15 is to be completed four questions must be answered.

1. How much of each sub-assembly is required (i.e. the net requirements)?
2. How long will it take to make all the order?
3. When will each sub-assembly need to be finished?
4. Do we have enough capacity to manufacture what is required?

The first three questions can be answered by using a time-phased requirement process chart as shown in Table 9.3. The day number is listed across the top of the chart (often this is referred to as time buckets) and the sub-assemblies are listed down the side. The first question is answered by putting all the inventory levels into the net requirement table. The net requirements are then calculated by working back from the total order. The amount in the first inventory is subtracted from the total order to give the first net requirement (2600) and so on until the last operation, *this must be done in order of dependence* as shown in Table 9.4.

Now that the net requirements and lead time to manufacture each sub-assembly is known, the time-phased requirement chart can be constructed. This chart utilises the net requirements and lead time information into a giant timetable of what needs to be manufactured and when.

The time-phased requirement processing chart can be constructed by starting at the first available day to start manufacturing and working forward utilising the net requirement information. As can clearly be seen if the timetable is followed the total order can be manufactured in 15 days if Western-Star Plc started manufacturing now; this answers the second question. The third question is answered by referring to the time-phased requirement chart (Table 9.3) which shows when each sub-assembly must be started and finished. The final question about capacity can now be addressed by looking at the capacity of each section of the company and the net requirements (see Table 9.5). A rough capacity check is undertaken to see whether any sub-assembly capacities are broken. The capacity constraints would be known and fixed as the maximum production that can take place. Work at or just below these figures can be dangerous.

Table 9.5   Capacity

Production stage	Net requirement	Capacity constraint
Package finished product	2660	2950
Assemble all components	2519	2950
Assemble screen	2285	2960
Manufacture screen	1294	2970

In this case no net requirement exceeds capacity therefore the order should be ready on day 15. If capacity is exceeded the company has a number of choices; it could:

- Sub-contract some of the work to a different company.

- Run an extra shift through the night.

- Ask if the customer would accept the order in two shipments one in 15 days and another shipment 15 days later.

- Refuse the order or reduce the order to within capacity levels.

(Also see section on capacity planning for more detailed discussion of capacity solutions.)

Whatever choice the company makes they can plan for the capacity problem. Without systems like this capacity problems become invisible until it is too late and customers end up waiting for goods that were promised weeks ago. If this does happen future orders are highly unlikely and customer satisfaction will be greatly reduced.

Obviously the example shown here is very simple as we have only one product and one customer, but it does illustrate many of the basic concepts involved in MRP systems. As the number of products and number of customers increases the calculations become more and more complex particularly if sub-assemblies can be used in different products. The answer is to use specialised computer software which can keep track of all the orders, net requirements and most importantly the timings of starting work on sub-assemblies. These software packages are normally very expensive and can often be tailor-made to companies' individual require-ments. In some firms a computer spreadsheet can be used to generate the time-phased requirement chart, however this can only be undertaken if the firm is fairly small and only manufactures a small number of different items. In practice MRP systems allow for forecasted demand, as well as what is on the order book in terms of firm orders, and plan two to three months into the future.

The great benefits of the use of MRP techniques are to increase due date performance, reduce inventory levels and therefore improve cash flow and reduce management stress as work is now correctly timetabled. However, it should be noted that the introduction of an MRP system is not easy and careful planning is required to maximise the benefits from this type of system.

Finally it is important to note a number of implicit assumptions which have been made in the above analysis:

- Perfect quality both in terms of manufacture and supply.

- No set-up or change over time.

- All resources are fully available when the company wants to use them, i.e. no workers are sick on leave/holiday.

- There will be no breakdowns or problems with the manufacturing process.

- No finished products will be stolen or lost.

Some firms hold a small inventory of completely finished goods to allow for these types of problems. However, allowances can be made for most of the above assumptions within the basic planning process by increasing the time to manufacture each batch of products.

The main advantages of using MRP are:

- Inventory levels will fall, leading to less warehouse space being required and less capital being tied up in the inventory.

- It provides a detailed plan of what to do and when, which in turn leads to better utilisation of resources.

- Less time is spent on emergency orders, so there is less stress on managers and workers alike.

- It assigns priorities to jobs on the production floor.

After MRP or MRP1 new pieces were added to the jigsaw puzzle – these included detailed capacity planning, capacity control and short-range scheduling. This led to MRP2 (Materials Resource Planning 2).

Optimised Production Technology

Optimised Production Technology (OPT) has been put forward in two books by Goldratt (1984, 1987) as a way of continuous ongoing improvement for companies. The idea of OPT is a new way of management thinking where a company seeks to maximise profits, minimise inventories and reduce operating expenses.

As can be seen from Figure 9.3, the effects of changes in the operational measures (throughput, inventory and operating expenses) will all have positive effects on the competitive edge and the customer's requirements. The basic principles of OPT can be viewed as a number of rules.

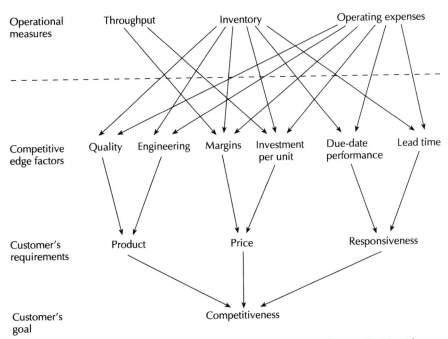

Operational measures: Throughput, Inventory, Operating expenses

Competitive edge factors: Quality, Engineering, Margins, Investment per unit, Due-date performance, Lead time

Customer's requirements: Product, Price, Responsiveness

Customer's goal: Competitiveness

Figure 9.3 Customer's and firm's goals interactions (*Source*: Rodriguez (1997) with permission)

1. *Balance flow not capacity* Production should plan to improve the flow of production rather than just minimise idle capacity. This rule means that there is no point in manufacturing items if there is no demand for them.

2. *The level of utilisation of a non-bottle-neck is not determined by its own potential but by some other constraint in the system* Bottle-necks illustrate where the constraint or weakest link in the system is and therefore determine the whole system's capacity. If you want more capacity, speed up the bottle-neck.

3. *Utilisation and activation of a resource are not synonymous* There is no point in producing more inventory from any machine which is not a bottle-neck as this will only result in more work in progress at the bottle-neck.

4. *An hour lost at a bottle-neck is an hour lost for the total system* As the bottle-neck's capacity defines the capacity of the whole system, any time lost at the bottle-neck for any reason will result in lost production for the whole system.

5. *An hour saved at a non-bottle-neck is just a mirage* Saving time at a non-bottle-neck process is of no use to the production system as there is already idle capacity there. Resources would be better spent in improving or speeding up the bottle-neck process instead.

6. *Bottle-necks govern both throughput and inventories* It is not possible to use parts which have passed through the bottle-neck any faster than the bottle-neck

can produce them. Therefore if the whole production system works at the pace of the bottle-neck no excess work-in-progress will be produced. Secondly, the whole production system will be more tidy as excess work-in-progress will disappear. This will in turn lead to a positive cash flow effect and it will also mean the company can react fast to changes.

In practice the whole production system should work to the beat of the drum from the bottle-neck, i.e. raw materials should only be released from the inventory at the speed the bottle-neck can produce them. If raw materials are released faster then the beat of the drum from the bottle-neck excess work in progress will build up.

7. *The transfer batch may not and many times should not be equal to the process batch* OPT allows and encourages flexibility in the production process, this means that there should not be a fixed level or number of products which are transferred between production stations. A high fixed transfer batch only maximises work-in-progress and increases waiting times.

8. *The processed batch should be variable not fixed* OPT allows and encourages flexibility in the production process; this means that there should not be a fixed number of products which are worked on at each production station. High batches of products will only increase work-in-progress and waiting times.

9. *Schedules should be established by looking at all the constraints simultaneously. Lead times are the result of a schedule and cannot be predetermined* OPT systems consider all the constraints of the whole production system simultaneously, which includes routeings, quantities, tooling, maintenance, staff shifts and changes in market demand.

These rules lead to the following rule:

> The sum of local optima is not equal to the optimum of the whole.

The above rules are only the starting point for applying OPT as the competitive race between companies never ends. New technology and improvements in product design will mean there will be a constant process of ongoing change.

One criticism often levelled at OPT is it is just common sense, however in the words of famous American writer Mark Twain 'common sense is not so common'. The power of OPT is only just being realised and numerous companies have benefited from its new way of managerial thinking. In many ways OPT and JIT achieve very similar goals, however the paths they follow to achieve this are very different.

Just-in-Time

Just-in-Time or JIT is commonly thought to have originated in Japan in the late 1960s. This was due to the steel industry greatly over expanding and having excess capacity which meant that the shipbuilding industry got their orders for steel fulfilled almost instantly. This resulted in the shipbuilding industry reducing their store of steel from an average of around one month to only three days. Therefore, steel was delivered as it was required or JIT. Once the great advantages of receiving goods and materials on a JIT basis were realised, the car industry was quick to adopt this new technique and one of the greatest advocates of this new philosophy was the vice-president of Toyota, Taiichi Ohno. However, it was an American, namely R.J. Schonberger (1982), who played a large role in bringing the ideas of JIT to the West.

In JIT systems, inventories are viewed as evil and all inventories are reduced to as low a level as possible. This goal is achieved by the reduction of excess (MURI), waste (MUDA) and unevenness in the production process (MURA).

MURI

A prime example of MURI is high levels of raw materials, often caused by ordering large quantities of raw materials in an attempt to reduce the purchase price through discounted prices. However, with short product life-cycles these large inventory stocks clog up the store room, tie up large levels of working capital and cause the company to be less dynamic and flexible. In a JIT system goods are delivered straight to the production line only when they are required, and manufactured only when they are needed. To achieve this you need to develop a mutual trust between you and your supplier. This does not necessarily mean that your supplier will be knee deep in stock. If you know when you will require supplies and in what quantities, you can tell the supplier so they can plan (e.g. 450 steel castings every day). To achieve this, detailed forward planning is required and forecasting can be used to predict future demand levels. Therefore lead times only become a problem if you do not plan for them.

MUDA

A prime example of MUDA is caused by accepting a certain percentage of production to be defective. This is totally unacceptable within a JIT system and perfect quality is seen as one of the most important goals of the company. Both suppliers and manufacturers within a JIT framework aim for zero defects.

MURA

A prime example of MURA is unevenness in the production line which can be caused by running all the machines within the production level at full capacity. This causes large levels of work-in-progress to build up where there are faster machines. This in turn causes the production system to clog up and wastes working capital, slows the production system down and often leads to high levels of finished goods which have not been demanded. Work by Toyota after years of ongoing improvement identified seven key types of waste. These seven types of waste need to be eliminated if the smooth flow of products through the system is to be established and improved. The seven types of waste are:

1. Waste from over production.
2. Waste from waiting time.
3. Transportation waste.
4. Processing waste.
5. Inventory waste.
6. Waste from motion.
7. Waste from product defects.

Waste from over production

This is possibly the worst form of waste and is also the most common found in factories. This problem is created by producing products in excess to that demanded by your customers and are visible as high levels of finished goods inventory. The reason some firms give for following this policy is to be ready for sudden increases in demand or viewing the inventory as an asset. Over production is a very dangerous policy particularly with falling product life-cycles. There are numerous negative side-effects of over production which can include:

- High levels of finished goods inventory.

- Extra space requirement to store all the products.

- Higher overheads.

- Higher number of workers required.

- Higher bank charges to be paid, due to working capital being used to fund high inventories.

- Higher levels of machinery are required to make all this excess production.

Waste from waiting times

Waste from waiting time is clearly visible within a production system as workers may be simply watching machines so that corrective action can be taken if abnormal conditions start. However, it would be much better to have a mechanism that automatically stops the process if it starts to go wrong (this could be linked to a light or a buzzer to alert an operator).

Transportation waste

This waste is from double- and sometimes triple-handling of materials; the problem is worst in factories with poor layout. In some factories materials are first put into store then taken to the production line and often returned to stores before being returned again to the production line to be finished. In order to eliminate this type of waste, optimal shop floor layout, optimal organisation and co-ordination of processes is required. In a well laid out factory transportation waste can be reduced to almost zero.

Processing waste
Often the way a product has been designed or is manufactured can cause process waste. For example if a product is allowed to go cold before being heat treated, this will require much more energy in reheating the product. It would be much better not to allow the product to go cold before going on to the next process.

Inventory waste
Excess inventory will increase the cost of the product (see the reasons listed under waste from over production). It will also make the firm less flexible and unable to change over to new products quickly. Therefore firms must seek to maximise their level of inventory turnover. The following formula can be used to calculate this.

$$\text{Inventory turnover} = \frac{\text{Annual turnover}}{\text{Inventory level}}$$

Levels of inventory turnover in excess of 30 are considered to be fairly good, however some companies in Japan have already produced inventory turnover levels of 100 or more (i.e. turning their inventory over every 3 to 4 days). To achieve levels of this type the following strategies should be adopted:

- Dispose of all obsolete materials.

- Tidy up the inventory and keep a careful check on what is in there and how it is used.

- Do not produce items which are not required at that time and look for line imbalances.

- Manufacture products in small lot sizes (i.e. 2 or 3) and reduce set-up time where ever possible.

As the level of the inventory starts to fall other problems will start to appear, common problems are:

- Poor scheduling.
- Communication problems.
- Supplier delivery problems.
- Quality problems.
- Breakdown problems.

These problems will need to be fully addressed and carefully solved if the process of 'ongoing improvement' is to be achieved. In JIT excess inventory is viewed as the root of all evil.

Waste from motion
Any time that is not spent in adding value to a product should be eliminated wherever possible and we should always remember that movement does not equal work. Walking can also be a waste caused by poor shop floor layout.

Waste from product defects
This type of waste is caused by poor quality and leads to problems of reworking defective items or time spent in sorting out defective items from good ones. More importantly poor quality will at its worst lead to the return of products from the customer under warranty for repair. This will cause lower levels of customer satisfaction for products and could lead to brand switching if customers are dissatisfied.

Basic Components of a JIT System

JIT can be seen on two levels: firstly, the philosophy of the operation and, secondly, as a set of tools and technques. However, all JIT systems have the following four basic components in common.

1. *Optimum layout (U-shaped cells)*   Within a JIT factory the layout of the production system is not designed in straight lines, instead the system is divided into a number of U-shaped production cells. This allows the flow line principles to be used, where materials flow in a smooth way through the system. There is also little waste in terms of materials travelling around the production system unnecessarily. Furthermore, the quality of the items being manufactured which enter and leave each production cell is guaranteed by the work-force in those production cells. Therefore, if any problems do occur there is very little work-in-progress to correct. The workers can also stop the production cell if any problems start to occur.

2. *Kanban control*   Kanban control is the use of cards or a signal to control the flow of materials. All materials are stored and moved in standard containers and a container can only be moved when it has a Kanban attached to it. When a work area requires more materials a Kanban is attached to an empty container and returned to the preceding work area. The Kanban is then attached to a full container and returned to the work area. Therefore, empty containers are signals for the preceding work area to start work on this material and stop when the container is full. Through the use of a Kanban system the amount of work-in-progress can be controlled by firstly, the number of Kanbans and secondly the size of the standard container.

    Another part of this control system is called *Andon* which shows where things are going wrong. Typically this uses three coloured lights above each work station.

A green light – everything is fine.

An amber light – work is falling a little bit behind.

A red light – there is a serious problem.

With this system it is very clear where the problems are, so action can be taken quickly to solve them.

3. *Total Quality Philosophy*   Within a JIT system the product and manufacturing facility are designed to avoid quality problems or waste and this is referred to as *Poka-Yoke* or idiot proof. This is achieved by the involvement of the workforce in product and quality improvements plus the use of statistical process control (SPC) and the use of quality circles.

4. *Supplier Integration*   The aim of supplier integration is to use the supplier as an extension of the company's own facilities. To achieve this, mutual trust is vital, and JIT manufacturers should use single or dual suppliers, if possible, with long-term contracts. The views and suggestions of suppliers are often sought at all the key stages from product design to manufacture. Suppliers are expected to make sure that their products have zero defects (this is referred to as *Jidoka*), so as to minimise inspection and delays after delivery. They are also expected to make deliveries straight to the work station at a very frequent rate (two or three times a day in some cases). To make this work, information systems, such as electronic data interchange (EDI), are developed and used. Finally, if there is a choice of suppliers, the closest one will be chosen.

The Harley-Davidson Case Study

In 1978 Harley-Davidson, an American motorcycle manufacturer, tried to prove in court that Japanese motorcycle companies (Honda, Yamaha, Suzuki and Kawasaki) were dumping motor cycles below the cost of production. However during these hearings, the Japanese companies proved that they had manufacturing costs 30% lower than Harley-Davidson. The main reason for this was their use of the JIT principle.

Harley-Davidson realised that the Japanese companies had a massive competitive advantage and adopted JIT in 1982. Like many other companies Harley-Davidson faced many problems in using this system. However, they stuck to the JIT principles and once again became a world competitive company. Over a five-year time-frame, after the introduction of JIT, Harley-Davidson reduced machine set-up times by 75%, reduced warranty and scrap costs by 60% and work-in-progress by a staggering $22million. Productivity during this period at Harley-Davidson rose by 30%.

Summary of JIT

Therefore, JIT does not mean working harder, it means working smarter. Firms which have introduced JIT have often found that it is very hard to change the original working practices of the company. However, those firms which have successfully achieved a full implementation of JIT have found great rewards. Improved quality, lower overhead costs, reduced set-up times, lower scrap levels and the exposure of problems. In fact, the effect of JIT will often have a snow-ball effect leading to constant improvements – this is sometimes referred to as *Kaizen*, which means ongoing improvements. JIT is a philosophy which embraces everyone.

CONCLUSION AND SUMMARY

This chapter has looked at four of the key areas in operations management, namely capacity management, inventory control, quality control and production management systems. These four areas should be understood by all managers and management students. This is due to their increasing importance to all areas of management in understanding the processes and systems used elsewhere in the company – *promises made by one section will have important knock-on effects on other sections.*

The pace of change over the last 20 years has been nothing short of dramatic with quality of produced items increasing, product life-cycles falling and competition reaching fever pitch. To succeed in today's market place you must not simply reach but exceed customers' expectations, incorporate technological change and innovate at a very fast rate. Companies which do not continually review and update will be left behind in this tornado of international competition. One very visible result of all this change has been the increase in management stress. The correct use and understanding of all four areas will increase the efficiency of any company who is not presently using it and will subsequently reduce the stress on the management team.

Two excellent videos on OPT and JIT are *The Goal*, published by Melrose Videos (duration 55 minutes) and *Just-In-Time*, published by BBC Enterprises Training Videos (duration 25 minutes). An excellent book on production systems and the motor industry is *The Machine that Changed the World* by Womack and Jones (1990).

Finally, the area of operations management is constantly changing, however this chapter has introduced you to a number of its key areas. Books such as Waters (1996) or Lee and Schniederjans (1994) provide an excellent and full introduction to this subject.

REFERENCES AND FURTHER READING

Crosby, P.B. (1979) *Quality is Free – The Art of Making Quality Certain*, New York: McGraw-Hill.

Deming, W.E. (1986) *Out of the Crisis*, Cambridge (Mass.): MIT Press.

Foss, M. (1963) 'The Utilisation of Capital Equipment', *Survey of Current Business*, **43**.

Goldratt, E.M. and Cox, J. (1993) *The Goal – A Process of Ongoing Improvement*, 2nd edition, Aldershot: Gower Publishing.

Goldratt, E.M. and Fox, R.E. (1986) *The Race*, New York: North River Press.

Jorgenson, D.W. and Grilliches, Z. (1967) 'The Explanation of Productivity Change', *Review of Economic Studies*, **XXXIV**.

Lee, S.M. and Schniederjans, M.J. (1994) *Operations Management*, Boston: Houghton Mifflin Company.

Morishima, M. (1982) *Why has Japan Succeeded? Western Technology and The Japanese Ethos*, Cambridge: Cambridge University Press.

Oliver, N. and Wilkinson, B. (1988) *The Japanization of British Industry*, Oxford: Basil Blackwell Ltd.

Powell, T.C. (1995) 'Total Quality Management As Competitive Advantage: A Review and Empirical Study', *Strategic Management Journal*, **16**, pp. 15–37.

Rodriguez, M. (1997) 'Operations Management' assignment, MBA (Cardiff).

Schonberger, R.J. (1982) *Japanese Manufacturing Techniques: Nine Hidden Lessons in Simplicity*, New York: Free Press; London: Collier Macmillan.

Suzaki, K. (1987) *The New Manufacturing Challenge: Techniques for Continuous Improvement*, New York: The Free Press.

Voss, C. (1982) *Just in Time Manufacture*, London: IFS.

Waters, D. (1996) *Operations Management, Producing Goods and Services*, Wokingham and Reading (Mass.): Addison-Wesley.

Wild, R. (1972) *Mass-Production Management: The Design and Operations of Production Flow-line Systems*, London: John Wiley and Sons.

Womack, J.P. and Jones, D.T. (1990) *The Machine that Changed the World*, New York: Rawson Associates.

PROBLEM: MANAGEMENT OF INVENTORY

Introductory Comments

The main purposes of stock holding are:

- To enable customer orders to be satisfied from stock.
- To act as a buffer between stages of production.
- To provide secure and regular supplies of materials.
- To secure economies of scale in purchasing materials and semi-finished goods.

The best stock control policy is sought which will give decision rules for the size and timing of replenishments and procedure in stock-outs.
    The classical static model assumes:

- A single item of stock.
- All parameters known and constant.
- Instantaneous replenishment of stock.
- No variable re-order costs.

Total costs in this model – sometimes called relevant or controllable costs – are given by:

$$C = \frac{1}{2}QH + \frac{FD}{Q} \tag{1}$$

where Q is the quantity re-ordered, H is the holding costs per unit per annum, F is the fixed costs per re-order and D is annual demand.
    Costs are minimised for:

$$\bar{Q} = \sqrt{\frac{2FD}{H}} \tag{2}$$

$\bar{Q}$ is the economic order quantity (EOQ) or economic lot size (ELS) and equation (2) is known as the square root rule. Q is robust with respect to errors or estimation of parameters – an important practical advantage. When unit costs (U) are included an amount UD must be added to equation (1) but the square root rule is unchanged.
    Lead time (L) – the delay between ordering and arrival of stock – is allowed for by triggering the replenishment process when stock has fallen to the re-order level or re-order point (R). The re-order level model is often implemented as a two-bin system. with buffer stock (B) – the average stock remaining at the end of each cycle – added, the re-order level is given by:

$$R = LW + B \tag{3}$$

where W is weekly demand. Where demand is a discrete random variable, enumeration may be used to determine the optimum buffer stock and hence re-order level from equation (3). The optimal buffer stock minimises 'uncertainty costs' X where:

$$X = BSHC + SOC \tag{4}$$

In equation (4) $BSHC$ is buffer stock holding costs and SOC is stockout costs. The costs X are additional to the relevant costs in equation (1). An average value of annual demand is first used to determine the EOQ from equation (2) and hence the number of cycles. Then the buffer stock is calculated to minimise equation (4).

Sensitivity analysis can be conducted on the estimated shortage cost figure or, at greater complexity, on holding or other costs. In service level approaches to stochastic demand, re-order level is set to provide a predetermined chance that customer orders can be satisfied from stock during the lead time. The $97\frac{1}{2}\%$ vendor service level is given by:

$$R = LW + 1.96\,\sigma\sqrt{L} \tag{5}$$

where σ is the standard deviation of weekly demand and where $1.96\,\sigma\sqrt{L}$ is the level of buffer stock. Sensitivity analysis is worthwhile on the stock-out cost figures. The unit normal loss integral or service function can also be used in a service level approach. Customer service level is defined as the percentage of demand met from stock (G) where:

$$G = \frac{100Q - 19.78\sigma}{Q}\sqrt{L} \tag{6}$$

In the build-up model the length of production run is considered. With a production rate of P units per annum the EOQ is increased by the factor $\sqrt{P/P - D}$.

When quantity discounts (or economies of scale) affect the unit cost figure, the EOQ will be either at Q given by equation (2) or at one of the price-break points – the value of Q at which a lower unit cost takes effect – above the EOQ.

The classical static model can be used in cash management with procurement and interest costs being the analogues of replenishment costs and holding costs respectively.

In inventory models with periodic review, stock-takings replace the constant monitoring required by the re-order level approach. If at the stock-taking inventory is at or below the re-order level a replenishment order of fixed sized is placed – otherwise there is no re-ordering. In this periodic review, model information costs are reduced in comparison to the re-order level policy but this is achieved at the expense of increased average stock level or increased stock-out costs.

In the re-order cycle model there is no re-order level and a replenishment order of size $S - I$ is placed at each review where I is the stock on hand at review and S is a predetermined maximum level. The re-order cycle model has the advantage of generally reducing stock-out costs but with increased re-order or holding costs in comparison to the periodic review model. In the S-model there is a periodic review with re-order only when stock is at or below re-order level, S, at review. Re-order quantity is $S - I$. This model frequently gives the best results.

Zero inventory is optimal when it is cheaper to undertake production to order. Where batches of size X are ordered N times per year for:

$$m = \sqrt{\frac{2NF}{XH}} \tag{7}$$

If $m < 1$ produce to order; if $m > 2$ stock the item; if $1 < m < 2$ further investigation is required.

In the ABC classification system (PARETO analysis), category A items (the 10% or so of product range that may account for 70% + of total turnover) warrant detailed forecasting and stock control methods; category B items (say the 30% of product range accounting for 20% or so of turnover) warrant simple forecasting methods with robust estimates of EOQs; category C items (the 60% of the product range that may account for just 10% of turnover) warrant basic methods only – say a two-bin re-order system.

In the lot size inventory management technique (LIMIT), account is taken of the cost of identifying holding costs. If holding cost H is expressible as a proportion L or unit costs U then the frequency of re-order should be N where:

$$N = \sqrt{\frac{UD}{K}} \tag{8}$$

where the parameter K is given by:

$$K = \sqrt{\frac{2F}{L}} \tag{9}$$

In practice K may be estimated company-wide and substituted directly into equation (8). In materials requirements planning (MRP) demand for a final assembled product (such as a car) is 'exploded' to determine the dependent demand for the components, stocks of which can be used to damp the fluctuations in these derived demands. Use of centralised stores at a few (or a single) locations enables lower stocks to be kept at retail outlets. Coverage analysis seeks to reduce capital tied up in inventory in multi-plant organisations.

Problem

Yatis Holding Company have a fifty-week working year. The demand for a particular product stocked by Yatis is subject to random variability. Demand for this product during any one week of the working year is described by the

Table 9.6

Units demanded (X)	Probability (P)
0	0.03
1	0.06
2	0.07
3	0.09
4	0.11
5	0.21
6	0.17
7	0.12
8	0.08
9	0.06

probability distribution in Table 9.6. Demand can only be satisfied (if at all) from stocks. The stock holding costs are £40 per unit held per annum. Each time that a re-order is made a cost of £50 is incurred irrespective of the re-order size and the cost of the item is £180 per unit. There is a lead time of one week. The cost of being out of stock is estimated as £20 per unit short. Yatis Holding Company desires to minimise annual inventory costs.

Questions

1. Determine the economic order quantity.
2. Find the optimal re-order level and size of buffer stock.
3. For what range of values of the shortage cost figure would the re-order level found in question 2 remain optimal? Assume all other data at their original values. Could a similar sensitivity analysis be conducted on the holding cost figure?

PROBLEM: DEVELOPING A MODEL WHICH WILL MINIMISE THE PURCHASING WORK LOAD WITHOUT INCREASING THE AVERAGE INVENTORY

Introductory Comments

It is possible to minimise the purchasing work load without altering the average level of inventory. In situations where temporary shortages of qualified purchasing personnel can greatly affect the policy and level of customer service, companies can make exploration of this alternative advantageous. The method to be illustrated represents a very practical alternative. Assume that information on carrying costs

Table 9.7 Inventory situation at Lynda's Boutique

SKU	Sterling value used annually	Number of items ordered/year	Sterling per order	Average inventory balance (£)
Decorator lamp	10,000	4	2,500	1,250
Rattan chair	8,000	4	2,000	1,000
Rope hammock	5,000	4	1,250	625
Brass chafing dish	1,000	4	250	125
Embroidered placemat	600	4	150	75
		20 = total purchasing work load		£3,075 = average inventory balance

and ordering costs is not available. We begin by first calling the following equation:

$$N_£ = X\sqrt{A} \tag{1}$$

As X is a constant for any single inventory item it is also a constant for an entire inventory of items. $N_£$ is the economic order quantity in sterling per order and A is the annual sterling use an item per year.

Suppose we have just walked into Lynda's Boutique. She has never made any attempt to apply EOQ models and she has no cost information on purchasing or carrying costs. Her past inventory policy on the five stock-keeping units (SKUs) she stocks was to purchase them quarterly. Table 9.7 illustrates Lynda's inventory situation.

Thus for the five inventory items of our Lynda's Boutique illustration, we can rewrite equation (1) to:

$$\Sigma N_£ = (X)\Sigma(\sqrt{A})$$

and solving for X we have:

$$X = \frac{\Sigma(N_£)}{\Sigma(\sqrt{A})} \tag{2}$$

Question

1. Apply the above equation in order to minimise Lynda's purchasing work load without increasing her average inventory and interpret the results. Purchasing work load is measured in terms of the number of orders processed per year.

PART 3

Future Trends and Conclusion

10
Future trends

COMPUTER-BASED INFORMATION SYSTEMS

In previous chapters of this book we have shown how various mathematical models can be used to help or support the decision-making process. Computer-based information systems have similar objectives. Such systems enable large volumes of different types of data to be handled more systematically, quickly and efficiently. Database technology allows data to be organised and retrieved in ways which are useful to management – for instance, summaries of sales by geographical areas, individual salespeople, product line, etc., or analyses of performance against targets or budgets. Such systems are known as management information systems (MIS), while those systems which go further and provide help and support for higher level strategic and tactical decisions are often called executive information systems (EIS). These are likely to integrate all information within an organisation, to include external data relevant to the company and its markets, and to allow viewing of information on different levels, from an overall perspective of the organisation down to detail of specific products or markets. Other types of information system have been developed to serve the needs of specific departments of a company – ideally, of course, all such systems should be a part of a company-wide integrated EIS.

Marketing Information Systems and Database Marketing

A marketing information system (MkIS) collects, organises and processes the data required for a company to effectively plan and control the marketing function – internal data on costs, sales, budgets, targets, etc., and on all aspects of the marketing mix, and external data on competitors, markets and the marketing environment. In the growing number of companies using database marketing, where individual customers' and prospects' details are held on a database, this database should be at the centre of the MkIS. Database marketing enables marketers to look at customers individually, look at purchase levels, response rates to promotions, demographic details and lifestyles, so that estimates can be made of long-term customer value. It also allows customers to be quickly grouped into target market segments using many different criteria. Typical applications of database marketing now include customer care and loyalty programmes, generating and assessing sales leads, cross-selling and price or promotion testing. However, with a good relational database and the commitment from senior management and the marketing team to use it to its full potential, database marketing may also be used to target users of competitive brands, to market to new consumers captured through promotions, to test and launch new brands and to differentiate new or existing brands by the addition of features or services which customers think important or desirable. Used properly, database marketing should result in better identification of the most valuable customers, better targeting, higher brand loyalty, better product differentiation and higher cost efficiency than most mass marketing programmes.

Marketing Decision Support Systems

Decision support systems (DSS) are computer-based information systems designed to provide support to a decision process, in the form of information and analysis necessary for making that decision. They do not automate decision making – they help the decision maker to come to a decision and thus usually have an interactive capability. They are generally used for unstructured or semistructured problems, and are able to evolve to meet changing needs or new applications. Some DSS that have been developed for marketing as follows

- STRATPORT, a system developed to help top managers and corporate planners in the assessment and formulation of business planning strategies (Larreche and Srinavasan 1981, 1982).

- A decision support system for planning marketing strategies and allocating resources for a multi-store retailer (Lodish 1982).

- BEII, a system for evaluating sales prospects and launch strategies for new products (Choffray and Lilien 1986).

- TANGIBILITY, a system designed to assist marketing communication departments in monitoring sales objectives (Evans 1986).

- A decision support tool for helping marketing managers of manufacturing companies and chief buyers of retail chains to examine strategic options in competitive situations (Ambrosiadou and Singh 1986).

- A decision support system that aids in defining businesses (Rita and Moutinho 1991), developed using Expert Choice (Dyer et al. 1988) and based on the Analytical Hierarchy Process, AHP (Saaty 1980; Wind and Saaty 1980), described below.

The Aanalytic Hierarchy Process (AHP)

This is a general-purpose method, due to Thomas Saaty (1980), for modelling decision making. It permits the whole of a problem to be analysed as one unit or block by using a tree-like structure which also permits easy visualisation of the problem. For instance, marketing planners in a certain company may decide that their marketing effectiveness is best measured by three factors: profits, market share, and company image. There are then two questions to be analysed: firstly, what is the required balance among these sometimes conflicting objectives to achieve optimum marketing effectiveness, and secondly, how much impact does the use of each marketing tool available to the planners have on each objective? Let us, for simplicity, consider only three marketing tools: customer data, market analysis and financial statements. The first step in the AHP method is then to construct a tree, from the goal node (marketing effectiveness) down to the leaf nodes (marketing tools) (see Figure 10.1).

The next step is to derive relative weights for each of the nodes, showing the extent of their contribution to the higher level node to which they are connected. On the first layer, we want to know the relative importance of the three factors market share, profit and image, in contributing to marketing effectiveness. To do this, the AHP uses a method based on pairwise comparisons, which are then converted into weights. Thus it would ask questions like 'Is profit moderately more important than market share?', offering the user a scale from strongly more important through equal to strongly less important. Similarly, on the lowest level, the user would have to consider the relative importance of all pairs in the set (customer data, market analysis, financial statements) to each of the first layer nodes. Once such pairwise comparisons have been carried out for each pair of nodes at each level, weights are derived for each node (summing to 1 at each level). Weights can then be combined over the different levels of the tree to show the relationship of each node to the goal node.

Figure 10.1   AHP tree structure

The AHP would normally be carried out using specialised software such as Expert Choice, although it is possible to carry out the procedure manually in simple cases. The method's benefits lie in its ability to handle an almost unlimited range of decision problems and its ease of use. The construction of an AHP tree represents the decision maker's own perception of a problem in a highly visual form, which often stimulates further thought leading to refinements and improvements.

Knowledge-Based Systems

Traditional decision support systems, and indeed AHP, are based on numeric approaches, requiring that all relevant aspects of a decision can be quantified in some way – whether as a number, a weighting or a probability. An interesting alternative to this can be found in the newer technologies of artificial intelligence (AI), in particular knowledge-based or expert systems. The aim of the expert systems' approach is to get the computer to emulate, as far as possible, human thought processes. The knowledge contained in the system is expressed in a form similar to natural language using If ... then rules which can be processed by the computer. A typical expert system can handle rules expressed both in words and numerically, thus a medical expert system might contain a rule such as:

> If patient has spots
> and temperature > 38 degrees
> Then possible diagnoses include 'measles'

Such rules can be easily processed using specialised programming languages such as LISP or PROLOG, or expert system shells such as LEONARDO or CRYSTAL. Major benefits of this approach include easily understandable programming and high quality interaction between system and user, in particular the facility for the system to explain its reasoning and how it arrives at its decisions.

In general, expert systems are most successful at problem solving or providing decision support in fairly small, well-defined, knowledge-intensive areas where frequent decision making is required, and where expert knowledge is readily available. Many areas of marketing satisfy these criteria and expert systems have been developed in the areas of market research, automated data analysis, forecasting, product management, new product development, pricing, advertising, sales promotion, sales management, strategy and planning, and international marketing. As an example of expert system development, we now examine the COMSTRAT model, a prototype expert system in strategic marketing developed by Moutinho, Curry and Davies (1993).

The COMSTRAT Model

This model was developed, using the expert system shell LEONARDO, as a decision support tool for helping marketing managers to analyse the position of their company relative to their competitors in a particular business or product area. Following its positional analysis, it gives advice on strategies to improve the current position. Initially, its knowledge base was gleaned from academic theory – it was then enhanced through interviews with potential users.

Data is input on the current state of the industry, the marketplace, the user company and its operations in that marketplace, and competitors and their operations. Broadly, such data could be categorised as either company data or environmental data. The output of the system is a set of recommended strategies, taken from a list of possible strategies, and further specific advice on different aspects of the marketing mix. The main set of system rules therefore take the form:

$$\text{If company.attribute(I)}$$
$$\text{and company.attribute(J)}$$
$$\text{and} \ldots \ldots$$
$$\text{and environment.attribute(I)}$$
$$\text{and environment.attribute(J)}$$
$$\text{and} \ldots \ldots$$
$$\text{Then recommended strategies include strategy(I)}$$

where company.attribute(I), etc. contain information relating to attributes of the company (e.g. size, return on investment, market share) and of the environment (e.g. industry life cycle stage, number of competitors, state of the economy). Such information may have been directly input or deduced from a combination of inputs.

Operation of the model
On the first two input screens (first screen shown in Figure 10.2), the user is asked to describe the current market structure in the industry, in terms of evolutionary stage, competitive intensity, market leadership, use of new technology, potential for deriving competitive advantage, and market share and return on investment for the top three firms in the market. The user is then asked to describe his/her own company and then major competitors, in terms of market share, market share rank, company growth rate, productivity, return on investment and degree of vertical integration.

Output is in three stages: firstly, graphical screens showing the company's and competitors' relative positioning on key variables, secondly, an 'Initial Advice' screen (Figure 10.3) giving general strategic advice based on the information input; and, finally, a 'Further Advice' screen allowing dialogue between system and user, where the system asks follow-up questions in order to be able to refine the recommended strategies.

Responses to COMSTRAT
The model was tested with senior marketing managers in twenty large and successful organisations. Responses were broadly favourable, although it was felt

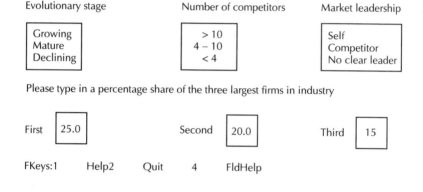

LEONARDO (c) 1986 – 1990 Creative Logic Ltd
Knowledge Base: Comstrat

THE MARKET

Please answer the following questions on the current market structure in your
industry by selecting the most appropriate option from each menu.

Evolutionary stage   Number of competitors   Market leadership

Growing		> 10		Self
Mature		4 – 10		Competitor
Declining		< 4		No clear leader

Please type in a percentage share of the three largest firms in industry

First | 25.0 | Second | 20.0 | Third | 15 |

FKeys:1   Help2   Quit   4   FldHelp

Figure 10.2   Input screen

Initial advice

The details given indicate the following general strategies are
suitable. Try to improve quality of your product or service –
quality is a major influence on profitability. Try to increase your
productivity and streamline costs. As the market is maturing,
there is likely to be more competition for customers, and
winners will be those who can produce good value through
efficient production. Introduction of new product lines often
increases market share of followers – but may decrease return
on investment. Increased marketing expenditure should increase
your market share – but may decrease return on investment.

More specific advice is available by answering the questions
which follow. Hit any key to continue.

Figure 10.3   Initial advice screen

that COMSTRAT was too general and systems designed for specific industries would be more useful. This led to the development of the BANKSTRAT model (Davies, Moutinho and Curry 1995a), advising on marketing strategy for banks and building societies.

Benefits of Expert Systems

Expert systems such as COMSTRAT can serve a number of important functions for marketing managers. Firstly, they stimulate and challenge managers to explore new options, challenge assumptions, play 'what-if?' games and critically assess their own strategic marketing expertise, all of which could improve their decision making. Secondly, these systems provide a means of bridging gaps between academics and practitioners, as well as transferring strategic marketing expertise between different organisational levels, thus allowing for more uniform implementation of policies. Thirdly, expert systems can serve as a vehicle for systematically accumulating organisational knowledge. Finally, they can be used as training tools for staff in specialised areas of marketing.

Neural Networks

Another application of artificial intelligence techniques which is becoming of increasing interest to marketers is that of neural networks (NN), an approach rooted in both physiology and psychology. The aim is to work with a direct analogy of the human brain as a set of interconnected processing nodes operating in parallel. Knowledge is acquired by the NN through a process of learning from examples presented to it.

The most basic NN model is the 'Perceptron' (Figure 10.4), originally suggested by Rosenblatt (1958) and further examined by Minsky and Papert (1969). This consists of a layer of input nodes each of which is potentially connected to each node in a layer of outputs. As this has serious limitations, the model was extended to allow one or more 'hidden layers', as in Figure 10.5.

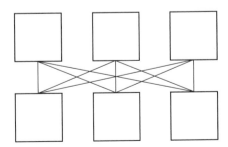

Figure 10.4   The 'Perceptron' model

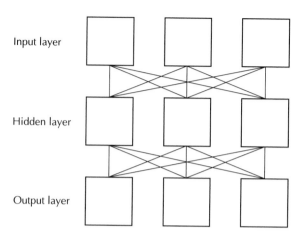

Input layer

Hidden layer

Output layer

Figure 10.5   A neural network with one hidden layer

Each node in the hidden layer may receive signals from each node in the input layer, in turn passing on signals to each node in the output layer. The most common scheme for learning is known as the 'backpropagation algorithm', an extension of an iterative procedure known as the 'Delta Rule', whereby the weights for each node are adjusted in proportion to the difference between the given values of the output nodes in the training set of examples and the values predicted by the network. For the hidden layer, the algorithm calculates imputed values for these errors at each stage by dividing the output layer error among the hidden nodes. An element of linearity is brought in through the use of threshold levels for each hidden layer node. The threshold effect is modelled by a suitable continuous function such as the Sigmoid function (Figure 10.6).

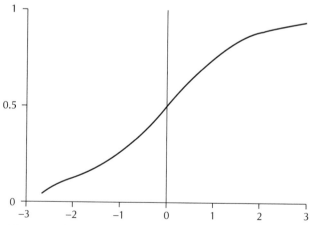

Figure 10.6   The Sigmoid function

Recently, researchers have begun to investigate the potential for using NNs in the prediction of consumer behaviour. The NN learns from a 'training set' of consumer data, the inputs being consumer opinions and characteristics and the outputs such variables as satisfaction with product, intention to purchase/repurchase, and likelihood of recommending product to others. It is hypothesised that the hidden layer nodes represent respondents' less easily articulated attitudes and beliefs which influence satisfaction and purchase decisions, and which can be identified and labelled. Examination of the network can thus provide deeper insights into consumer behaviour, and help marketers in market segmentation and in developing appeals to different consumer types.

An example of this research is a study carried out on user satisfaction with automated teller machines (ATMs) (Davies, Moutinho and Curry, 1995b). Training data was gathered from 380 consumers and input variables for the NN were expectations of ATMs, perceived risk from using ATMs, confidence in functioning of ATMs, respondent age and value for money – a rating of ATM service in terms of the charges paid to use it. Outputs were overall satisfaction with ATM use, likelihood of recommendation to others, extent of ATM use in terms of services offered and frequency of ATM use. Data was analysed using the NN software NeuralWorks, from NeuralWare, Inc., on a network with a single hidden layer of four nodes. After running the network until it appeared that no further improvement could be made to the quality of its predictions, the network connection weights were established as shown in Table 10.1.

Table 10.1 Network connection weights

To hidden node	From input node				
	Expectations	Perceived risk	Confidence	Age	Value for money
1	−0.60	0.37	−0.97	−1.44	0.55
2	−1.22	0.59	−0.65	1.14	−1.63
3	1.58	−0.76	1.27	−0.42	1.50
4	0.88	−0.18	0.77	−0.92	−0.34

To output node	From hidden node			
	1	2	3	4
Satisfaction	−0.71	−0.66	0.92	0.44
Recommend to others	−0.46	−0.04	1.61	0.41
Full use of services	−0.03	−0.91	0.58	−0.53
Frequency of use	0.77	−0.82	0.63	0.53

The signs (+ or −) and values of the network connection weights were used to deduce suitable intermediate attributes with which to label the hidden nodes, i.e.

- Disaffected youth.

- Technophobic.

- Pro-technology.

- Cost conscious.

Thus the analysis pointed to four different attitudinal types of ATM users. Only the pro-technology segment appeared fully satisfied with ATM services. The disaffected youth segment was linked with low expectations and confidence and high perceived risk, linked negatively with age but positively with value for money. Looking at the outputs, it was linked positively with frequency of use but negatively with other outputs. This led to a characterisation of the attitude of a segment of young consumers (possibly students or others who have free banking) who use ATMs frequently but often experience problems with their use.

The node labelled 'technophobic' was the only one linked positively with age, and linked with low expectations, low confidence, high perceived risk and an opinion that ATMs did not give value for money. Connections to all output nodes were negative. This node was thought to characterise an attitude of mistrust of technology, often found among older consumers.

The last two nodes showed a more positive attitude towards ATMs, linking with high expectations, high confidence and low perceived risk. Where the link from 'value for money' was also positive (hidden node 3), this led to all positive outputs – an attitude of satisfaction with, and willingness to use, ATMs, which was labelled 'pro-technology'. Where the link from 'value for money' was negative (hidden node 4), this led to positive outputs on all but 'full use of services'. It was felt that the perception of not getting value for money could well be linked with the limited extent of service use, and the attitude was characterised as 'cost conscious'.

The insights gained into consumer attitudes by this analysis can obviously be used by bank marketing managers to develop marketing programmes for different attitudinal types. Analysis of the network as a whole can also indicate relationships between different variables – in this case, there is a correlation between 'satisfaction' and 'recommendation to others', and it can be said that high expectations which are confirmed lead to satisfaction, while low expectations which are confirmed lead to dissatisfaction.

Much work has yet to be done regarding neural network techniques in behavioural analysis. In particular, results need to be compared to those obtained from more traditional statistical methods of analysis, and different types of network need to be tested.

Optimisation Techniques Using Approximate Algorithms

The final section of this chapter looks at a new generation of optimisation techniques – genetic algorithms, tabu search and simulated annealing. These techniques are, so far, relatively unknown in the field of marketing management, but show much potential for use in practical applications.

Genetic Algorithms

Genetic algorithms, invented by Holland (1975), attempt to mimic some of the processes of natural evolution and selection. The first step is to represent a valid or legal solution to the problem under consideration by a string of genes that can take on some value from a specified range or alphabet. This string of genes is called a chromosome. Then an initial population of legal chromosomes is constructed at random and the fitness of each chromosome measured – high fitness values indicate better solutions than low fitness values. The fitter chromosomes are then selected to produce 'offspring' to form the next generation – these inherit the best characteristics of both parents. After this process has been repeated many times, the resulting population should be substantially fitter than the original population – i.e. the population is likely to include optimal or near-optimal solutions. A complete and detailed description of the technique can be found in Goldberg (1989).

Example

A multi-outlet retail company has three existing outlets and wishes to build at least two further stores. The company has a choice of four sites. Which should it use in order to create the best network of stores in terms of profitability, attractiveness to customers, or other important criteria? Here we could represent the possible networks of stores by chromosomes, each containing seven genes, each of which represents one existing or possible site. If the individual gene is represented by 1, this indicates the site is used; if it is represented by 0, the site is not used. Thus the chromosome {1 1 1 0 1 1 0} represents a network where sites 1, 2 and 3 (the existing network) and sites 5 and 6 are used, while sites 4 and 7 remain unused. We will assume for the purposes of the example that the company would consider closing existing sites, if not required for the optimal network.

There are different fitness functions which could be used, depending on the most important factors to the company. They would be likely to include variables such as the population within a specified radius of the site, mean household expenditure on the company's products in that area and number of competitors. We will assume that the company has found a suitable function. For simplicity, let us consider a population of six chromosomes:

C1	1010011	fitness	=	145
C2	0110101	fitness	=	376
C3	1110001	fitness	=	203
C4	1101100	fitness	=	178
C5	1101001	fitness	=	329
C6	0010011	fitness	=	124

The fittest chromosomes are C2 and C5 so they will be selected for reproduction. The main way of generating offspring is by using a crossover operator, e.g. a one-point crossover at position 3 would mean that the new chromosomes would take the first three genes of one parent and the last four genes of the other, thus producing the new chromosomes

C7	0111001
C8	1100101

If the fitness values calculated for one or both of these chromosomes were greater than 376 (C2), then we have found a better network than any in the original population.

The advantages of using genetic algorithms for this problem are: (a) they find an optimal or near-optimal network in reasonable time, (b) the strength of alternative networks can be easily compared and (c) poor networks can be easily identified and thus avoided. However, the performance of genetic algorithms is highly dependent on the suitability of the fitness function used.

Tabu Search

Tabu search is an iterative procedure for solving discrete combinatorial optimisation problems. It has been used very successfully in the areas of production planning, job-shop scheduling and vehicle routeing. The basic idea (Glover, Taillard and de Werra, 1993) is to explore the search space of all feasible solutions by a sequence of moves from one solution to another, each move seeking a better solution. However, for each iteration, some moves are classified as tabu (or taboo) – this stops the procedure cycling endlessly through particular move sequences, and moves it on from locally optimal but not globally optimal solutions. In certain circumstances, however, the tabu may be overridden. Hurley, Stephens and Moutinho (1994) consider the application of tabu search to market segmentation, in particular, the deriving of a most likely product-market structure from scanner panel data.

Simulated Annealing

Simulated annealing is a computational technique for finding near globally-minimum-cost solutions to large optimisation problems. Derived from statistical mechanics, the method has an analogy with the way that liquids freeze and crystallise, or metals cool and anneal. At high temperatures, the molecules of a liquid move freely, but at lower temperatures movement is restricted and the atoms are often able to line themselves up and form a completely regular crystal – the state of minimum energy for the system, corresponding to the optimal solution in an optimisation problem. To use this method for mathematical problems, one needs:

- A method of representing possible solutions as system configurations.

- A generator of random changes, known as moves, in a configuration; such moves typically involve changing one of the solution parameters.

- An objective function whose minimisation or maximisation is the goal of the problem.

- A control parameter (analog of temperature) and an annealing schedule which indicates when and how this parameter is lowered from high values to lower values.

The general principle is that, from an initial solution, the system goes through a succession of moves to enable it to arrive at the optimal solution. A move which lowers the objective function will always be accepted, while moves which do not will still have a probability of acceptance to ensure that the system does not stick at a local minimum. This probability may be changed by the annealing schedule.

Example

Simulated annealing can be used to design an optimal allocation of sales territories over a large geographical area. We assume that the area can be divided into small sales coverage units (SCUs) for each of which relevant statistical information is obtainable. The territory design must be such that each territory is a block of contiguous SCUs and all territories have approximately equal sales workload and sales potential. In order to satisfy these last two constraints, we will need to derive formulae for sales workload and sales potential.

For each customer, sales workload can be expressed as:

no. of calls × (average length of call + travelling time)

and this can be summed over all customers in each SCU.

Sales potential for an existing customer can be measured by:

(sales for preceding time period) × (likelihood customer remains loyal)

while sales potential for prospects can be measured by:

(estimated value of sales if prospect converted) × (likelihood of conversion)

These can likewise be summed over all customers in each SCU.

An expression will also be required for the profit associated with each customer – this is the margin on sales to that customer, less the cost of servicing the customer. Thus the profit per SCU can be derived.

The simulated annealing model would then commence with an initial territory design, where the contiguity condition was satisfied and where sales workloads and potentials were equal to within an acceptable margin of error. The system would compute the profit for this design, then consider a move of transferring one SCU from one territory to another. If the profit for the new design was higher and the equality of workload and potential constraints were satisfied, the move would be accepted. The move would also have a probability of acceptance if it did not increase profit. This process would continue until the control parameter had been reduced, in accordance with the annealing schedule, to its lowest level at which point an optimal design should be achieved. The exact values of the control parameter and the annealing schedule would have to be determined by experimentation.

CONCLUSION

This chapter has covered some of the main advances that are being made in the use of computer models in marketing. Research is constantly continuing to discover new ways in which computer analysis can aid the marketer in researching the marketplace.

REFERENCES

Ambrosiadou, V. and Singh, M. (1986) 'Strategic Decision Making in Competitive Marketing Channels Using a Differential Games Framework', *IEEE Proceedings*, July, pp. 301–10.

Choffray, J. and Lilien, G. (1986) 'A Decision Support System for Evaluating Sales Prospects and Launch Strategies for New Products', *Industrial Marketing Management*, **15**, pp. 75–85.

Davies, F., Moutinho, L. and Curry, B. (1995a) 'Construction and Testing of a Knowledge-based System in Retail Bank Marketing', *The International Journal of Bank Marketing*, **13** (2), pp. 4–14.

Davies, F., Moutinho, L. and Curry, B. (1995b) 'ATMs – Linking Consumer Perceptions and Behaviour: A Neural Network Approach', *Proceedings of the Marketing Education Group Annual Conference*, Bradford.

Dyer, R., Forman, E., Forman, E. and Douglas, G. (1988) *Marketing Decisions Using Expert Choice*, Pittsburgh: Decision Support Systems, Inc.

Evans, M. (1986) 'Software system monitors sales objectives', *Marketing News*, **20** (6), 14 March, p. 1

Glover, F., Taillard, E. and de Werra, D. (1993) 'A User's Guide to Tabu Search', *Annals of Operations Research*, **41**, pp. 3–28.

Goldberg, D.E. (1989) *Genetic Algorithms in Search, Optimization and Machine Learning*, Reading (Mass.): Addison Wesley.

Holland, J.H. (1975) *Adaption in Natural and Artificial Systems*, Ann Arbor: University of Michigan Press.

Hurley, S., Stephens, N.M. and Moutinho, L. (1994) 'Approximate Algorithms for Marketing Management Problems', *Proceedings of the Marketing Education Group Annual Conference*, **II**, pp. 522–31.

Larreche, J.C. and Srinavasan, V. (1981) 'STRATPORT: A Decision Support System for Strategic Planning', *Journal of Marketing*, **45** (4), Fall, pp. 39–52.

Larreche, J.C. and Srinavasan, V. (1982) 'STRATPORT: A Model for the Evaluation and Formulation of Business Portfolio Strategies', *Management Science*, **28** (9), September, pp. 979–1001.

LEONARDO (Expert System Shell), Copyright Software Directions (London) 1992, Creative Logic Ltd 1986–91.

Lodish, L. (1982) 'A Marketing Decision Support System for Retailers', *Marketing Science*, **1** (1), Winter, pp. 31–56.

Minsky, M. and Papert, S. (1969) *Perceptrons*, Cambridge (Mass.): MIT Press.

Moutinho, L., Curry, B. and Davies, F. (1993) 'The COMSTRAT Model: Development of an Expert System in Strategic Marketing', *Journal of General Management*, **18** (4), Autumn, pp. 32–47.

Rita, P. and Moutinho. L. (1991) 'The Use of the Analytic Hierarchy Process (AHP) in Business Definition: A Marketing Decision Support System', University of Wales, Cardiff Business School.

Rosenblatt, F. (1958) 'The Perceptron: A Probability Model for Information Storage and Organisation in the Brain', *Psychological Review*, **65** (6).

Saaty, T.L. (1980) *The Analytic Hierarchy Process*, New York: McGraw Hill.

Wind, Y. and Saaty, T.L. (1980) 'Marketing Applications of the Analytic Hierarchy Process', *Management Science*, July, pp. 641–58.

Conclusion

This book has attempted to draw together the many different types of quantitative techniques, taken from various disciplines, which the marketing student or practitioner is likely to need at some time during his or her career. Due to the length of the book and the number of areas included, detailed coverage of particular areas has not been possible, so the reader needing more detail of particular methods or further guidance on how to use them is referred to the bibliographies at the end of each chapter. The marketing world continues to adapt techniques from other disciplines to its own needs (particularly, nowadays, computer-based techniques) and the reader wishing to keep up with current developments is referred to one of the excellent marketing journals available in most university libraries (e.g. *Journal of Marketing, Marketing Science, Marketing Letters, International Journal of Research in Marketing, Journal of the Academy of Marketing Science, European Journal of Marketing*), or to journals more specific to their field (e.g. *Journal of Marketing Research, Journal of Services Marketing, Journal of Consumer Research, Journal of Direct Marketing, Journal of Interactive Marketing, Journal of Database Marketing, Journal of Advertising, Journal of Advertising Research, Journal of Product Innovation Management, Industrial Marketing Management*).

We hope that you have found this book useful, and wish you the best of luck in your marketing career!

Appendix A
Formulae and statistical tables

Contents

The tables on pages 303–14 have been reproduced from Kmietowicz, Z.W. and Yannoulis, Y., *Statistical Tables for Economics, Business and Social Studies*, Harlow: Longman, with permission. The original sources for pages 313 and 314 respectively are Glasser, G.J. and Winters, R. 'Critical values of the coefficient of rank correlations for testing the hypothesis of independence', *Biometrika*, **48**, 1961 and Durbin, J. and Watson, G.S. 'Testing for serial correlation in least squares regression', *Biometrika*, **38**, pp. 159–77, 1951.

FORMULAE FOR SIMPLE RANDOM SAMPLING

Mean $\bar{x} = \dfrac{\sum x}{n}$

Variance $\sigma^2 = \dfrac{\sum_{i=1}^{N}(X_i - \mu)^2}{N}$

Standard deviation σ is the square root of the variance

Standard error of sample mean $s_{\bar{x}} = \dfrac{s}{\sqrt{n}} = \dfrac{\sqrt{\sum_{i=1}^{n}(x_i - \bar{x})^2 / n - 1}}{\sqrt{n}}$

95% confidence interval is $\bar{x} \pm 1.96\dfrac{s}{\sqrt{n}}$

Precision of estimate of sample mean (at 95% level of confidence) $= \pm 1.96\dfrac{s}{\sqrt{n}}$.

NORMAL DISTRIBUTION (AREAS)

Example

$$Pr(0 \le z \le 1.96) = 0.4750$$
$$Pr(z \ge 1.96) = 0.5 - 0.4750$$
$$= 0.025$$

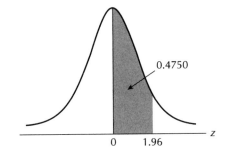

z \ z	.00	.01	.02	.03	.04	.05	.06	.07	.08	.09
0.0	.0000	.0040	.0080	.0120	.0160	.0199	.0239	.2979	.0319	.0359
0.1	.0398	.0438	.0478	.0517	.0557	.0596	.0636	.0675	.0714	.0753
0.2	.0793	.0832	.0871	.0910	.0948	.0987	.1026	.1064	.1103	.1141
0.3	.1179	.1217	.1255	.1293	.1331	.1368	.1406	.1443	.1480	.1517
0.4	.1554	.1591	.1628	.1664	.1700	.1736	.1772	.1808	.1844	.1879
0.5	.1915	.1950	.1985	.2019	.2054	.2088	.2123	.2157	.2190	.2224
0.6	.2257	.2291	.2324	.2357	.2389	.2422	.2454	.2486	.2517	.2549
0.7	.2580	.2611	.2642	.2673	.2704	.2734	.2764	.2794	.2823	.2852
0.8	.2881	.2910	.2939	.2967	.2995	.3023	.3051	.3078	.3106	.3133
0.9	.3159	.3186	.3212	.3238	.3264	.3289	.3315	.3340	.3365	.3389
1.0	.3413	.3438	.3461	.3485	.3508	.3531	.3554	.3577	.3599	.3621
1.1	.3643	.3665	.3686	.3708	.3729	.3749	.3770	.3790	.3810	.3830
1.2	.3849	.3869	.3888	.3907	.3925	.3944	.3962	.3980	.3997	.4015
1.3	.4032	.4049	.4066	.4082	.4099	.4115	.4131	.4147	.4162	.4177
1.4	.4192	.4207	.4222	.4236	.4251	.4265	.4279	.4292	.4306	.4319
1.5	.4332	.4345	.4357	.4370	.4382	.4394	.4406	.4418	.4429	.4441
1.6	.4452	.4463	.4474	.4484	.4495	.4505	.4515	.4525	.4535	.4545
1.7	.4554	.4564	.4573	.4582	.4591	.4599	.4608	.4616	.4625	.4633
1.8	.4641	.4649	.4656	.4664	.4671	.4678	.4686	.4693	.4699	.4706
1.9	.4713	.4719	.4726	.4732	.4738	.4744	.4750	.4756	.4761	.4767
2.0	.4772	.4778	.4783	.4788	.4793	.4798	.4803	.4808	.4812	.4817
2.1	.4821	.4826	.4830	.4834	.4838	.4842	.4846	.4850	.4854	.4857
2.2	.4861	.4864	.4868	.4871	.4875	.4878	.4881	.4884	.4887	.4890
2.3	.4893	.4896	.4898	.4901	.4904	.4906	.4909	.4911	.4913	.4916
2.4	.4918	.4920	.4922	.4925	.4927	.4929	.4931	.4932	.4934	.4936
2.5	.4938	.4940	.4941	.4943	.4945	.4946	.4948	.4949	.4951	.4952
2.6	.4953	.4955	.4956	.4957	.4959	.4960	.4961	.4962	.4963	.4964
2.7	.4965	.4966	.4967	.4968	.4969	.4970	.4971	.4972	.4973	.4974
2.8	.4974	.4975	.4976	.4977	.4977	.4978	.4979	.4979	.4980	.4981
2.9	.4981	.4982	.4982	.4983	.4984	.4984	.4985	.4985	.4986	.4986
3.0	.4987	.4987	.4987	.4988	.4988	.4989	.4989	.4989	.4990	.4990

χ^2-DISTRIBUTION CRITICAL POINTS

Example

$Pr(\chi^2 > 23.8277) = 0.25$
$Pr(\chi^2 > 31.4104) = 0.05$
   for $df = 20$
$Pr(\chi^2 > 37.5662) = 0.01$

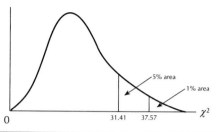

	Pr						
df	0.250	0.100	0.050	0.025	0.010	0.005	0.001
1	1.32330	2.70554	3.84146	5.02389	6.63490	7.87944	10.828
2	2.77259	4.60517	5.99146	7.37776	9.21034	10.5966	13.816
3	4.10834	6.25139	7.81473	9.34840	11.3449	12.8382	16.266
4	5.38527	7.77944	9.48773	11.1433	13.2767	14.8603	18.467
5	6.62568	9.23636	11.0705	12.8325	15.0863	16.7496	20.515
6	7.84080	10.6446	12.5916	14.4494	16.8119	18.5476	22.458
7	9.03715	12.0710	14.0671	16.0128	18.4753	20.2777	24.322
8	10.2189	13.3616	15.5073	17.5345	20.0902	21.9550	26.125
9	11.3888	14.6837	16.9190	19.0228	21.6660	23.5894	27.877
10	12.5489	15.9872	18.3070	20.4832	23.2093	25.1882	29.588
11	13.7007	17.2750	19.6751	21.9200	24.7250	26.7568	31.264
12	14.8454	18.5493	21.0261	23.3367	26.2170	28.2995	32.909
13	15.9839	19.8119	22.3620	24.7356	27.6882	29.8195	34.528
14	17.1169	21.0641	23.6848	26.1189	29.1412	31.3194	36.123
15	18.2451	22.3071	24.9958	27.4884	30.5779	32.8013	37.697
16	19.3689	23.5418	26.2962	28.8454	31.9999	34.2672	39.252
17	20.4887	24.7690	27.5871	30.1910	33.4087	35.7185	40.790
18	21.6049	25.9894	28.8693	31.5264	34.8053	37.1565	42.312
19	22.7178	27.2036	30.1435	32.8523	36.1909	38.5823	43.820
20	23.8277	28.4120	31.4104	34.1696	37.5662	39.9968	45.315
21	24.9348	29.6151	32.6706	35.4789	38.9322	41.4011	46.797
22	26.0393	30.8133	33.9244	36.7807	40.2894	42.7957	48.268
23	27.1413	32.0069	35.1725	38.0756	41.6384	44.1813	49.728
24	28.2412	33.1962	36.4150	39.3641	42.9798	45.5585	51.179
25	29.3389	34.3816	37.6525	40.6465	44.3141	46.9279	52.618
26	30.4346	35.5632	38.8851	41.9232	45.6417	48.2899	54.052
27	31.5284	36.7412	40.1133	43.1945	46.9629	49.6449	55.476
28	32.6205	37.9159	41.3371	44.4608	48.2782	50.9934	56.892
29	33.7109	39.0875	42.5570	45.7223	49.5879	52.3356	58.301
30	34.7997	40.2560	43.7730	46.9792	50.8922	53.6720	59.703
40	45.6160	51.8051	55.7585	59.3417	63.6907	66.7660	73.402
50	56.3336	63.1671	67.5048	71.4202	76.1539	79.4900	86.661
60	66.9815	74.3970	79.0819	83.2977	88.3794	91.9517	99.607
70	77.5767	85.5270	90.5312	95.0232	100.425	104.215	112.317
80	88.1303	96.5782	101.879	106.629	112.329	116.321	124.839
90	98.6499	107.565	113.145	118.136	124.116	128.299	137.208
100	109.141	118.498	124.342	129.561	135.807	140.169	149.449
$Z^\dagger$	+0.6745	+1.2816	+1.6449	+1.9600	+2.3263	+2.25758	+3.0902

For df greater than 100, the expression

$$\sqrt{2\chi^2} - \sqrt{(2k-1)} = Z$$

follows the standardised normal distribution, where k represents the degrees of freedom.

STUDENT'S *t*-DISTRIBUTION CRITICAL POINTS

Example

$\Pr(t > 2.086) = 0.025$

$\Pr(t > 1.725) = 0.05$

for $df = 20$

$\Pr(|t| > 1.725) = 0.10$

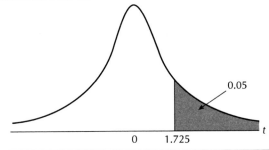

df \ Pr	0.25 0.50	0.10 0.20	0.05 0.10	0.025 0.05	0.01 0.02	0.005 0.010	0.001 0.002
1	1.000	3.078	6.314	12.706	31.821	63.657	318.31
2	0.816	1.886	2.920	4.303	6.965	9.925	22.327
3	0.765	1.638	2.353	3.182	4.541	5.841	10.214
4	0.741	1.533	2.132	2.776	3.747	4.604	7.173
5	0.727	1.476	2.015	2.571	3.365	4.032	5.893
6	0.718	1.440	1.943	2.447	3.143	3.707	5.208
7	0.711	1.415	1.895	2.365	2.998	3.499	4.785
8	0.706	1.397	1.860	2.306	2.896	3.355	4.501
9	0.703	1.383	1.833	2.262	2.821	3.250	4.297
10	0.700	1.372	1.812	2.228	2.764	3.169	4.144
11	0.697	1.363	1.796	2.201	2.718	3.106	4.025
12	0.695	1.356	1.782	2.179	2.681	3.055	3.930
13	0.694	1.350	1.771	2.160	2.650	3.012	3.852
14	0.692	1.345	1.761	2.145	2.624	2.977	3.787
15	0.691	1.341	1.753	2.131	2.602	2.947	3.733
16	0.690	1.337	1.746	2.120	2.583	2.921	3.686
17	0.689	1.333	1.740	2.110	2.567	2.898	3.646
18	0.,688	1.330	1.734	2.101	2.552	2.878	3.610
19	0.688	1.328	1.729	2.093	2.539	2.861	3.579
20	0.687	1.325	1.725	2.086	2.528	2.845	3.552
21	0.686	1.323	1.721	2.080	2.518	2.831	3.527
22	0.686	1.321	1.717	2.074	2.5098	2.819	3.505
23	0.685	1.319	1.714	2.069	2.500	2.807	3.485
24	0.685	1.318	1.711	2.064	2.492	2.797	3.467
25	0.684	1.316	1.708	2.060	2.485	2.787	3.450
26	0.684	1.315	1.706	2.056	2.479	2.779	3.435
27	0.684	1.314	1.703	2.052	2.473	2.771	3.421
28	0.683	1.313	1.701	2.048	2.467	2.763	3.408
29	0.683	1.311	1.699	2.045	2.462	2.756	3.396
30	0.683	1.310	1.697	2.042	2.457	2.750	3.385
40	0.681	1.303	1.684	2.021	2.423	2.704	3.307
60	0.679	1.296	1.671	2.000	2.390	2.660	3.232
120	0.677	1.289	1.658	1.980	2.358	2.167	3.160
∞	0.674	1.282	1.645	1.960	2.326	2.576	3.090

Note: The smaller probability shown at the head of each column is the area in one tail; the larger probability is the area in both tails.

F - DISTRIBUTION

Example

$\Pr(F > 1.59) = 0.25$
$\Pr(F > 2.42) = 0.10$
$\quad$ for df $N_1 = 10$
$\Pr(F > 3.14) = 0.05$
$\quad$ and $N_2 = 9$
$\Pr(F > 5.26) = 0.01$

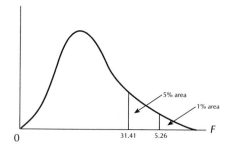

df for denominator						df for numerator N_1						

N_2	Pr	1	2	3	4	5	6	7	8	9	10	11	12
	.25	5.83	7.50	8.20	8.58	8.82	8.98	9.10	9.19	9.26	9.32	9.36	9.41
1	.10	39.9	49.5	53.6	55.8	57.2	58.2	58.9	59.4	59.9	60.2	60.5	60.7
	.05	161	200	216	225	230	234	237	239	241	242	243	244
	.25	2.57	3.00	3.15	3.23	3.28	3.31	3.34	3.35	3.37	3.38	3.39	3.39
2	.10	8.53	9.00	9.16	9.24	9.29	9.33	0.35	9.37	9.38	9.39	9.40	9.41
	.05	18.5	19.0	19.2	19.2	19.3	19.3	19.4	19.4	19.4	19.4	19.4	19.4
	.01	98.5	99.0	99.2	99.2	99.3	99.3	99.4	99.4	99.4	99.4	99.4	99.4
	.25	2.02	2.28	2.36	2.39	2.41	2.42	2.43	2.44	2.44	2.44	2.45	2.45
3	.10	5.54	5.46	f.39	5.34	5.31	5.28	5.27	5.25	5.24	5.23	5.22	5.22
	.05	10.1	9.55	9.28	9.12	9.01	8.94	8.89	8.85	8.81	8.79	8.76	8.74
	.01	34.1	30.8	29.5	28.7	28.2	27.9	27.7	27.5	27.3	27.2	27.1	27.1
	.25	1.81	2.00	2.05	2.06	2.07	2.08	2.08	2.08	2.08	2.08	2.08	2.08
4	.10	4.54	4.32	4.19	4.11	4.05	4.01	3.98	3.95	3.94	3.92	3.91	3.90
	.05	7.71	6.94	6.59	6.39	6.26	6.16	6.09	6.04	6.00	5.96	5.94	5.91
	.01	21.2	18.0	16.7	16.0	15.5	15.2	15.0	14.8	14.7	14.5	14.4	14.4
	.25	1.69	1.85	1.88	1.89	1.89	1.89	1.89	1.89	1.89	1.89	1.89	1.89
5	.10	4.06	3.78	3.62	3.52	3.45	3.40	3.37	3.34	3.32	3.30	3.28	3.27
	.05	6.61	5.79	5.41	5.19	5.05	4.95	4.88	4.82	4.77	4.74	4.71	4.68
	.01	16.3	13.3	12.1	11.4	11.0	10.7	10.5	10.3	10.2	10.1	9.96	9.89
	.25	1.62	1.76	1.78	1.79	1.79	1.78	1.78	1.78	1.77	1.77	1.77	1.77
6	.10	3.78	3.46	3.29	3.18	3.11	3.05	3.01	2.98	2.96	2.94	2.92	2.90
	.05	5.99	5.14	4.76	4.53	4.39	4.28	4.21	4.15	4.10	4.06	4.03	4.00
	.01	13.7	10.9	9.78	9.15	8.75	8.47	8.26	8.10	7.98	7.87	7.79	7.22
	.25	1.57	1.70	1.72	1.72	1.71	1.71	1.70	1.70	1.69	1.69	1.69	1.68
7	.10	3.59	3.26	3.07	2.96	2.88	2.83	2.78	2.75	2.72	2.70	2.68	2.67
	.05	5.59	4.47	4.35	4.12	3.97	3.87	3.79	3.73	3.68	3.64	3.60	3.57
	.01	12.2	9.55	8.45	7.85	7.46	7.19	6.99	6.84	6.72	6.62	6.54	6.47
	.25	1.54	1.66	1.67	1.66	1.66	1.65	1.64	1.64	1.63	1.63	1.63	1.62
8	.10	3.46	3.11	2.92	2.81	2.73	2.67	2.62	2.59	2.56	2.54	2.52	2.50
	.05	5.32	4.46	4.07	3.84	3.69	3.58	3.50	3.44	2.39	2.35	3.31	3.28
	.01	11.3	8.65	7.59	7.01	6.63	6.37	6.18	6.03	5.91	5.81	5.73	5.67
	.25	1.51	1.62	1.63	1.63	1.62	1.61	1.60	1.60	1.59	1.59	1.58	1.58
9	.10	3.36	2.01	2.81	2.69	2.61	2.55	2.51	2.47	2.44	2.42	2.40	2.38
	.05	5.12	4.26	3.86	3.63	3.48	3.37	3.29	3.23	3.19	3.14	3.10	3.07
	.01	10.6	8.02	6.99	6.42	6.06	5.80	5.61	5.47	5.35	5.26	5.18	5.11

F - DISTRIBUTION (continued)

15	20	24	30	40	50	60	100	120	200	500	∞	Pr	N_2
				df for numerator N_1									*df* for denominator
9.49	9.58	9.63	9.67	9.71	9.74	9.76	9.78	9.80	9.82	9.84	9.85	.25	
61.2	61.7	62.0	62.3	62.5	62.7	62.8	63.0	63.1	63.2	63.3	63.3	.10	1
246	248	249	250	251	252	252	253	253	254	254	254	.05	
3.41	3.43	3.43	3.44	3.45	3.45	3.46	3.47	3.47	3.48	3.48	3.48	.25	
9.42	9.44	9.45	9.46	9.47	9.47	9.47	9.48	9.48	9.49	9.49	9.49	.10	2
19.4	19.4	19.5	19.5	19.5	19.5	19.5	19.5	19.5	19.5	19.5	19.5	.05	
99.4	99.4	99.5	99.5	99.5	99.5	99.5	99.5	99.5	99.5	99.5	99.5	.01	
2.46	2.46	2.46	2.47	2.47	2.47	2.47	2.47	2.47	2.47	2.47	2.47	.25	
5.20	5.18	5.18	5.17	5.16	5.15	5.15	5.14	5.14	5.14	5.14	5.13	.10	3
8.70	8.66	8.64	8.62	8.59	8.58	8.57	8.55	8.55	8.54	8.53	8.53	.05	
26.9	26.7	26.6	26.5	26.4	26.4	26.3	26.2	26.2	26.2	26.1	26.1	.01	
2.08	2.08	2.08	2.08	2.08	2.08	2.08	2.08	2.08	2.08	2.08	2.08	.25	
3.87	3.84	3.83	3.82	3.80	3.80	3.79	3.78	3.78	3.77	3.76	3.76	.10	4
5.86	5.80	5.77	5.75	5.72	5.70	5.69	5.66	5.66	5.65	5.64	5.63	.05	
14.2	14.0	13.9	13.8	13.7	13.7	13.7	13.6	13.6	13.5	13.5	13.5	.01	
1.89	1.88	1.88	1.88	1.88	1.88	1.87	1.87	1.87	1.87	1.87	1.87	.25	
3.24	3.21	3.19	3.17	3.16	3.15	3.14	3.13	3.12	3.12	3.11	3.10	.10	5
4.62	4.56	4.53	4.50	4.46	4.44	4.43	4.41	4.40	4.39	4.37	4.36	.05	
9.72	9.55	9.47	9.38	9.29	9.24	9.20	9.13	9.11	9.08	9.04	9.02	.01	
1.76	1.76	1.75	1.75	1.75	1.75	1.74	1.74	1.74	1.74	1.74	1.74	.25	
2.87	2.84	2.82	2.80	2.78	2.77	2.76	2.75	2.74	2.73	2.73	2.72	.10	6
3.94	3.87	3.84	3.81	3.77	3.75	3.74	3.71	3.70	3.69	3.68	3.67	.05	
7.56	7.40	7.31	7.23	7.14	7.09	7.06	6.99	6.97	6.93	6.90	6.88	.01	
1.68	1.67	1.67	1.66	1.66	1.66	1.65	1.65	1.65	1.65	1.65	1.65	.25	
2.63	2.59	2.58	2.56	2.54	2.52	2.51	2.50	2.49	2.48	2.48	2.47	.10	7
3.51	3.44	3.41	3.38	3.34	3.32	3.30	3.27	3.27	3.25	3.24	3.23	.05	
6.31	6.16	6.07	5.99	5.91	5.86	5.82	5.75	5.74	5.70	5.67	5.65	.01	
1.62	1.61	1.60	1.60	1.59	1.59	1.59	1.58	1.58	1.58	1.58	1.58	.25	
2.46	2.42	2.40	2.38	2.36	2.35	2.34	2.32	2.32	2.31	2.30	2.29	.10	8
3.22	3.15	3.12	3.08	3.04	3.02	3.01	2.97	2.97	2.95	2.94	2.93	.05	
5.52	5.36	5.28	5.20	5.12	5.07	5.03	4.96	4.95	4.91	4.88	4.86	.01	
1.57	1.56	1.56	1.55	1.55	1.54	1.54	1.53	1.53	1.53	1.53	1.53	.25	
2.34	2.30	2.28	2.25	2.23	2.22	2.21	2.19	2.18	2.17	2.17	2.16	.10	9
3.01	2.94	2.90	2.86	2.83	2.80	2.79	2.76	2.75	2.73	2.72	2.71	.05	
4.96	4.81	4.73	4.65	4.57	4.52	4.48	4.42	4.40	4.36	4.33	4.31	.01	

(continued)

F - DISTRIBUTION (continued)

df for denominator N_2	Pr	1	2	3	4	5	6	7	8	9	10	11	12
						df for numerator N_1							
10	.25	1.49	1.60	1.60	1.59	1.59	1.58	1.57	1.56	1.56	1.55	1.55	1.54
	.10	3.29	2.92	2.73	2.61	2.52	2.46	2.41	2.38	2.35	2.32	2.30	2.28
	.05	4.96	4.10	3.71	3.48	3.33	3.22	3.14	3.07	3.02	2.98	2.94	2.91
	.01	10.0	7.56	6.55	5.99	5.64	5.39	5.20	5.06	4.94	4.85	4.77	4.71
11	.25	1.47	1.58	1.58	1.57	1.56	1.55	1.54	1.53	1.53	1.52	1.52	1.51
	.10	3.23	2.86	2.66	2.54	2.45	2.39	2.34	2.30	2.27	2.25	2.23	2.21
	.05	4.84	3.98	3.59	3.36	3.20	3.09	3.01	2.95	2.90	2.85	2.82	2.79
	.01	9.65	7.21	6.22	5.67	5.32	5.07	4.89	4.74	4.63	4.54	4.46	4.40
12	.25	1.46	1.56	1.56	1.55	1.54	1.53	1.52	1.51	1.51	1.50	1.50	1.49
	.10	3.18	2.81	2.61	2.48	2.39	2.33	2.28	2.24	2.21	2.19	2.17	2.15
	.05	4.75	3.89	3.49	3.26	3.11	3.00	2.91	2.85	2.80	2.75	2.72	2.69
	.01	9.33	6.93	5.95	5.41	5.06	4.82	4.64	4.50	4.39	4.30	4.22	4.16
13	.25	1.45	1.55	1.55	1.53	1.52	1.51	1.50	1.49	1.49	1.48	1.47	1.47
	.10	3.14	2.76	2.56	2.43	2.35	2.28	2.23	2.20	2.16	2.14	2.12	2.10
	.05	4.67	3.81	3.41	3.18	3.03	2.92	2.83	2.77	2.71	2.67	2.63	2.60
	.01	9.07	6.70	5.74	5.21	4.86	4.62	4.44	4.30	4.19	4.10	4.02	3.96
14	.25	1.44	1.53	1.53	1.52	1.51	1.50	1.49	1.48	1.47	1.46	1.46	1.45
	.10	3.10	2.73	2.52	2.39	2.31	2.24	2.19	2.15	2.12	2.10	2.08	2.05
	.05	4.60	3.74	3.34	3.11	2.96	2.85	2.76	2.70	2.65	2.60	2.57	2.53
	.01	8.86	6.51	5.56	5.04	4.69	4.46	4.28	4.14	4.03	3.94	3.86	3.80
15	.25	1.43	1.52	1.52	1.51	1.49	1.48	1.47	1.46	1.46	1.45	1.44	1.44
	.10	3.07	2.70	2.49	2.36	2.27	2.21	2.16	2.12	2.09	2.06	2.04	2.02
	.05	4.54	3.68	3.29	3.06	2.90	2.79	2.71	2.64	2.59	2.54	2.51	2.48
	.01	8.68	6.36	5.42	4.89	4.56	4.32	4.14	4.00	3.89	3.80	3.73	3.67
16	.25	1.42	1.51	1.51	1.50	1.48	1.47	1.46	1.45	1.44	1.44	1.44	1.43
	.10	3.05	2.67	2.46	2.33	2.24	2.18	2.13	2.09	2.06	2.03	2.01	1.99
	.05	4.49	3.63	3.24	3.01	2.85	2.74	2.66	2.59	2.54	2.49	2.46	2.42
	.01	8.53	6.23	5.29	4.77	4.44	4.20	4.03	3.89	3.78	3.69	3.62	3.55
17	.25	1.42	1.51	1.50	1.49	1.47	1.46	1.45	1.44	1.43	1.43	1.42	1.41
	.10	3.03	2.64	2.44	2.31	2.22	2.15	2.10	2.06	2.03	2.00	1.98	1.96
	.05	4.45	3.59	3.20	2.96	2.81	2.70	2.61	2.55	2.49	2.45	2.41	2.38
	.01	8.40	6.11	5.18	4.67	4.34	4.10	3.93	3.79	3.68	3.59	3.52	3.46
18	.25	1.41	1.50	1.49	1.48	1.46	1.45	1.44	1.43	1.42	1.42	1.41	1.40
	.10	3.01	2.62	2.42	2.29	2.20	2.13	2.08	2.04	2.00	1.98	1.96	1.93
	.05	4.41	3.55	3.16	2.93	2.77	2.66	2.58	2.51	2.46	2.41	2.37	2.34
	.01	8.29	6.01	5.09	4.58	4.25	4.01	3.84	3.71	3.60	3.51	3.43	3.37
19	.25	1.41	1.49	1.49	1.47	1.46	1.44	1.43	1.42	1.41	1.41	1.40	1.40
	.10	2.99	2.61	2.40	2.27	2.18	2.11	2.06	2.02	1.98	1.96	1.94	1.91
	.05	4.38	3.52	3.13	2.90	2.74	2.63	2.54	2.48	2.42	2.38	2.34	2.31
	.01	8.18	5.93	5.01	4.50	4.17	3.94	3.77	3.63	3.52	3.43	3.36	3.30
20	.25	1.40	2.49	1.48	1.46	1.45	1.44	1.43	1.42	1.41	1.40	1.39	1.39
	.10	2.97	2.59	2.38	2.25	2.16	2.09	2.04	2.00	1.96	1.94	1.92	1.89
	.05	4.35	3.49	3.10	2.87	2.71	2.60	2.51	2.45	2.39	2.35	2.31	2.28
	.01	8.10	5.85	4.94	4.43	4.10	3.87	3.70	3.56	3.46	3.37	3.29	3.23

F - DISTRIBUTION (continued)

15	20	24	30	40	50	60	100	120	200	500	∞	Pr	N_2
				df for numerator N_1									*df* for denominator
1.53	1.52	1.52	1.51	1.51	1.50	1.50	1.49	1.49	1.49	1.48	1.48	.25	
2.24	2.20	2.18	2.16	2.13	2.12	2.11	2.09	2.08	2.07	2.06	2.06	.10	10
2.85	2.77	2.74	2.70	2.66	2.64	2.62	2.59	2.58	2.56	2.55	2.54	.05	
4.56	4.41	4.33	4.25	4.17	4.12	4.08	4.01	4.00	3.96	3.93	3.91	.01	
1.50	1.49	1.49	1.48	1.47	1.47	1.47	1.46	1.46	1.46	1.45	1.45	.25	
2.17	2.12	2.10	2.08	2.05	2.04	2.03	2.00	2.00	1.99	1.98	1.97	.10	11
2.72	2.65	2.61	2.57	2.53	2.51	2.49	2.46	2.45	2.43	2.42	2.40	.05	
4.25	4.10	4.02	3.94	3.86	3.81	3.78	3.71	3.69	3.656	3.62	3.60	.01	
1.48	1.47	1.46	1.45	1.45	1.44	1.44	1.43	1.43	1.43	1.42	1.42	.25	
2.10	2.06	2.04	2.01	1.99	1.97	1.96	1.94	1.93	1.92	1.91	1.90	.10	12
2.62	2.54	2.51	2.47	2.43	2.40	2.38	2.35	2.34	2.32	2.31	2.30	.05	
4.01	3.86	3.78	3.70	3.62	3.57	3.54	3.47	3.45	3.41	3.38	2.36	.01	
1.46	1.45	1.44	1.43	1.42	1.42	1.42	1.41	1.41	1.40	1.40	1.40	.25	
2.05	2.01	1.98	1.96	1.93	1.92	1.90	1.88	1.88	1.86	1.85	1.85	.10	13
2.53	2.46	2.42	2.38	2.34	2.31	2.30	2.26	2.25	2.23	2.22	2.21	.05	
3.82	3.66	3.59	3.51	3.43	3.38	3.34	3.27	3.25	3.22	3.19	3.17	.01	
1.44	1.43	1.42	1.41	1.41	1.40	1.40	1.39	1.39	1.39	1.38	1.38	.25	
2.01	1.96	1.94	1.91	1.89	1.87	1.86	1.83	1.83	1.82	1.80	1.80	.10	14
2.46	2.39	2.35	2.31	2.27	2.24	2.22	2.19	2.18	2.16	2.14	2.13	.05	
3.66	3.51	3.43	3.35	3.27	3.22	3.18	3.11	3.09	3.06	3.03	3.00	.01	
1.43	1.41	1.41	1.40	1.39	1.39	1.38	1.38	1.37	1.37	1.36	1.36	.25	
1.97	1.92	1.90	1.87	1.85	1.83	1.82	1.79	1.79	1.77	1.76	1.76	.10	15
2.40	2.33	2.29	2.25	2.20	2.18	2.16	2.12	2.11	2.10	2.08	2.07	.05	
3.52	3.37	3.29	3.21	3.13	3.08	3.05	2.98	2.96	2.92	2.89	2.87	.01	
1.41	1.40	1.39	1.38	1.37	1.37	1.36	1.36	1.35	1.35	1.34	1.34	.25	
1.94	1.89	1.87	1.84	1.81	1.79	1.78	1.76	1.75	1.74	1.73	1.72	.10	16
2.35	2.28	2.24	2.19	2.15	2.12	2.11	2.07	2.06	2.04	2.02	2.01	.05	
3.41	3.26	3.18	3.10	3.02	2.97	2.93	2.86	2.84	2.81	2.78	2.75	.01	
1.40	1.39	1.38	1.37	1.36	1.35	1.35	1.34	1.34	1.34	1.33	1.33	.25	
1.91	1.86	1.84	1.81	1.78	1.76	1.75	1.73	1.72	1.71	1.69	1.69	.10	17
2.31	2.23	2.19	2.15	2.10	2.08	2.06	2.02	2.01	1.99	1.97	1.96	.05	
3.31	3.16	3.08	3.00	2.92	2.87	2.83	2.76	2.75	2.71	2.68	2.65	.01	
1.39	1.38	1.37	1.36	1.35	1.34	1.34	1.33	1.33	1.32	1.32	1.32	.25	
1.89	1.84	1.81	1.78	1.75	1.74	1.72	1.70	1.69	1.68	1.67	1.66	.10	18
2.27	2.19	2.15	2.11	2.06	2.04	2.02	1.98	1.97	1.95	1.93	1.92	.05	
2.23	3.08	3.00	2.92	2.84	2.78	2.75	2.68	2.66	2.62	2.59	2.57	.01	
1.38	1.37	1.36	1.35	1.34	1.33	1.33	1.32	1.32	1.31	1.31	1.30	.25	
1.86	1.81	1.79	1.76	1.73	1.71	1.70	1.67	1.67	1.65	1.64	1.63	.10	19
2.23	2.16	2.11	2.07	2.03	2.00	1.98	1.94	1.93	1.91	1.89	1.88	.05	
3.15	3.00	2.92	2.84	2.76	2.71	2.67	2.60	2.58	2.55	2.51	2.49	.01	
1.37	1.36	1.35	1.34	1.33	1.33	1.32	1.31	1.31	1.30	1.30	1.29	.25	
1.84	1.79	1.77	1.74	1.71	1.69	1.68	1.65	1.64	1.63	1.62	1.61	.10	20
2.20	2.12	2.08	2.04	1.99	1.97	1.95	1.91	1.90	1.88	1'.86	1.84	.05	
3.09	2.94	2.86	2.78	2.69	2.64	2.61	2.54	2.52	2.48	2.44	2.42	.01	

(continued)

F - DISTRIBUTION (continued)

N_2	Pr	1	2	3	4	5	6	7	8	9	10	11	12
						df for numerator N_1							
22	.25	1.40	1.48	1.47	1.45	1.44	1.42	1.41	1.40	1.39	1.39	1.38	1.37
	.10	2.95	2.56	2.35	2.22	2.13	2.06	2.01	1.97	1.93	1.90	1.88	1.86
	.05	4.30	3.44	3.05	2.82	2.66	2.55	2.46	2.40	2.34	2.30	2.26	2.23
	.01	7.95	5.72	4.82	4.31	3.99	3.76	3.59	3.45	3.35	3.26	3.18	3.12
24	.25	1.39	1.47	1.46	1.44	1.43	1.41	1.40	1.39	1.38	1.38	1.37	1.36
	.10	2.92	2.54	2.33	2.19	2.10	2.04	1.98	1.94	1.91	1.88	1.85	1.83
	.05	4.26	3.40	3.01	2.78	2.62	2.51	2.42	2.36	2.30	2.25	2.21	2.18
	.01	7.82	5.61	4.72	4.22	3.90	3.67	3.50	3.36	3.26	3.17	3.09	3.03
26	.25	1.38	1.46	1.45	1.44	1.42	1.41	1.39	1.38	1.37	1.37	1.36	1.35
	.10	2.91	2.52	2.31	2.17	2.08	2.01	1.96	1.92	1.88	1.86	1.84	1.81
	.05	4.23	3.37	2.98	2.74	2.59	2.47	2.39	2.32	2.27	2.22	2.18	2.15
	.01	7.72	5.53	4.64	4.14	3.82	3.59	3.42	3.29	3.18	3.09	3.02	2.96
28	.25	1.38	1.46	1.45	1.43	1.41	1.40	1.39	1.38	1.37	1.36	1.35	1.34
	.10	2.89	2.50	2.29	2.16	2.06	2.00	1.94	1.90	1.87	1.84	1.81	1.79
	.05	4.20	3.34	2.95	2.71	2.56	2.45	2.36	2.29	2.24	2.19	2.15	2.12
	.01	7.64	5.45	4.57	4.07	3.75	3.53	3.36	3.23	3.12	3.03	2.96	2.90
30	.25	1.38	1.45	1.44	1.42	1.41	1.39	1.38	1.37	1.36	1.35	1.35	1.34
	.10	2.88	2.49	2.28	2.14	2.05	1.98	1.93	1.88	1.85	1.82	1.79	1.77
	.05	4.17	3.32	2.92	2.69	2.53	2.42	2.33	2.27	2.21	2.16	2.13	2.09
	.01	7.56	5.39	4.51	4.02	3.70	3.47	3.30	3.17	3.07	2.98	2.91	2.84
40	.25	1.36	1.44	1.42	1.40	1.39	1.37	1.36	1.35	1.34	1.33	1.32	1.31
	.10	2.84	2.44	2.23	2.09	2.00	1.93	1.87	1.83	1.79	1.76	1.73	1.71
	.05	4.08	3.23	2.84	2.61	2.45	2.34	2.25	2.18	2.12	2.08	2.04	2.00
	.01	7.31	5.18	4.31	3.83	3.51	3.29	3.12	2.99	2.89	2.80	2.73	2.66
60	.25	1.35	1.42	1.41	1.38	1.37	1.35	1.33	1.32	1.31	1.30	1.29	1.29
	.10	2.79	2.39	2.18	2.04	1.95	1.87	1.82	1.77	1.74	1.71	1.68	1.66
	.05	4.00	3.15	2.76	2.53	2.37	2.25	2.17	2.10	2.04	1.99	1.95	1.92
	.01	7.08	4.98	4.13	3.65	3.34	3.12	2.95	2.82	2.72	2.63	2.56	2.50
120	.25	1.34	1.40	1.39	1.37	1.35	1.33	1.31	1.30	1.29	1.28	1.27	1.26
	.10	2.75	2.35	2.13	1.99	1.90	1.82	1.77	1.72	1.68	1.65	1.62	1.60
	.05	3.92	3.07	2.68	2.45	2.29	2.17	2.09	2.02	1.96	1.91	1.87	1.83
	.01	6.85	4.49	3.95	3.48	3.17	2.96	2.79	2.66	2.56	2.47	2.40	2.34
200	.25	1.33	1.39	1.38	1.36	1.34	1.32	1.31	1.29	1.28	1.27	1.26	1.25
	.10	2.73	2.33	2.11	1.97	1.88	1.80	1.75	1.70	1.66	1.63	1.60	1.57
	.05	3.89	3.04	2.65	2.42	2.26	2.14	2.06	1.98	1.93	1.88	1.84	1.80
	.01	6.76	4.71	3.88	3.41	3.11	2.89	2.73	2.60	2.50	2.41	2.34	2.27
∞	.25	1.32	1.39	1.37	1.35	1.33	1.31	1.29	1.28	1.27	1.25	1.24	1.24
	.10	2.71	2.30	2.08	1.94	1.85	1.77	1.72	1.67	1.63	1.60	1.57	1.55
	.05	3.84	3.00	2.60	2.37	2.21	2.10	2.01	1.94	1.88	1.83	1.79	1.75
	.01	6.63	4.61	3.78	3.32	3.02	2.80	2.64	2.51	2.41	2.32	2.25	2.18

df for denominator

F - DISTRIBUTION (continued)

15	20	24	30	40	50	60	100	120	200	500	∞	Pr	N₂
1.36	1.34	1.33	1.32	1.31	1.31	1.30	1.30	1.30	1.29	1.29	1.28	.25	
1.81	1.76	1.73	1.70	1.67	1.65	1.64	1.61	1.60	1.59	1.58	1.57	.10	22
2.15	2.07	2.03	1.98	1.94	1.91	1.89	1.85	1.84	1.82	1.80	1.78	.05	
2.98	2.83	2.75	2.67	2.58	2.53	2.50	2.42	2.40	2.36	2.33	2.31	.01	
1.35	1.33	1.32	1.31	1.30	1.29	1.29	1.28	1.28	1.27	1.27	1.26	.25	
1.78	1.73	1.70	1.67	1.64	1.62	1.61	1.58	1.57	1.56	1.54	1.53	.10	24
2.11	2.03	1.98	1.94	1.89	1.86	1.84	1.80	1.79	1.77	1.75	1.73	.05	
2.89	2.74	2.66	2.58	2.49	2.44	2.40	2.33	2.31	2.27	2.24	2.21	.01	
1.34	1.32	1.31	1.30	1.29	1.28	1.28	1.26	1.26	1.26	1.25	1.25	.25	
1.76	1.71	1.68	1.65	1.61	1.59	1.58	1.55	1.54	1.53	1.51	1.50	.10	26
2.07	1.99	1.95	1.90	1.85	1.82	1.80	1.76	1.75	1.73	1.71	1.69	.05	
2.81	2.66	2.58	2.50	2.42	2.36	2.33	2.25	2.23	2.19	2.16	2.13	.01	
1.33	1.31	1.30	1.29	1.28	1.27	1.27	1.26	1.25	1.25	1.24	1.24	.25	
1.74	1.69	1.66	1.63	1.59	1.57	1.56	1.53	1.52	1.50	1.49	1.48	.10	28
2.04	1.96	1.91	1.87	1.82	1.79	1.77	1.73	1.71	1.69	1.67	1.65	.05	
2.75	2.60	2.52	2.44	2.35	2.30	2.26	2.19	2.17	2.13	2.09	2.06	.01	
1.32	1.30	1.29	1.28	1.27	1.26	1.26	1.25	1.24	1.24	1.23	1.23	.25	
1.72	1.67	1.64	1.61	1.57	1.55	1.54	1.51	1.50	1.48	1.47	1.46	.10	30
2.01	1.93	1.89	1.84	1.79	1.76	1.74	1.70	1.68	1.66	1.64	1.62	.05	
2.70	2.55	2.47	2.39	2.30	2.25	2.21	2.13	2.11	2.07	2.03	2.01	.01	
1.30	1.28	1.26	1.25	1.24	1.23	1.22	1.21	1.21	1.20	1.19	1.19	.25	
1.66	1.61	1.57	1.54	1.51	1.48	1.47	1.43	1.42	1.41	1.39	1.38	.10	40
1.92	1.84	1.79	1.74	1.69	1.66	1.64	1.59	1.58	1.55	1.53	1.51	.05	
2.52	2.37	2.29	2.20	2.11	2.06	2.02	1.94	1.92	1.87	1.83	1.80	.01	
1.27	1.25	1.24	1.22	1.21	1.20	1.19	1.17	1.17	1.16	1.15	1.15	.25	
1.60	1.54	1.51	1.48	1.44	1.41	1.40	1.36	1.35	1.33	1.31	1.29	.10	60
1.84	1.75	1.70	1.65	1.59	1.56	1.53	1.48	1.47	1.44	1.41	1.39	.05	
2.35	2.20	2.12	2.03	1.94	1.88	1.84	1.75	1.73	1.68	1.63	1.60	.01	
1.24	1.22	1.21	1.19	1.18	1.17	1.16	1.14	1.13	1.12	1.11	1.10	.25	
1.55	1.48	1.45	1.41	1.37	1.34	1.32	1.27	1.26	1.24	1.21	1.19	.10	120
1.75	1.66	1.61	1.55	1.50	1.46	1.43	1.37	1.35	1.32	1.28	1.25	.05	
2.19	2.03	1.95	1.86	1.76	1.70	1.66	1.56	1.53	1.48	1.42	1.38	.01	
1.23	1.21	1.20	1.18	1.16	1.14	1.12	1.11	1.10	1.09	1.08	1.06	.25	
1.52	1.46	1.42	1.38	1.34	1.31	1.28	1.24	1.22	1.20	1.17	1.14	.10	200
1.72	1.62	1.57	1.52	1.46	1.41	1.39	1.32	1.29	1.26	1.22	1.19	.05	
2.13	1.97	1.89	1.79	1.69	1.63	1.58	1.48	1.44	1.39	1.33	1.28	.01	
1.22	1.19	1.18	1.16	1.14	1.13	1.12	1.09	1.08	1.07	1.04	1.00	.25	
1.49	1.42	1.38	1.34	1.30	1.26	1.24	1.18	1.17	1.13	1.08	1.00	.10	∞
1.67	1.57	1.52	1.46	1.39	1.35	1.32	1.24	1.22	1.17	1.11	1.00	.05	
2.04	1.88	1.79	1.70	1.59	1.52	1.47	1.36	1.32	1.25	1.15	1.00	.01	

The header spanning: *df* for numerator N_1 (over columns 15–∞); *df* for denominator (over Pr, N₂).

THE CORRELATION COEFFICIENT

Values of the Correlation Coefficient for Different Levels of Significance

For a total correlation, ν is 2 less than the number of pairs in the sample; for a partial correlation, the number of eliminated variates should also be subtracted. The probabilities at the head of the columns refer to the two-tail test of significance and give the chance that $|r|$ will be greater than the tabulated values given that the true product moment correlation coefficient, ρ, is zero. For a single-tail test the probabilities should be halved.

Example: In a test for a significant positive correlation between two variables, the observed correlation coefficient of ten pairs of observations would have to exceed the value +0.7155 to be significant at the 1% level.

	.1	.05	.02	.01	.001
$\nu = 1$	.98769	.99692	.999507	.999877	.9999988
2	.90000	.95000	.98000	.990000	.99900
3	.8054	.8783	.93433	.95873	.99116
4	.7293	.8114	.8822	.91720	.97406
5	.6694	.7545	.8329	.8745	.95074
6	.6215	.7067	.7887	.8343	.92493
7	.5822	.6664	.7498	.7977	.8982
8	.5494	.6319	.7155	.7646	.8721
9	5214	.6021	.6851	.7348	.8471
10	.4973	.5760	.6581	.7079	.8233
11	.4762	.5529	.6339	.6835	.8010
12	.4575	.5324	.6120	.6614	.7800
13	.4409	.5139	.5923	.6411	.7603
14	.4259	.4973	.5742	.6226	.7420
15	.4124	.4821	.5577	.6055	.7246
16	.4000	.4683	.5425	.5897	7084
17	.3887	.4555	.5285	.5751	.6932
18	.3783	.4436	.5155	.5614	.6787
19	.3687	.4329	.5034	.5487	.6652
20	.3598	.4227	.4921	.5368	.6524
25	.3233	.3809	.4451	.4869	.5974
30	.2960	.3494	.4093	.4487	.5541
35	.2746	.3246	.3810	.4182	.5189
40	.2573	.3044	.3578	.3932	.4896
45	.2428	.2875	.3384	.3721	.4648
50	.2306	.2732	.3218	.3541	.4433
60	.2108	.2500	.2948	.3248	.4078
70	.1954	.2319	.2737	.3017	.3799
80	.1829	.2172	.2565	.2830	.3568
90	.1726	.2050	.2422	.2673	.3375
100	.1638	.1946	.2301	.2540	.3211

SPEARMAN RANK CORRELATION COEFFICIENT

Percentage Points of Spearman Rank Correlation Coefficient

The coefficient r_s is calculated as $1 - \dfrac{6 \sum d^2}{n(n^2 - 1)}$ where n is the number of observations in each of two series and d is the difference between the ranks of the corresponding observations in each series.

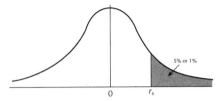

An observed value of r_s greater than or equal to that tabulated indicates a significant positive correlation between the ranks of the two series of observations at the level indicated (5% or 1%). For a two-sided test the probabilities should be doubled. For a significant negative correlation between ranks, an observed r_s should be negative but numerically greater than or equal to the tabulated value.

n	α 5%	(One-tailed test) 1%
4	1.000	—
5	0.900	1.000
6	0.829	0.943
7	0.714	0.893
8	0.643	0.833
9	0.600	0.783
10	0.564	0.746
12	0.506	0.712
14	0.456	0.645
16	0.425	0.601
18	0.399	0.564
20	0.377	0.534
22	0.359	0.508
24	0.343	0.485
26	0.329	0.465
28	0.317	0.448
30	0.306	0.432

When n is large (greater than about 10 say), the significance of an observed value of r_2 under the null hypothesis may be tested using:

$$t \simeq r_2 \sqrt{\frac{n - 2}{1 - r_s^2}}$$

where t is Student's t with $n - 2$ degrees of freedom.

DURBIN–WATSON TABLES

Five percent significance points of d_l and d_u for Durbin–Watson Test

N	k = 1		k = 2		k = 3		k = 4		k = 5	
	d_l	d_u	d_l	d_u	d_l	d_u	d_l	d_u	d_l	d_u
15	1.08	1.36	.95	1.54	.82	1.75	.69	1.97	.56	2.21
16	1.10	1.37	.98	1.54	.86	1.73	.74	1.93	.62	2.15
17	1.13	1.38	1.02	1.54	.90	1.71	.78	1.90	.67	2.10
18	1.16	1.39	1.05	1.53	.93	1.69	.82	1.87	.71	2.06
19	1.18	1.40	1.08	1.53	.97	1.68	.86	1.85	.75	2.02
20	1.20	1.41	1.10	1.54	1.00	1.68	.90	1.83	.79	1.99
21	1.22	1.42	1.13	1.54	1.03	1.67	.93	1.81	.83	1.96
22	1.24	1.43	1.15	1.54	1.05	1.66	.96	1.80	.86	1.94
23	1.26	1.44	1.17	1.54	1.08	1.66	.99	1.79	.90	1.92
24	1.27	1.45	1.19	1.55	1.10	1.66	1.01	1.78	.93	1.90
25	1.29	1.45	1.21	1.55	1.12	1.66	1.04	1.77	.95	1.89
26	1.30	1.46	1.22	1.55	1.14	1.65	1.06	1.76	.98	1.88
27	1.32	1.47	1.24	1.56	1.16	1.65	1.08	1.76	1.01	1.86
28	1.33	1.48	1.26	1.56	1.18	1.65	1.10	1.75	1.03	1.85
29	1.34	1.48	1.27	1.56	1.20	1.65	1.12	1.74	1.05	1.84
30	1.35	1.49	1.28	1.57	1.21	1.65	1.14	1.74	1.07	1.83
31	1.36	1.50	1.30	1.57	1.23	1.65	1.16	1.74	1.09	1.83
32	1.37	1.50	1.31	1.57	1.24	1.65	1.18	1.73	1.11	1.82
33	1.38	1.51	1.32	1.58	1.26	1.65	1.19	1.73	1.13	1.81
34	1.39	1.51	1.33	1.58	1.27	1.65	1.21	1.73	1.15	1.81
35	1.40	1.52	1.34	1.53	1.28	1.65	1.22	1.73	1.16	1.80
36	1.41	1.52	1.35	1.59	1.29	1.65	1.24	1.73	1.18	1.80
37	1.42	1.53	1.36	1.59	1.31	1.66	1.25	1.72	1.19	1.80
38	1.43	1.54	1.37	1.59	1.32	1.66	1.26	1.72	1.21	1.79
39	1.43	1.54	1.38	1.60	1.33	1.66	1.27	1.72	1.22	1.79
40	1.44	1.54	1.39	1.60	1.34	1.66	1.29	1.72	1.23	1.79
45	1.48	1.57	1.43	1.62	1.38	1.67	1.34	1.72	1.29	1.78
50	1.50	1.59	1.46	1.63	1.42	1.67	1.38	1.72	1.34	1.77
55	1.53	1.60	1.49	1.64	1.45	1.68	1.41	1.72	1.38	1.77
60	1.55	1.62	1.51	1.65	1.48	1.69	1.44	1.73	1.41	1.77
65	1.57	1.63	1.54	1.66	1.50	1.70	1.47	1.73	1.44	1.77
70	1.58	1.64	1.55	1.67	1.52	1.70	1.49	1.74	1.46	1.77
75	1.60	1.65	1.57	1.68	1.54	1.71	1.51	1.74	1.49	1.77
80	1.61	1.66	1.59	1.69	1.56	1.72	1.53	1.74	1.51	1.77
85	1.62	1.67	1.60	1.70	1.57	1.72	1.55	1.75	1.52	1.77
90	1.63	1.68	1.61	1.70	1.59	1.73	1.57	1.75	1.54	1.78
95	1.64	1.69	1.62	1.71	1.60	1.73	1.58	1.75	1.56	1.78
100	1.65	1.69	1.63	1.72	1.61	1.74	1.59	1.76	1.57	1.78

N = number of observations; k = number of explanatory variables (excluding the constant term).

DISCOUNT TABLE I

					Discount Rate (%)					
Year	1	2	3	4	5	6	7	8	9	10
0	1.0000	1.0000	1.0000	1.0000	1.0000	1.0000	1.0000	1.0000	1.0000	1.0000
1	0.9901	0.9804	0.9709	0.9615	0.9524	0.9434	0.9346	0l.9259	0.9174	0.9091
2	0.9803	0.9612	0.9426	0.9246	0.0070	0.8900	0.8734	0.8573	0.8417	0.8264
3	0.9706	0.9423	0.9151	0.8890	0.8638	0.8396	0.8163	0.7938	0.7722	0.7513
4	0.9610	0.9238	0.8885	0.8548	0.8227	0.7921	0.7629	0.7350	0.7084	0.6830
5	0.9515	0.9057	0.8626	0.8219	0.7835	0.7473	0.7130	0.6806	0.6499	0.6209
6	0.9420	0.8880	0.8375	0.7903	0.7462	0.7050	0.6663	0.6302	0.5963	0.5645
7	0.9327	0.8706	0.8131	0.7599	0.7107	0.6651	0.6227	0.5835	0.5470	0.5132
8	0.9235	0.8535	0.7894	0.7307	0.6768	0.6274	0.5820	0.5403	0.5019	0.4665
9	0.9143	0.8368	0.7664	0.7026	0.6446	0.5919	0.5439	0.5002	0.4604	0.4241
10	0.9053	0.8203	0.7441	0.6756	0.6139	0.5584	0.5083	0.4632	0.4224	0.3855
11	0.8963	0.8043	0.7224	0.6496	0.5847	0.5268	0.4751	0.4289	0.3875	0.3505
12	0.8874	0.7885	0.7014	0.6246	0.5568	0.4970	0.4440	0.3971	0.3555	0.3186
13	0.8787	0.7730	0.6810	0.6006	0.5303	0.4688	0.4150	0.3677	0.3262	0.2897
14	0.8700	0.7579	0.6611	0.5775	0.5051	0.4423	0.3878	0.3405	0.2992	0.2633
15	0.8613	0.7430	0.6419	0.5553	0.4810	0.4173	0.3624	0.3152	0.2745	0.2394
16	0.8528	0.7284	0.6232	0.5339	0.4581	0.3036	0.3387	0.2919	0.2519	0.2176
17	0.8444	0.7142	0.6050	0.5134	0.4363	0.3714	0.3166	0.2703	0.2311	0.1978
18	0.8360	0.7002	0.5874	0.4936	0.4155	0.3503	0.2959	0.2502	0.2120	0.1799
19	0.8277	0.6864	0.5703	0.4746	0.3957	0.3305	0.2765	0.2317	0.1945	0.1635
20	0.8195	0.6730	0.5537	0.4567	0.3769	0.3118	0.2584	0.2145	0.1794	0.1486

DISCOUNT TABLE II

					Discount Rate (%)					
Year	11	12	13	14	15	16	17	18	19	20
0	1.0000	1.0000	1.0000	1.0000	1.0000	1.0000	1.0000	1.0000	1.0000	1.0000
1	0.9009	0.8929	0.8850	0.8772	0.8696	0.8621	0.8547	0.8475	0.8403	0.8333
2	0.8116	0.7972	0.7831	0.7695	0.7561	0.7432	0.7305	0.7182	0.7062	0.6944
3	0.7312	0.7118	0.6931	0.6750	0.6575	0.6407	0.6244	0.6086	0.5934	0.5787
4	0.6587	0.6355	0.6133	0.5921	0.5718	0.5523	0.5337	0.5158	0.4987	0.4823
5	0.5935	0.5674	0.5428	0.5194	0.4972	0.4761	0.4561	0.4371	0.4190	0.4019
6	0.5346	0.5066	0.4803	0.4556	0.4323	0.4104	0.3898	0.3704	0.3521	0.3349
7	0.4817	0.4523	0.4251	0.3996	0.3759	0.3538	0.3332	0.3139	0.2959	0.2791
8	0.4339	0.4039	0.3762	0.3506	0.3269	0.3050	0.2848	0.2660	0.2487	0.2326
9	0.3909	0.3606	0.3329	0.3075	0.2843	0.2630	0.2434	0.2255	0.2090	0.1938
10	0.3522	0.3220	0.2946	0.2697	0.2472	0.2267	0.2080	0.1911	0.1758	0.1615
11	0.3173	0.2875	0.2607	0.2366	0.2149	0.1954	0.1778	0.1619	0.1476	0.1346
12	0.2858	0.2567	0.2307	0.2076	0.1869	0.1685	0.1520	0.1372	0.1240	0.1122
13	0.2575	0.2292	0.2042	0.1821	0.1625	0.1452	0.1299	0.1163	0.1042	0.0935
14	0.2320	0.2046	0.1807	0.1597	0.1413	0.1252	0.1110	0.0985	0.0876	0.0779
15	0.2090	0.1827	0.1599	0.1401	0.1229	0.1079	0.0949	0.0835	0.0736	0.0649
16	0.1883	0.1631	0.1415	0.1229	0.1069	0.0930	0.0811	0.0708	0.0618	0.0541
17	0.1696	0.1456	0.1252	0.1078	0.0929	0.0802	0.0693	0.0600	0.0520	0.0451
18	0.1528	0.1300	0.1108	0.0946	0.0808	0.0691	0.0592	0.0508	0.0437	0.0376
19	0.1377	0.1161	0.0981	0.0829	0.0703	0.0596	0.0506	0.0431	0.0367	0.0313
20	0.1240	0.1037	0.0868	0.0728	0.0611	0.0514	0.0433	0.0365	0.0308	0.0261

Created by the authors using a standard computer spreadsheet; this is contained on the computer software disk which is available separately – see details at the end of the book.

Appendix B
Famous statisticians

This appendix lists some of the more important statisticians and their contribution to statistical thinking and theory. These statisticians are listed in order of their date of birth with their major contributions shown in italics.

James BERNOULLI (1654–1705)

Bernoulli's major contributions to statistics were in the areas of *combinations, permutations, Bernoulli trials and probability theory*. The binomial distribution is derived from the process known as a Bernoulli trial. He also carried out work on calculus and introduced the idea of integration (the inverse of differentiation). Most of Bernoulli's important work was published in the book *Ars Conjectandi* shortly after his death in 1713.

Pierre Simon LAPLACE (1749–1827)

Laplace's major work in statistics was in the field of probability and *the discovery of the Central Limits Theorem*, an important building block for inferential statistics. However, Laplace also carried out extensive research in the field of astronomy proving that the planets' average angular velocities are invariable and periodic. This was the most important astronomic discovery since the work of Isaac Newton.

Carl Frederick GAUSS (1777–1855)

Gauss's two major contributions to statistics were the method of *least squares* and *the normal distribution* (sometimes called the *Gaussian distribution* in his honour).

Two other mathematicians have also been linked to this distribution namely Abraham de Moivre (1667–1754) and Pierre Simon Laplace (1749–1827). Gauss also made important discoveries in the fields of mathematics, physics and astronomy. In 1833 at Göttingen University, with Wilhelm Weber, Gauss invented a working version of the electric telegraph, some five years before Samuel Morse.

Simeon Denis POISSON (1781–1840)

Poisson's work included the discrete distribution called the *Poisson distribution* and its derivation was published in 1837. It is important to note that two other statisticians have been linked to the discovery of the Poisson distribution, namely Abraham de Moivre (1667–1754) and Ladislaus von Bortkiewicz. Bortkiewicz is known for the application of this distribution to the study of deaths of Prussian soldiers from horses' kicks. The Poisson distribution has many applications particularly in queuing theory and in the demand for products.

Sir Francis GALTON (1822–1911)

Galton's work in statistics covers the fields of *regression* and *correlation* as tools for estimating the influence of heredity. Galton never held a professional or academic position and most of his research was undertaken at home. He also researched into many other areas including meteorology, biology, psychology and genetics. In his later life Galton was associated with Karl Pearson and was a co-founder of the journal *Biometrika*. Galton was knighted in 1909.

Karl PEARSON (1857–1936)

Pearson's extensive work in statistics covered the *chi-squared goodness of fit test* (using data generated by roulette wheels), the development of *the measure of correlation coefficients* and he introduced *the term standard deviation* and *measures of skewness*. Most of Pearson's work was carried out at University College London. Pearson worked with Galton and Weldon to found the statistical journal *Biometrika*, of which Pearson was editor from 1901 to 1936.

William Sealy GOSSET (1876–1937)

Gosset's major work in statistics was the *students' t-distribution*. After graduating from Oxford, Gosset started work with Arthur Guinness and Sons, a brewery company in Dublin. Gosset saw a need for accurate statistical analysis of numerous parts of the brewing process and requested that the company get expert mathematical advice. Instead the company sent Gosset to University College London to work under Karl Pearson and in the next few years the seminal work on the students' *t*-distribution was carried out. As Guinness forbids employees from publishing any of their research Gosset published this work under a pseudonym 'Student'. Gosset remained with Guinness for his whole working life. The use of the students' *t*-distribution has many different applications.

Sir Ronald FISHER (1890–1962)

Fisher's major contribution to statistics was the work on *ANOVA, exact tests of significance for small samples* and *maximum-likelihood solutions*. Most of his experimental work was carried out on biological research. Fisher was knighted in 1952.

Jerzy NEYMAN (1894–1981)

Neyman's major work in statistics covered the areas of *hypothesis testing, confidence intervals* and *survey sampling*. This work transformed both the theory and practice of statistics. Neyman is considered to be one of the principal founders of modern statistical thinking. His work was honoured by numerous awards and election to the United States National Academy of Sciences.

Andrei KOLMOGOROV (1903–1987)

Kolmogorov's work revolutionised probability theory and he formally proved many of the fundamental theories. He also worked in the field of non-parametric statistics and in particular the *Kolmogorov–Smirnov* test.

Appendix C
Exponential smoothing formulae

This appendix is of a technical nature; you can miss this section out if you wish without loss of continuity.

'Psychological help may be required if you get lost in this section!'.

As mentioned in the chapter on forecasting there are two methods of generating the initial value for exponential smoothing. The first method of simply taking the first value for the series and using it for the first F_{t+1} value was shown in Chapter 5 on forecasting. However, another method also exists which utilises backward substitution and is described below. The exponential smoothing equation (A.1) is repeatedly lagged by one period to produce equations (A.2), (A.3) and (A.4).

$$F_{t+1} = \alpha Y_t + (1 - \alpha) F_t \qquad \text{(A.1)}$$

$$F_t = \alpha Y_{t-1} + (1 - \alpha) F_{t-1} \qquad \text{(A.2)}$$

$$F_{t-1} = \alpha Y_{t-2} + (1 - \alpha) F_{t-2} \qquad \text{(A.3)}$$

We can now substitute (A.2) into equation (A.1) to create equation (B.1)

$$F_{t+1} = \alpha Y_t + (1 - \alpha)[\alpha Y_{t-1} + (1 - \alpha) F_{t-1}] \qquad \text{(B.1)}$$

which simplifies to:

$$F_{t+1} = \alpha Y_t + (1 - \alpha)\alpha Y_{t-1} + (1 - \alpha)^2 F_{t-1} \qquad \text{(B.1)}$$

We can now substitute (A.3) into (B.1) to create equation (B.2)

$$F_{t+1} = \alpha Y_t + (1 - \alpha)\alpha Y_{t-1} + (1 - \alpha)^2[\alpha Y_{t-2} + (1 - \alpha) F_{t-2} \qquad \text{(B.2)}$$

which simplifies to:

$$F_{t+1} = \alpha Y_t + (1 - \alpha)\alpha Y_{t-1} + (1 - \alpha)^2 \alpha Y_{t-2} + (1 - \alpha)^2 F_{t-2} \qquad \text{(B.2)}$$

As can be seen, a pattern is building up as the equation expands with the coefficient on Y_{t-i} being $(1 - \alpha)^i \alpha$. As the coefficient α varies between zero the coefficient on Y_{t-i} will decline the further back it goes. The following two tables, for α equals 0.33 and 0.88 illustrates this process.

$$\alpha = 0.33$$

Coefficient			Value
α	0.33	=	0.3300
$(1-\alpha)\alpha$	$(1-0.33){*}0.33$	=	0.2211
$(1-\alpha)^2\alpha$	$(1-0.33)^2{*}0.33$	=	0.1481
$(1-\alpha)^3\alpha$	$(1-0.33)^3{*}0.33$	=	0.0993
$(1-\alpha)^4\alpha$	$(1-0.33)^4{*}0.33$	=	0.0665

$$\alpha = 0.88$$

Coefficient			Value
α	0.88	=	0.8800
$(1-\alpha)\alpha$	$(1-0.88){*}0.88$	=	0.1056
$(1-\alpha)^2\alpha$	$(1-0.88)^2{*}0.88$	=	0.0126
$(1-\alpha)^3\alpha$	$(1-0.88)^3{*}0.88$	=	0.0015
$(1-\alpha)^4\alpha$	$(1-0.88)^4{*}0.88$	=	0.0002

Therefore the larger the value of α the quicker the decay in the coefficient $(1 - \alpha)^i \alpha$. How far back you need to go depends on two factors, firstly, the value of α and secondly the magnitude of your data. The following table illustrates this using two data sets and α equals 0.88.

$$\alpha = 0.88$$

Coefficient		Value	Time	Data set 1	E1	2	E2
α	=	0.8800	t	10	8.80	1000	8800
$(1-\alpha)\alpha$	=	0.1056	$t-1$	12	1.26	1200	127
$(1-\alpha)^2\alpha$	=	0.0126	$t-2$	13	0.16	1300	16
$(1-\alpha)^3\alpha$	=	0.0015	$t-3$	14	0.02	1400	2
$(1-\alpha)^4\alpha$	=	0.0002	$t-4$	17	0.00	1700	0

The values to E1 and E2 are found by multiplying the data set by its component in the value column (i.e. the first value in the column E1 is found by multiplying 0.8800 by 10 = 8.80).

Columns E1 and E2 are the effects on the calculation of F_{t+1}, with the first data set measured in tens you only need to go back to $t - 1$ with $\alpha = 0.88$ as the incremental effect of $t - 2$ has fallen to almost zero. However, with the second data set, which is measured in thousands, you need to go back to $t - 3$ before the incremental effect has fallen to zero.

To summarise, if the second method of backward substitution is used to generate the initial value of F_{t+1}, you will need to calculate how far into the past the exponential structure needs to go so the effect of $(1 - \alpha)^i \alpha$ decays to zero. Once you have calculated this you can calculate F_{t+1}, where i is the length of the exponential structure. The use of the backward substitution method will always yield accurate estimates of F_t; this is not the case with the first method $(F_{t+1} = Y_t)$ as early values in the F_t vector will be inaccurate. However, as the F_t vector progresses for the first method, the estimates of F_t will become more accurate and the difference between the two approaches will fall to zero.

Index